TWAYNE'S
RULERS AND STATESMEN OF THE WORLD
SERIES

Hans L. Trefousse, Brooklyn College
General Editor

Tom B. Jones, University of Minnesota
Ancient World Editor

ALEXANDER THE GREAT

TROW 4

Alexander The Great

By JOHN W. SNYDER

Indiana University

Twayne Publishers, Inc.   ::   New York

To Marg

Contents

Chronology

against the Scyths. Winter: Alexander enters winter quarters in Bactria.

328 Spring and summer: the main Sogdian campaign. Fall: the murder of Cleitus. Winter: army quarters at Nautaca; the death of Spitamenes.

327 Spring: seizure of Oxyartes' stronghold; Alexander's marriage with Roxane. Late spring: the *proskynesis* episode; the trial of Hermolaus; Callisthenes imprisoned. Summer: the army moves out for India. Winter: in quarters at Taxila.

326 June: the army enters Punjab. Summer: the battle against Porus. Fall: trouble with the army at the Beas; November: the beginning of the voyage down the Indus. Winter: the battle with the Malli.

325 Late winter: continuing down the Indus. July: the army reaches Pattala. August (?): Alexander marches into Gedrosia. November: the army reaches Carmania. December: Persis.

324 Spring: the mass marriages at Susa. Summer: the army mutinies at Opis. Fall: the march into Ecbatana; death of Hephaestion.

323 Spring: Alexander returns to Babylon; exploration of southern Mesopotamia. June 13: Alexander's death.

Introduction

Alexander's conquests opened the way for an eastward diffusion of Greek trade, art, and thought; but soon afterward Babylonian science, Persian gold, and the new kind of power politics devised by the Macedonians swept westward with an even greater effect. Alexander functioned as a catalyst: he altered a world that was ready for change. The ultimate result of his achievements, moreover, was to magnify a classical miniature into the colossal *oecumene* of Hellenistic times. It might almost be said that Alexander laid the foundation on which the Romans built their empire.

Despite his fame and the voluminous literature devoted to it, Alexander remains something of a mystery. This is in large part due to the character of the ancient literary works on which we must rely for accounts of his reign. There is some irony in this, considering that Alexander was unusually conscious of the value of public relations and deliberately sought to keep records as no one had before him. Yet the daily *Journal* and the work of his official historian, Callisthenes, have been lost. Further, even before Alexander died, a tradition hostile to him was developing in Greece, particularly among the philosophers. This was to color later writings about Alexander, but it was no more unhistorical than the popular, romantic tradition which began to grow soon after Alexander's death and became very widespread. The latter was characterized mainly by exaggerated assertions about his abilities, an acceptance of the philosophers' views concerning his alleged moral deterioration, and eager recitals of debauchery and massacre bearing little relation to reason, let alone fact. Cleitarchus is best known and the earliest important figure in fashioning this Alexander Romance. He wrote in the middle of the third century B.C., though his work too is lost. The Alexander Romance, however, continued to develop, influenced from East and West alike and growing more favorable to the king as it became even more fanciful. The last contributions to the Romance are the product of the Middle Ages.

The earliest extant source for Alexander is a portion of Diodorus Siculus' *World History,* written in the last half of the first century B.C. Diodorus' seventeenth book is a history of the Macedonian king, drawn in part from the then still available writings of Alexander's associates, but also largely influenced by Cleitarchus. The next oldest source is the Latin work of Quintus Curtius Rufus, who wrote in the second half of the first century A.D. Curtius is something of a puzzle himself in that he has some genuine and good information about Alexander, but often lazily repeated what was nearest to hand from genuine, hostile, and romantic works in an irritating mixture. He was unable or unwilling to be consistent in the picture he presented and, like Diodorus, must be used with great care.

The one good source for Alexander still in our possession is the work of Flavius Arrianus, who served as governor of Cappadocia in Asia Minor under the Roman emperor Hadrian. A successful military commander in his own right, Arrian ultimately retired from imperial service to write. His *Anabasis,* the history of Alexander, was written near the middle of the second century A.D. Arrian used the memoirs of Ptolemy, one of Alexander's generals, as his primary source, augmented at times by the work of Aristobulos, a Greek technician at Alexander's headquarters. Occasionally he also reported the popular tradition and usually identified it with the phrase "they say." It is normally safe to assume that unless he specifies otherwise, Arrian gives Ptolemy's version of events. The problems stemming from this reliance upon Ptolemy, who later became King of Egypt, will be discussed as they arise. What we know of Ptolemy's and Aristobulos' works comes to us almost entirely from Arrian.

Plutarch's *Life of Alexander* and his *On the Abilities and Fortune of Alexander* were written near the end of the first century A.D. They rely on the author's extremely wide reading, but are heavily influenced by his tendency to moralize. Consequently they too must be used with care and rank well below Arrian. Finally, we have the *Epitome* of Pompeius Trogus' *Historiae Philippicae* written by Marcus Junianus Justinus in the third century A.D. Although there are many passages in Justin which refer to genuine events, there is nothing that cannot be more reliably gained from other sources. In addition to the major literary

sources just described, there are countless fragments of now missing works that consist largely of quotations of earlier writings by
later authors. These have been collected by Felix Jacoby in his
Fragmente der griechischen Historiker.

While employing the traditional materials, this treatment will
rely heavily upon what can be learned from Eastern sources. Pro-
fessional readers will perhaps be most interesting in the ways in
which the Middle Eastern information has led to departures from
the usual views of Alexander. Cases in point are the pattern of
the campaigns in Asia Minor, the decision to acquire the whole
Persian Empire, taken between the Battle of Issus and the siege
of Tyre, the problem posed by the inability to defeat the Persian
cavalry, the importance of Babylon, and Alexander's realization
of the value of an Arabian expedition. The assertion that he did
not intend to be deified is not original here, but Middle Eastern
materials have thrown additional light on the matter.

Modern works on Alexander are numerous. As indicated by
the notes, I am immeasurably indebted to previous efforts, some
of which must be mentioned here. W. W. Tarn's *Alexander* and
F. Schachermeyr's *Alexander der Gross* are the most obvious
among general studies. H. Berve's *Alexanderreich* has been a constant reference because of the author's assemblage of the evidence
for the people who figure in the campaigns. H. Bengtson's *Griechische Geschichte* offers the easiest way to get at the general literature, both ancient and modern, on Alexander up to the time
of its writing. The study by G. Walzer can be used to bring the
materials up to date. J. F. C. Fuller's *The Generalship of Alexander the Great* provides the best current account of tactical military problems. L. Pearson, *The Lost Histories of Alexander the
Great,* is vital to any work with the original sources. A. R. Bellinger's *Essays on the Coinage of Alexander the Great* has provided valuable support concerning fiscal policies, just as V.
Ehrenberg's *Alexander and the Greeks* has offered comment on
matters of political policy. Because almost every aspect of Alexander's career is discussed in the journal literature, often as matters
for controversy, space forbids any listing here. All works used for
points about which there is no common agreement in modern
histories of Alexander are cited in the notes, as are all points in
the ancient sources about which there might be some question of
special interpretation.

Finally, I am indebted to the Graduate School of Indiana University, to the University's Program of Non-Western Studies and the Ford Foundation, and to the American Philosophical Society for generous grants with which to pursue this study. Professor Henri Seyrig and Miss Margaret Thompson have been most helpful in conversations about special problems. Professor Glanville Downey has made equally helpful comments on the manuscript. I have used their aid wherever it was available, but all mistakes are my own.

Alexander The Great

CHAPTER I

Alexander of Macedon

1. Boyhood

THE ISLAND OF SAMOTHRACE BROODS LIKE A DARK AND HULKING cloud in the distance off the Thracian shore in the North Aegean Sea, in antiquity an age-old source of myth and mystery to the fierce but simple tribesmen of the mainland. In mid-fourth century B.C., the mystery had tangible form in the celebration of the rites of the Kabirioi, the details of whose worship have long been lost. Among the spectators at the celebration of these erotic mysteries in 357 B.C., two stood out. One was the newly crowned king of Macedonia, Philip II. Already at twenty-six he had withstood rival claimants to the throne inside his land and pressures against its borders from without. Even at this moment, he was actively engaged in an increasingly successful effort to remove Athenian influence from the coast of Thrace. Many loves—and four wives— had made him a man of the world in other ways as well. The second spectator, set apart from the crowd by station and appearance alike, was Olympias, eighteen-year-old Molossian princess from Epirus. Later behavior leads to the suspicion that she had more than a passing interest in the celebration, despite the difficult position into which political change had lately thrust her. An uncle scheming to make himself king of Epirus after the death of her father had shouldered Olympias and her brother aside, and there remained effective claim to little save assassination should she attempt to force the situation in Epirus.

As Philip looked at the Molossian princess, his stare was amorous, yet perhaps it held a thought or two of policy and the advantage of acquiring through this girl an interest in the throne of Epirus. It was a glance that changed the world, for with their marriage, Olympias, unlike Philip's four previous wives, became the legitimate queen of Macedonia. The son born to this union in the following year possessed a claim to the throne that initially

stood without challenge. His name was Alexander, recalling earlier kings of Macedonia.

Much later, when Alexander of Macedon had amazed his world
by conquering a good share of it, observers and chroniclers remembered (or invented) many indications of divine interest in
this famous birth. Plutarch tells of dreams that came to both parents. The fact that she later kept snakes in her room lent some
credence to the suggestion that Zeus had visited the queen in ser-
pent form. Admittedly, Olympias was different. Her excesses and
her excitable temperament were known to all at the court. Some
also knew of her acts of jealous hatred directed against any other
member of the royal household whom she might regard as a
threat to her own position or that of her son. Olympias, often
wildly erratic, was queen and wife of the obviously blessed and
increasingly successful Philip. Little wonder that speculation
arose about the divine or unusual nature of Alexander's birth.
Divinity found greatest favor with the more credulous. A boast
tossed over a juvenile shoulder could have touched off the flattery
that, in after years, was destined to follow Alexander's steps each
time he reached a new triumph. There are reasons to think that
he regretted suggestions of divine parentage. Though the question is much debated, Alexander may never have believed he was
divine. Yet he was not averse to utilizing the concept when it
could help to achieve his ends.

Under Olympias' frequently unpredictable behavior, Philip's
ardor rapidly cooled, hastened no doubt by the snakes. Excess
begat excess in Olympias' dislike of Philip's wandering eye, and
soon the early felicity of the proud pair gave way to estrange-
ment. While Philip was heavily engaged in affairs of state, Olympias let neither her religious peculiarities nor her active interest
in the affairs of Epirus interfere with her efforts to alienate young
Alexander from his father.

In the beginning, the two persons Alexander saw most were his
mother and his nurse, Lanice. The tender affection Olympias
withheld from all others to lavish on the boy might have had
unfortunate results, had she not counteracted it by the appointment of an Epirote relative, Leonidas, as supervisor of the young
Prince's education. Leonidas never forgot his Spartan namesake.
Although he recognized his own limitations in philosophy and
literature, he determined to stamp out every indication of softness and love of luxury in his young charge. The fierce tutor fol-

lowed his zeal with such abandon that Olympias and Lanice smuggled sweets to the youth to fortify him against meager meals and all-night marches.

Leonidas' assistant in the early training of Alexander was Lysimachus. Plutarch says Lysimachus' chief recommendation was that he hit upon the lucky device of calling Alexander Achilles; Philip, Peleus; and himself, Phoenix. Alexander held all these friends of his childhood—Lysimachus, Leonidas, Lanice, and his mother Olympias—in highest esteem throughout his life. Much later in gentle irony he sent crusty old Leonidas the handsome present of some eighteen tons of aromatics—enough to make him rich.

The young Prince early began to attract the attention of people about him. He was not tall and handsome. Later the more royal appearance of Hephaestion was to confuse the Persian dowager when the two men appeared unannounced in her tent. Yet the sharpness of Alexander's eye and its direct glance from a slightly lowered face caught everyone's notice, as did his curly hair, long straight nose, light complexion, firm chin, head inclined slightly to the left, and great physical stamina. Alexander was fond of hunting, fleet of foot, yet contemptuous of athletic contests. Impatience with violent but unproductive physical activity is interesting in one with such natural prowess.

Two reported episodes of Alexander's early youth, if true, are worth notice. Quite early the young man happened to be at his father's court when some Persian friends also were present.[1] The boy engaged them in conversation about the nature of the Persian Empire: its great distances, and the character and abilities of its king. The Persians, more willing to answer such questions from a boy than from the father who was well on his way into Greece, went off marveling at the sagacity of the child. The other episode involved the horse Bucephalus. The owner had brought the beautiful but fractious animal to Philip in the hope of a handsome sale. After a few unsuccessful attempts to ride it by his best trainers, Philip was about to dismiss both seller and horse. He only then became aware of Alexander's repeated observation that they were about to lose an exceptional horse for want of someone with sufficient ability to ride him. The King good-humoredly let the youth try where professionals had failed. The boy led the animal away from the group and turned him to the sun so he could no longer see and start at his shadow. Then, carefully mounting, he stayed with the horse, giving it free rein until the end of the course. As he returned amid cries of admiration, the boy overheard his father remark that Macedon was too small a kingdom for one who showed such promise of ability. Philip spoke in jest, but Alexander laid the remark to rest on the ambition growing within his soul.

Meanwhile, Philip moved ahead in a fascinating schedule of conquest. In the year 343 B.C. he was rounding out control over Thrace and Thessaly, and Isocrates had begun to recognize him as ideal leader of the Greeks against the Persians.[2] The Macedonian king was already in a position to think less in terms of military action and intrigue and more of statesmanship. Once won, something would have to be done with these territories.

Perhaps this was the reason why Philip brought the philosopher Aristotle to Macedonia to be Alexander's tutor. He planned to have pupil, teacher, and suitable companions together and far from court life at Pella. The royal villa in the upland meadow of Mieza was chosen to be the site of the boy's finishing school. Alexander at thirteen probably already had all the education his father had enjoyed, and more. When the three years at Mieza came to a close, his own formal training ended. We do not know precisely what the philosopher taught Alexander during those three years at Mieza, but it is safe to assume that the boy learned much from the "master of those who know."

Aristotle's thought had always made utility an important issue in definition. He taught that the "final cause" of anything must be the purpose which that thing serves by nature or design. Alexander tended later to view political and military institutions in light of the purposes they could serve. The Prince was an apt pupil, finding greater compatibility with his own nature here than in the more speculative thought of, say, Plato. Aristotle's work also was a culmination of efforts among the Greeks to split knowledge and investigation into manageable categories. When so analyzed, information might be gathered in great quantities without confusion and applied without conflict. Our own systems of science and scholarship are so firmly organized around this device of ancient Greece that we tend to regard systems not so constructed as primitive.

In ancient times, Aristotelian logic was most useful. One of Alexander's chief sources of strength was the superior information he supplied himself about everything he came against. Allied to this was the boundless curiosity the young King exhibited towards all the new world, into which his army was penetrating. He frequently dispatched information and specimens back to Aristotle. One field of knowledge was essential to the campaigns: geography. Good information concerning land forms and distances was as important for communications and supply along the route already passed as it was for determining future plans and movements. Alexander gathered data from all possible sources: from accurate measurements of areas covered; from specimens of natural phenomena; and from native informants wherever they could be found.

Still, Alexander was no slavish imitator of Aristotle's system. He was known to take exception to some of Aristotle's public pronouncements; he disagreed categorically with the philosopher's estimate of conquered "barbarians"; in time, he was even to reward his teacher by executing Callisthenes, Aristotle's nephew, who had been with the young Prince in the pleasant years at Mieza.

That Alexander had a mind of his own in intellectual matters was shown early by his consuming interest in the poems of Homer. Plato had criticized the poets, and Aristotle had agreed that they were inconsistent and often ignored serious problems in order to engage in trivialities. Though one now may wonder just how profound the Homeric poems were intended to be, ancient philosophers disliked them. They found the aristocratic, military virtues of the Homeric heroes—athletic prowess, fearlessness in the face of a potentially successful enemy, and disdain for the physically less fortunate—pretty thin stuff alongside the Socratic definitions of virtue that so concerned Plato and Aristotle. For them, rigorous definition, logic, and complete intellectual honesty were to point the way toward understanding the Good and the Beautiful, perhaps even the Ultimate. Aristotle had a noticeably more practical approach to these problems than Plato; but Alexander slept with a copy of Homer's *Iliad* under his pillow and dreamed of outfighting Achilles.

Perhaps it was the continuing influence of Leonidas. If Aristotle gave Alexander many of the techniques of the philosophers, Leonidas gave him a large part of his own value system. Here the traditional Greek idea of *arete* must have had strong effect during the formative years of the young Prince. The boy grew up with this old idea of virtue as the ability to be or do something supremely well and sought to acquire the combination of many abilities, which made the true aristocrat.

Alexander's personality greatly conditioned his reactions to the life of the mind. From childhood, he had every bit of the strength of purpose, not to say wilfulness, which those who knew his parents must have expected. He viewed his father with mixed feelings. Though mistrustful under Olympias' tutelage, the Prince admired his father's abilities and sought to emulate them. As he grew old enough to acquire an idea of how to do things, he began to intersperse emulation with envy and the conviction that he could do as well or better. Occasionally, he was alarmed by the thought that Philip's Greek successes would leave him with nothing to do when he himself became king.

At the age of sixteen, Alexander left the company of Aristotle to assume the regency of Macedonia while his father was on campaign against Perinthus. Here was a new turn to his life, away from contemplation and theoretical things to the life of action. The new regent immediately used his opportunity to take the field against some of the barbarian tribes on the upper Strymon River. He quelled them and founded there the first of many cities to bear his name, Alexandropolis. The lad had the tactful advice of Eumenes while on this campaign, but it is nevertheless clear indication that, while Leonidas had been teaching him physical endurance and courage and Aristotle philosophy, Philip's influence had produced some awareness of the affairs of state.

2. Philip and the Conquest of Greece

It was a swirling political life for the young Alexander as he watched his father's combinations and collisions. Philip had come a long way. He had begun his career as a hostage from Macedonia at Thebes. In those years of Theban hegemony over all Greece, the young man had opportunity to learn much of Greek military tactics, strategy, and intrigue. Returning to Macedonia, he put his lessons to good use in various administrative capacities, and when King Perdiccas died in 359, Philip was in position as chief claimant for the regency of the minor child of Perdiccas, Amyntas. In swift succession, rival claims to the regency were brushed aside; their holders were killed or exiled. The barbarian Illyrian tribes to the northwest were tamed with similar speed.

Combining dissimulation with bribery, trickery, and lightning attack when necessary, the new regent reduced them to the status of vassals.

Philip used the respite thus gained to make sweeping changes in the organization of the Macedonian army. He added a well-outfitted and trained infantry to the former predominant reliance upon a cavalry made up of members of the nobility, the so-called Companions. The new infantry became the Foot Companions of the King. Their tightly organized units replaced the motley levies of near-irregulars that once had confused the edges of battle. These foot troops formed the infantry phalanx, new to Macedon, while they also underwent changes in individual armament. Compared with the standard for the usual Greek hoplite infantryman, the shield was lighter, the sword shorter, and there were fewer accessories. In compensation for these sacrifices to mobility, the spear was increased in length from eight to twelve, or thirteen, feet: a genuine pike. This *sarissa* could engage the enemy while keeping beyond range of short spears and swords. Philip's phalanx functioned even better than its Greek predecessors in the one chief task for which it was designed: holding the enemy stationary until cavalry, light infantry, or archers could carry the charge. Philip's improvements in armament made the phalanx more maneuverable. His training exercise, tactics, rewards, and promotions made both cavalry and infantry move as one, revelling in success. The King[3] also developed a system of military roads and fortifications to complement the army. Macedonia was stronger than ever before.

The new Macedonia provided a position from which Philip could move toward the control of the entire Greek peninsula. At first, his moves had been eastward toward Thrace, where Athens' superiority had long been recognized. The area was important to the Athenians for a number of reasons. Attic traders called at Thracian coastal cities, and these cities flanked the even more important trade route through the Dardanelles into the Black Sea. With the cities in unfriendly hands, Athenian losses might be great. And not the least sensitive of these potential losses was Athens' long-standing but unsuccessful claim on the city of Amphipolis and the gold mines near it. Initially, the Athenians had encouraged Philip's fledgling efforts at expansion. They hoped to use this Madedonian tool to control half-wild Thracian chieftains whose irrational raids damaged trade and security

alike. As their dupe, Philip could risk his army and life to stabilize the back country beyond Athenian trade stations. Reason to
doubt the wisdom of this policy, however, came when Philip
showed himself as willing to move against Athens' friends as her
foes.

So long as Philip confined his activities to Thrace, only Athens
was the loser. Later, when he became involved in the Sacred War
of Central Greece, other cities began also to feel the threat. The
war had begun as a result of Phocian resentment against Thebes's
efforts to control Central Greece by means of the Delphic Amphictiony, an organization of states established to administer the
oracles of Apollo at Delphi. After having seized it, the Phocians
were able to use the wealth of Delphi to sustain a war effort of
sufficient scope to bring almost all of Greece into the fray. Later,
finding themselves in difficulty, the Phocians invited Philip to
come south to their aid. With characteristic decisiveness, he used
the opportunity to move into central Greece as far as the defile
between mountain and sea at Thermopylae, where he was halted
without a fight by the presence of Athenian troops.

Philip's action was more helpful to himself than it was to the
Phocians. His forces now were in north-central Greece, but without his active further assistance, the fighting in the Phocians' Sacred War declined to a series of border skirmishes. But now
Athens felt herself seriously threatened. For, even before the rise
of Philip, Athenian policy for central Greece was directed against
the re-establishment of Theban hegemony in the area. So long as
Thebes and Phocis fought each other, with Thebes and her Boeotian partisans in a superior position, the two chief aims of Athenian policy were realized: Thebes was limited by the Sacred War,
and Philip was kept from coming south below Thermopylae by a
strong Boeotia.

The Macedonian king, however, continued his efforts to expand, now in open conflict with Athenian forces in Thrace and
the area eastward toward the Dardanelles. Attic fears seemed
realized, and many Athenians were somewhat relieved when
Philip turned his attention to the Chalcidice for his next major
effort. The dominant city of the area was Olynthus, erstwhile ally
of Macedon, but lately hostile to Philip to the extent of hiding
two of Philip's exiled rivals and treating with Philip's enemy,
Athens. Twice Philip protested, and in 348 began his invasion of
the Chalcidice. Possible Athenian inclination to help Olynthus

was put off when Macedonian agents stirred up rebellion against Attic possessions in Euboea. While Athenian forces rushed to that island, unfortunately without success, Philip moved to the destruction of Olynthus. Soon the city lay ruined and abandoned, its inhabitants slaves as Philip went on to vent his ire upon other cities of the Chalcidice as well. Now all spirit of resistance lay scorched and smoking in the ruins of the cities or was hobbling off in chains to Macedonian slavery.

Athens sought peace, and Philip's respect for Athenian naval superiority led him to agree in 346. He used the peace, however, to continue his encroachments in Central Greece, aided by local divisions there. When war was renewed in 340, the Athenians found their position growing steadily worse. The situation reached a climax in 339 as the members of the Delphic Amphictiony appealed to Athens and Thebes to chastise the neighboring Amphissans for sacrilege in farming certain lands belonging to the temple precincts. When the Athenians and Thebans refused to answer the appeal, the other members of the Amphictiony turned to Philip.

The decision of Thebes and Athens to remain aloof was perhaps the last major decision they were to take as free cities. Philip acted with characteristic speed to convert opportunity into new advance. Instead of moving immediately against Amphissa he seized Elatea, which the Phocians once had used in conflict with the Boeotians. The abandoned fortress commanded the approach to Boeotia from the west and was now Philip's temporary headquarters as he sent word to Thebes that he intended to invade Attica. He invited the Thebans to join. Failing that, he hoped they could allow free passage through their territory.

This presented the Athenians with the choice of fighting alone or attempting agreement with their old enemies, the Boeotians. Either way, traditional Athenian policy for central Greece was ended. Demosthenes proposed an embassy to Thebes. There, its members nervously debated with Macedonian envoys before the Theban assembly. Under Demosthenes' leadership the Athenians pieced together an offer the Thebans could not refuse: Athens would pay two thirds of the cost of their combined military venture against Philip, leaving supreme command of the forces to Thebes. The offer had a mark of desperation, and the Thebans allowed themselves to accept it.

Demosthenes also strove to strengthen the Athenian position

elsewhere. His efforts to awaken resistance in the Peloponnesus were, as usual, disappointing. At Athens, the fund for religious expenditure, about which Demosthenes had been arguing in assembly for years, was now earmarked for military expenditures. After these arrangements, and the few allies who agreed to participate were organized, the Greeks began their countermeasures.

The positions of the combatants prior to the Battle of Chaeronea are as important as their tactics to the understanding of its outcome. Greeks occupied the passes leading into Boeotia from the west with exception of Elatea, which apparently was screened by taking up positions in the pass of Parapotami some miles to the south of the fortress. Ten thousand mercenaries under Chares went to bar the roads from Doris into Amphissa and on to the Gulf of Corinth. Philip calmly permitted these measures as he awaited reinforcement from Macedonia. Well into the spring of 338, he moved with the swiftness that always left his opponents breathless. With the bulk of the enemy concentrated in Boeotia to the east, he struck south against Amphissa, running over Chares and the mercenaries on the way. Then he moved on to the gulf, seizing Naupactus. This one rapid campaign accomplished what the Athenians had been seeking for years to prevent: Philip had access to the Gulf of Corinth. He could isolate all Attica. The allies were left with nothing to strike but their tents. Philip, on the gulf to the south, had only to cross the Isthmus of Corinth to come up behind the enemy positions in western Boeotia. They would have to fall back. Withdrawal was orderly as the allies moved onto the plain near Chaeronea, where they took up a position employing the river Cephisus to secure their right flank. The time taken to accomplish this maneuver permitted Philip to leave Naupactus under garrison by the Aetolians and to return to Elatea. He then advanced along the Parapotami in the footsteps of the lately withdrawn allies. On about August 2, 338 B.C., he came out onto the great plain where the enemy had drawn up their full lines awaiting him.

Tradition tells us that after the battle the elated Philip was given pause for a moment when he realized that Demosthenes had maneuvered him into risking his entire army in one fight. Philip generally had been careful not to commit so much of his power. But if the risk was great, so were the rewards. Philip entered the plain with some 30,000 infantry and 2,000 cavalry along with an unknown number of allies. We are not told the numbers he faced. On the right, the Thebans had massed their infantry, much superior to that of Athens or the allies. Smaller-state contingents were in the center; Athens' forces were on the left. Philip took command of his right, opposite the Athenians; and the eighteen-year-old Alexander commanded the left, against Thebes. Philip ordered his infantry to do what hoplites could do only with great difficulty: they retired, simulating flight under the Athenians' jubilant attack, without losing their order. Meantime, Alexander drove against the superior Theban forces and finally broke through. Just as this happened, Philip gave the order to wheel and attack the now widely separated and hence virtually isolated Athenians. His phalanx completed this change of tactic in a manner bespeaking their superlative training, and once the Athenians had begun to retire in confusion Philip wheeled left while Alexander wheeled right. This obliterated the allied center. Larger contingents suffered heavily. Many of those who lived, including Demosthenes, fled the scene. Southern Greece lay open.

Chaeronea was a military triumph, but it left Philip with new problems. Whatever the relative merits of Theban and Athenian fighting men, Thebes, more than Athens, was defeated that day in August. The city lay open, the bulk of its resources committed to the failure on the plain. Because he was more angered at their part in the fight, since they once had been his allies; or perhaps simply because he was able to do so, Philip deprived Thebes of her commanding voice in the Boeotian League. He expelled the anti-Macedonian party in the city and turned its government over to an oligarchy whose members he could control.

Athens presented a different situation. The city had withstood the continuous onslaught of the Peloponnesians for years during the great war with Sparta because the Spartans could not meet the Athenian navy on equal terms. Philip, also lacking a navy, could not hope to take the city without a siege of many years. For Philip this would have been temperamentally difficult. For his men, trained on successes, it might have been impossible. Yet Athens had steadfastly resisted his own efforts to expand. We can —for Demosthenes did— accuse the Athenians of vacillation, inept diplomacy, perhaps even of moral cowardice, but it was Athens that had aroused opposition against the king in Thrace; Athens had been duped of Amphipolis, feinted away from Olynthus, beguiled away from Phocis. Moreover, at Athens, largely under the oratory of Demosthenes, opposition had stiffened against the Macedonian king, resulting in repeated attempts to put together a coalition of southern states to resist him. It was Athens that detached Thebes from Philip and then met defeat with the rest at Chaeronea. And Athens alone was still able to resist when that great day was over. The Peloponnesians, although they had failed to help at Chaeronea, were also a possibly hostile force about which Philip surely had no illusions. Without Athens, he could not hope to go on to the south; with Attica, he could threaten southern Greece with invasion at will, and control the South with this threat. Philip must have pondered, as long as he was sober after the battle of Chaeronea, how to control Athens without taking the city.

The ease with which the answer to these questions came may well argue for Philip's having thought the problems through long before coming into central Greece. He extended a completely unexpected leniency to Athens. The Athenians looked for a siege, but their wildly desperate preparations to resist ended when Philip informed them of his attitude by repatriating without ransom the two thousand Attic prisoners taken in the battle (having sold his Theban prisoners into slavery). The Athenian maritime confederacy was to disband, though many of the island allies of Athens might remain friends. The King sent Alexander to Athens at the head of an embassy to return the ashes of those men who had fallen in the battle. It was Alexander's only visit to the city. By now, all Greece save Sparta had flocked to accept Philip's hegemony.

Sometime close to the end of the year 338, Philip turned to the next move in his plan for control of the Greeks: the King of Macedonia summoned a congress of all Greeks to meet at Corinth early in 337. There he laid a plan for alliance before the assembled delegates; only the Spartans were absent. The member states were to ally with Philip, not with each other. To Philip went supreme command in case of war; to them, the privilege and duty of furnishing troops and ships. There were provisions with which to keep the peace within the group of states formed by this alliance system—the so-called League of Corinth. Each member state agreed to permit no tampering with affairs of other states, no constitutional alteration, no redistribution of land, and no sudden enfranchisement of slaves to aid rebellion. Each member agreed to enforce these provisions among all signatories.

Philip then announced his intention to carry out a full-scale invasion of Asia Minor and called upon the league members to furnish military support. Assent came immediately, although the members acted later with some reluctance and only partial fulfilment. With Sparta isolated by intransigence, Thebes defeated and occupied, and Athens party to the league of whose armed forces Philip was hegemon, the wily King of Macedon had provided a basis for the control of Greece which his arms and diplomacy had won. As a complete realist, he well knew that the league would have to function for some purpose besides his own royal benefit. The leader must lead, and for Philip the solution of this problem had been suggested eight years earlier when Isocrates had called upon him to lead the Greeks against the Persians in order to free Asia Minor. In doing this, Isocrates was sounding an older theme, which Herodotus tells us went back to the Trojan War, when conflict between East and West first began. Such war could be revenge against the eastern barbarians who had devastated Greece and burned the Acropolis at Athens a century and a half earlier. Now Philip's activist statesmanship combined vengeance on the East with the need for stability in Greece. The League of Corinth was at once a peace and an alliance; perhaps the two ideas never had been separate. But now also Philip, who before Chaeronea had been moving on two fronts, northeast and south, could profit from the alliance and strengthen his hold on the south by a northeastern campaign to Asia Minor.

Philip and Alexander thereupon returned to Macedonia and to the quarrel that had lain uneasily below the surface of their relations for some years.

3. *The Assassination of Philip*

The tale of Philip and Alexander, father and son, teacher (in some respects) and student, came to an end in violence—the assassination of Philip.

The facts, as we have them, are easy to state. Philip, long since wearied of Olympias, her snakes, her Maenad frenzies, her attempted domination over their son, had returned to his series of feminine alliances, from which Olympias at best had provided an interlude. There is little profit now in attempting to determine which came first, wandering or resentment. By 337, both had worked their way to the surface to fuel the bitter quarrel that broke out when Philip sought momentary relief from the cares of conquest and preparation by marrying the sixteen-year-old Eurydice, niece of Attalus, one of Philip's most able field commanders.

During the wedding feast, Attalus, no doubt under the combined influence of what he had drunk and what he expected from his new relation with the royal house, proposed that Macedonians pray to the gods for a legitimate heir to the throne. Resentment fostered by his mother, uneasiness about his father, and distaste for the idea of illegitimacy implicit in occasional suggestions of divine parentage may all have crowded into Alexander's thoughts as he faced this taunt. There was a dark scene. He threw his wine cup at Attalus, demanding to know what the general meant. Philip jumped to his feet, intending to impale the Prince on his sword. But from temper, wine—or design—his foot slipped and he fell to the floor before he could reach the young man. Alexander then uttered his own famous taunt: the man who prepared to leave Europe for Asia could not cross from one chair to the next. Immediately, the young Prince and his mother withdrew. Olympias remained in Epirus, while Alexander went to Illyria. A reconciliation that was at least formal between the King and his son came some months later.

Family trouble for Philip was also simmering outside Macedonia. For years, the question of Epirus had been solved for the King by his acceptance as suzerain there. Olympias, nearly as ambitious for her family's dynasty in Epirus as for her son in Macedonia, had been constantly urging the claims of her brother, Alexander of Epirus, who finally had acquired the throne. The greater the breach between Philip and Olympias, the more intractable this Alexander became, and the greater the danger that the façade of Macedonian imperialism would crumble.

For Philip, it was time to mend some family fences. The attempt proved fatal. Soon after the reconciliation of Alexander of Macedon with his father, perhaps as part of it, Alexander's sister and only legitimate sibling, Cleopatra, married the king of Epirus, her uncle. The wedding ceremony included a procession from the palace into the theater. Philip, unwisely walking alone, ahead of his guards, met an assassin—one Pausanias, a disgruntled member of the hypaspist guards, seeking redress for the King's failure to right a personal wrong suffered at the hands of someone else.

Philip lay dead in the entrance to the theater. Alexander stood alone.

Few details come to us about the days that followed. The assassin was cut down immediately; some said his body was nailed to a cross. There is a vague indication that Olympias was solicitous about his burial. Had she been party to the act, or at least aware of its planning?

Surely, there was no lack of possible claimants to the throne. Among those whose presence threatened Alexander was Amyntas, whom Philip had set aside nearly twenty years before as he moved from regent to king. There was also Alexander's half brother, Caranus. Arrhidaeus, another half brother, did not come into question, apparently, for which he could thank the animosity of Olympias whose ominous attention (allegedly by poison) had robbed him of half his reason years before. Beyond Amyntas and Caranus there was the whole house of Lyncestis. The situation was tense.

For all practical purposes, however, the questions of Alexander's claim, his legitimacy, and his freedom from any guilt of complicity in his father's assassination were settled when the elder general of highest rank, Antipater, declared for him. Parmenion and Attalus were in Asia Minor at the time of the assassination, and they hurried back. Parmenion joined Antipater in supporting Alexander. These two most important of Philip's generals provided Alexander with the strength he needed to meet the remainder of his problems at Pella. The eldest of the family of Lyncestis had saved himself by being among the first to hail Alexander as the new king. Amyntas and Caranus were killed. Attalus soon was accused of conniving with the Athenians in a minor revolt movement and executed. Much later, the niece of Attalus, who upon marrying Philip had changed her name from Eurydice to Cleopatra, was murdered. This was the doing of Olympias, who also required that Cleopatra's infant daughter be struck dead while sitting on her mother's lap. Alexander, off in Asia at the time, is reported to have been angered by these excesses but let them pass without reprimand.

The mystery of Philip's assassination was never solved to anyone's satisfaction. That the Lyncestian house, a Persian plot, and Olympias all were mentioned, though doubtless not all with the same candor, shows that the facts were not known or at least were successfully suppressed. People took positions on the question in line with their attitudes towards the royal house and its policies. Alexander's later query concerning the assassination, addressed to the oracle of Ammon at Siwah, may, if genuine, have been in part an effort to limit factionalism at the Macedonian court.

4. *King Alexander*

As soon as departure from Pella was possible, Alexander moved into Greece at the head of his army to secure the position created there by his father. Need to do so was apparent in the restiveness that had greeted news of Philip's death. Alexander was a mere twenty years old. Who could say to what extent his campaign in Thrace at age sixteen, his cavalry charge at Chaeronea at eighteen, his leadership of the embassy to Athens had been assisted by the presence of older and wiser hands at his elbow? The Greeks did not wait to learn the truth of the matter, if ever they had questioned it, for resistance faded as the Macedonian army drew near. Alexander was accepted in his father's place as hegemon of the League of Corinth and, in effect, renewed the mandate for invasion of Asia Minor.

The threat of rebellion also appeared in Thrace and necessitated something more than a show of force. In 335, Alexander began the first real campaign for his independent leadership. He left Amphipolis for Philippi and then turned north. Away from the coast he approached free Thracians, not subjected by Philip, and their allies, the Triballians. These people held the high ground inland, and, as the Macedonians neared the center of resistance, they found themselves coming up a narrow defile leading to a ridge over which they would have to cross. As they climbed toward the enemy stationed just under the ridge, the ground grew steeper. The Triballians had screened their positions with a line of wooden carts, which they planned to use for fortification or, as a last desperate measure, to loosen the carts so they would roll downhill into the face of the advancing army. Alexander, relying upon the maneuverability of the phalanx, ordered those men with sufficient room to open ranks and let the carts roll past. Others were to lie flat with their shields interlocked over their heads. Arrian says the carts bounded harmlessly over the prone soldiers. But averting the carts with shields is unlikely; stones or a

shallow embankment just above the positions, to make them
bound outward would be more believable. The wagons past, Alexander's troops surged through the pass, killing some 1,500 of
the enemy and taking all camp followers and gear.

The next obstacle was the Danube River. Reaching it, Alexander met a large population of Celts, new and foreign to Macedonians and Greeks. Specifically, these were the Getae. When Alexander reached the river he met a few ships, sent upriver from
Byzantium and the Black Sea by arrangement. He first flung
these against the Getae positions on an island in the river, without success. The mighty stream seemed an equal barrier to enemy
and friend, and the Getae drew up ranks on the opposite side to
glory in their immunity.

Alexander ceased his attempt against the island, marched upstream, and moved his army across under cover of night. He had
commandeered all small boats in the area, in addition to the
ships from Byzantium. One other device enabled him to surprise
the enemy, who did not expect him to cross in force. This was his
order for the men to roll up hay in their tents and, after tying the
ends, to use them as air bottles with which to paddle across the
river. On the other side, as cavalry and phalanx screened their
advance by proceeding through a barley field, they were able to
surprise the Getae who melted at the first cavalry charge. The
victory was so decisive, and Alexander so amazing in his ability to
get a whole army across the river in one night without visible
means of ferrying them, that an embassy of the Celts approached
him with a request for pledges and friendship. The subsequent
agreement was honored for nearly sixty years, well after Alexander's death.

The last phase of this preliminary campaign was against the
Illyrians, who had used Alexander's absence to attack Macedonia.
Right after his conversations with the Celts, the King learned
that Cleitus, a king of Illyrians formerly subservient to Philip,
had rebelled. The Macedonians moved off on a forced march
along the river Erigon toward Cleitus' position at Pelium, where
the enemy held the heights before the town. Suddenly, Alexander
was in a difficult position. He had been marching with a part of
his troops towards Pelium through a narrow defile that broadened before narrowing again in front of hills he now discovered
were strongly held. To turn and retreat through the same defile
would require lengthening his column to no more than four

abreast, thus enabling the enemy—who had come around on the hills to link up with those at his rear—to enjoy great advantage when they attacked, as surely they would if he withdrew. But the young King used the widening of the defile to deploy his infantry in mass formation, with some 200 cavalry even beyond them on the wings.

A peculiar formation for attack past the heights; an impossible one for retreat! Giving his men the order for complete silence, he commanded the infantry first to raise their spears vertically, then forward in charge position, then to the right and to the left, all smartly together. The phalanx wheeled and countermarched on command as one man, completing complicated maneuvers with great rapidity. Then without warning, the left formed a wedge and stormed to the attack. Arrian tells us that the Illyrians were so startled at what they had seen they abandoned the lower heights even before the attack began. The Macedonian army moved on, and some five days later Cleitus was decisively defeated.

No sooner was he finished with the Illyrians than news came to Alexander that Thebes had rebelled under exiled democratic leaders who had infiltrated the city. The Macedonian garrison on the Cadmeia (the Theban acropolis) was under siege. Success by Thebes stood to undo all Philip had accomplished at Chaeronea and after, for it could screen the rebellions sure to follow at Athens, not to mention the already obvious hostility of Sparta. Alexander determined to meet the threat. Thirteen days later he was entering Boeotia with full army. He delayed the attack as long as he could, hoping the rebels would reconsider. Their leaders seem to have bolstered the city's will to resist with the argument that the young King would spare even fewer than his father had, if indeed it was Alexander. For, there had been great reluctance to believe that it was. Rumor had it that he was dead in the north; that his army was under Antipater; and that the "Alexander" surely must be Alexander the son of Aeropus of Lyncestis.

Arrian credits Ptolemy with the information that a rash attack by Perdiccas precipitated the onslaught against the city. The battle moved back and forth for a time, then the Macedonians broke into the city. Macedonians and their Boeotian allies, the Phocians, Plataeans, and others who had grudges of long-standing, began a merciless sack of the city and the slaughter of its inhabitants. The carnage was so great that it became customary to compare it with the losses of the Athenians on their ill-fated Sicilian Expedition of 413 B.C. Those other Greeks who had profited from the example in time to keep from joining the revolt tended to credit the disaster to the will of the gods, just repayment to Thebes for past treachery. The more they thought about it, the longer grew the list of those past sins. Thebes's Boeotian enemies took this opportunity, under command of Alexander and aided by Macedonian troops, to make the city pay for pride and insolence exhibited from the time of the Persian Wars to the tangled period of Theban hegemony over all Greece. Alexander had erased Thebes, center of resistance, largely self-supporting in men and matériel, arbiter of Boeotia. As the father had done at Olynthus, the son now removed both intransigence and potential threat by an act of sheer desolation.

Athens saw the meaning of this act. Despite former alliances and the persuasion that Attica too might look for the heavy hand of Macedon, Athenians rushed to congratulate Alexander on victory over the Theban revolt and safe return from the north. Other Greek cities followed this lead, save Sparta. Alexander allowed himself to accept all these indications of loyalty. He ceased to press for the surrender of Demosthenes and most of the others he held responsible for troubles at Athens and elsewhere. With Greece again pacified and the renewed Corinthian League now tested in conflict at Thebes, Alexander retired to Macedonia, there to spend the winter months in preparation for his coming invasion of Asia Minor.

CHAPTER II

The Conquest of Asia Minor

1. The Beginnings

BEFORE DEPARTING WITH HIS ARMY IN THE SPRING OF 334, ALEXander gave careful attention to Macedonia and its problems. Antipater was left behind with some 9,000 troops, the major share of the royal income, and responsibility for maintaining the home front. He must supervise the Corinthian alliances, defend and administer Macedonia, and keep a watchful eye on Olympias. Petulant complaints from the Queen to her son showed that the watch was close, though not close enough to prevent the murder of Philip's latest wife and infant child. Despite difficulties with Olympias, which never subsided, the old general kept tight rein on Greeks and Macedonians alike. He maintained security at home with few exceptions during the entire course of Alexander's Persian campaigns.

After leaving Macedon, the army made its way along the Thracian coast to the Chersonese, then doubled south along the peninsula to Sestus, the narrowest crossing from Europe to Asia west of Byzantium. With 150 triremes as a screen, Parmenion directed the maneuver without difficulty. Alexander and a small party employed this delay to sail westward down the Hellespont to a spot near Ilium. Midway, Alexander sacrificed a bull to Poseidon and poured libations of wine to the Nereids. Then, as they approached the beach at Ilium, the King cast a javelin into the sand and declared Asia conquered by the spear. When the royal party came to Ilium itself Alexander sacrificed at the tomb of Achilles, his supposed ancestor, and then ran naked around the city in commemoration of the famous combat of Hector and Achilles. Later, when leaving the city, he exchanged his armor for a set reportedly belonging to Achilles, left in a temple of Athene.

As Alexander emerged from the darkened interior of the temple into brilliant spring sunlight lighting the wind-tossed green of the ancient Trojan plain, the significance of launching an attack directly at the Persian Empire must have been borne in upon him. Such a moment crackled with echoes from the past for one as steeped as he in Homeric tradition. Somewhere on this plain Greeks had left the wooden horse that was to bring ten years of conflict between champions to a close with the destruction of Troy. That struggle had come to be seen as the first major event in an unending conflict between East and West.

Other events had followed in time. Greeks who had colonized the west coast of Asia Minor, Ionia, found themselves under the domination of the Persians by the middle of the sixth century B.C., and after they tried unsuccessfully to revolt in 499, they continued to dream of liberation. The Persian Wars of 490-480 B.C. brought the problem directly to the shores of Greece itself. The last episode of these wars occurred when the Achaemenid Persian king Xerxes in 480 crossed the Hellespont, sacrificing en route to the gods, and then went on to seize Athens and burn its Acropolis. The expedition met disaster in the straits between the barren rocks of Salamis and Attica, and this Greek naval victory was soon followed by one on land at Plataea. Persia had learned that Greece would not fall by outright military invasion.

Still, Ionia remained under Persian control, and Greek soil as far south as Attica had been violated, the Acropolis sacrilegiously burned. Athenians immediately sounded the note of revenge, for they had suffered most. Cost of the war and reparations, they said, should come from campaigns carried directly to Persian territory in Asia Minor. From the organization of this effort grew the Delian League, made up of states allied with Athens. Problems of maintaining the system limited Athens to naval efforts against Persia. But Sparta was temporarily successful in campaigns actually conducted on Persian soil.

The Achaemenid answer to these threats was to interfere in Greek internal affairs, not by military action, but by monetary subsidy. This indirect intervention served to encourage local differences and turn Greek military action inward upon mainland problems. Persian gold bought Sparta a fleet that helped to defeat Athens at the close of the Peloponnesian War. It paid for part of Sparta's short-lived bid for superiority in Greece, and a few years later did nearly as much for Thebes. The subsidies proved successful enough for the Persian throne to dictate the terms of the peace between Greek states in the year 387, the settlement known as the King's Peace. Thereafter, Greeks made regular visits to the Persian capital for more money and support. But the very success of the plan tended to broaden interest in action against Persia. The Great King loomed in the affairs of all, and revenge and liberation were a concern of all Greeks, not merely the Athenians.

Isocrates had been sounding this double note for years in his plan for the unification of Greece under Philip. He proposed a combined military effort under Macedonian leadership against the Persian Empire. Urging Philip to invade Ionia, Isocrates called attention to current Persian problems suggesting Greeks, Cypriotes, Phoenicians, and Egyptians as potential allies and helpers against Persia.

Philip had responded with an invasion of Asia Minor. His principal motive may have been to use the campaign to increase and prolong his control over mainland Greeks, but the invasion was well planned and adequately supported. He would have joined it himself had he lived. Attalus and Parmenion had gone as far as Ephesus in 336. The Ephesian welcome was enthusiastic, and the citizens promptly set up a statue of Philip in the market place. Enthusiasm spread to Caria where Pixodarus prepared to offer his daughter to Philip Arrhidaeus. At this juncture, however, Memnon, Greek mercenary chieftain from Rhodes, replaced his brother Mentor in Persian graces to become commander-in-chief of the western provinces. When Parmenion advanced south of Ephesus to the Maeander, Memnon defeated him at Magnesia. Persian forces soon pushed the Macedonians back to the Troad, where they were able only to hold a bridgehead. Philip's statue in Ephesus toppled even as he fell victim to the assassin's knife. But now the cry of revenge also had a Macedonian ring to it.

Alexander's behavior before Ilium shows his awareness of traditional history. Point by point, his propaganda would erase the symbols of Persian conquest. Xerxes had crossed the Hellespont and sacrificed to the gods, and so had Alexander. Persia had controlled Greece with gold; Alexander declared Asia Minor taken by the spear. And by going directly to Troy, he called attention to his own alleged descent from Achilles. Greek rights to freedom lay deeper in the past than even the existence of Persia.

Philip's previous expedition under Parmenion and Attalus had shown the readiness of the Greeks and the Carian dynasts to accept liberation so long as it demonstrated sufficient military ability to offer promise of permanent success. It also had added greatly to Macedonian intelligence, a point that cannot have been far from Alexander's mind as he surveyed Ilium. A story is told that once the young Alexander was asked what he would do when confronted with certain circumstances. He replied that he would have to await those circumstances to see what he should do. This does not make Alexander a towering opportunist; it does show him to have had a healthy respect for the intelligence of the moment as a factor in decision-making. A glance at the geography of Asia Minor will illustrate the kinds of information Parmenion brought back to Pella. Alexander's later actions make it clear that he understood his informant.

Two categories of land predominated in the Persian Empire west of the Iranian mountains. Rural areas were the direct property of the King, administered for him by barons, farmed by virtual serfs. Against these lands there was a relatively heavy tribute. The second kind of land was attached to cities. As geography, agriculture, and trade patterns combined to permit the development of a large settlement, the empire invariably realized an advantage. The wealth and stability such cities could produce was rewarded by the privilege of administering the agricultural land in the vicinity, by generally lower tribute rates, and by some degree of local self-determination. There could be interference in all these by the King, and this almost always occurred with respect to political organization. The Persian throne strove wherever possible to maintain its voice in city affairs through a local oligarchy or tyrant whose position depended upon royal support and whose obedience was thus assured. There was great variation in the degree of royal control. The stronger and wealthier cities were most valuable to the Crown because they made for greater stability. Yet they also were more able to resist Achaemenid meddling. Their relations with Miletus, Tyre, and Babylon must always have disturbed the Persian kings.

Officials known as satraps handled territorial administration within the Persian Empire. There were between twenty and thirty satrapies from the Troad to the Hindu Kush mountains. Each was a large territory under direct supervision of the satrap, who was a member of the Persian nobility, or even a relative of the King. In most known cases, the satrap was primarily a civil administrator. In those satrapies where there was need for military action, a general commanded the armies. This general was subject directly and only to the King.[1] Separation of powers was a device learned at great cost by Assyrians and Persians alike and existed primarily to keep a strong satrap from considering rebellion in this vast area where distance made immediate punitive action from the throne impossible. Xenophon's *Anabasis* is the tale of a satrap who was allowed to recruit a strong army of Greek mercenaries and then used them to attack his brother, the King.

The land forms of western Asia Minor were as important to the course of the young King's campaign as was the nature of Persian control. The area consists of a series of narrow and sharply divided small coastal plains, some of which lead by relatively easy stages through the mountains and up to the interior plateau. Everywhere this terrain is broken by ridges, but following any one of the larger rivers and negotiating one or more of the low passes easily gains access to the interior. These coastal valleys provided locations for most of the Greek city-states of Ionia, the primary object of Macedonian conquest. In most instances the cities lay on the coast; in some, especially those whose population originally had been non-Greek, the city was some way inland to take advantage of a defensible hill or ridge to form an acropolis around which the later city grew. This pattern of city formation was predominantly in the south. Farther north, there was more of the open crown land already mentioned. Since cities were fixed in location, any defense of them would have also to be fixed. In the more open areas of the north, Persian defensive operations would have the advantage of mobility.

Parmenion and Attalus once had taken most of the cities of the south. Taken and lost them. But the expedition had shown that it was possible to liberate these cities. Thereafter, the Macedonian general staff must have known that the often difficult coastline had encouraged the establishment of maritime trade between cities. Since they had come to rely upon the sea for communication, clearing the seas could easily isolate one from another. Still, although the cities could be isolated by sea and picked off one at a time by an army coming down the coast, they were also subject to attack from the interior. And Memnon, in fact, defeated Parmenion at Magnesia in the Maeander Valley, some twenty-five miles inland at a point to which the low pass south of Ephesus funneled the Macedonians, and to which also Memnon had easy access by coming down the valley from the interior. Alexander was one to take a lesson from such mistakes.

The resources in men and matériel with which the Macedonians began their conquest of the east have long been debated.[2] Alexander inherited an army whose training, organization, and logistical support made it superior to anything the ancient world had previously witnessed. His own experience in the northern campaigns showed that the troops were trained to obey instantly the most complicated commands, that their drill, stamina, and devotion to duty and commander allowed them to operate as one man when the occasion demanded. Details of their supply are missing, but the King's campaigns show the procurement command to have been the equal of the rest.

Four divisions are recognizable among Alexander's troops. The largest of these was the 24,000 infantry under the command of Parmenion. The central core of the infantry consisted of the Foot Companions of the King, the Macedonian phalanx of 9,000 in six battalions. Each soldier was armed primarily with shield and long pike, the *sarissa*. This heavy armor is responsible for the name "hoplite," used of such soldiers to distinguish them from the light infantry. In addition to the phalanx, there were the Macedonian hypaspists, 3,000 strong, under the command of Nicanor, a son of Parmenion. The precise nature of these troops and their peculiar armament is a mystery, but they are always mentioned separately and often bore some of the heaviest fighting. There also were 12,000 Greeks. Of these, 7,000 were allies, ultimately to be commanded by Ptolemy; and 5,000 were mercenaries. The foot included 7,000 light-armed archers, often referred to as barbarians, made up of Thracians, Cretans, and others. Finally, 1,000 Agrianians, whose chief weapon was the spear, constituted the remainder.

The second major division of combat troops was the cavalry. Mounted troops, along with archers and light infantry, served to carry the attack against the enemy by charging at the right moment into the field held by the infantry phalanx. The horses often were also used to screen the phalanx while it moved into position. The most important group of the cavalry were 1,800 Macedonian Companions of the King, commanded by Philotas, another son of Parmenion. Part of these were the royal squadron under Cleitus. They had the privilege always of remaining closest to Alexander when the situation would permit. A second group of 1,800 horse were the Thessalian cavalry under Calas. This section included 600 Greeks under Antigonus, whom Ergyius later replaced. Finally, there were 900 Thracian scouts.

Alexander's personal staff made up the third division. It included his bodyguard, whose members, like the infantry commanders, often were used for important special details. The King usually made his decisions after consultation with an informal council. Parmenion, whose sons Nicanor and Philotas also held high commands, stood foremost in this council. It also included a number of personal friends of the King: Nearchus, who later commanded naval contingents returning from India; Hephaestion, Alexander's constant companion and closest friend until his demise shortly before the death of Alexander himself; Ptolemy, who later seized Egypt and wrote the memoirs that were Arrian's chief source; Harpalus, relative of the Thessalian cavalry commander Calas. Harpalus was physically unfit for military duty but came along as a civilian and Alexander's chief adviser in financial affairs, until his final disgrace and flight.

The last division of the forces is perhaps the least known to us. These were the Greek technicians and the other members of what at times must have been a large siege train. There were sappers, engineers, architects, surveyors, and the *bematists*, who kept track of the itinerary and distances traversed. From among these people and those engaged in scribal activities come some additional names worth noting: Aristobulus, Arrian's other chief source of information; Eumenes of Cardia, who kept the daily *Journal*, which formed the basis for official histories of the expedition; Callisthenes, nephew of Aristotle, philosopher, and official historian, whose difficulties with Alexander were to end in imprisonment and death. Quite clearly, many of these were frequently involved in Alexander's counsels. It is equally clear that the King would listen to the views of all and then make his own decisions, occasionally in conflict with his advisers.

Alexander's resources in funds were amazingly slight, if we may believe the literary sources. We are told he gave away almost everything of personal value before he left Macedon. Philip had left a debt of 500 talents despite his phenomenal income. Some writers place this figure even higher. Most crucial of all, Alexander is alleged to have had only 70 talents with him when he left. And this in the face of a payroll amounting to some 300 talents per month. The problems posed are obvious. It is true that he must have realized some funds from his conquests, and many have stressed that the rural crown lands were much more important to Alexander for this purpose than were the cities he conquered. Yet, he made his first genuinely important financial gains only after Parmenion seized the Persian war chest at Damascus, and that well after the Battle of Issus. Since at that time Alexander ordered Parmenion to send him only the important Greeks he had captured on the coast, and to keep all else in Damascus for him, it could have been at least eighteen months, possibly more than two years, before Alexander's coffers received any such large contributions from Achaemenid resources. Further, his grants of political freedom, democratic government, and freedom from tribute to the cities of Asia Minor are well known.

This traditional picture needs some change. There can be little doubt that the Macedonians were operating on a shoestring. But the largess attributed to the King before he left his homeland cannot have been limitless, for Macedonian royal lands did not at this time pass out of existence; indeed, Antipater's position would need considerable support of this kind. Even a shoestring must be long enough to reach, however slim it may be. Seventy talents would not meet the 3,500 or 4,000 talents in payroll and gifts demanded of Alexander in the period before his seizure of Damascus. To have organized the resources of the crown lands in usable form to support a large and expensive army would have demanded more time if it could have been done at all. Gifts to the cities would have been meaningless if actual collections canceled them. Funds may have been short and have required economizing, but the temper of the Macedonian army and its allies was not such to go very long without pay.[3]

2.　*Coastal Asia Minor*

Prior to the arrival of the Macedonians, the Persian leaders had held a conference. Memnon urged all to retire in front of Alexander, leaving him only ruined villages and scorched earth. The satraps, however, rejected this plan despite Memnon's position as supreme commander and chose instead to make their defense at the Granicus River. Their purpose was to select a point from which they could attack the Macedonian king. Their position was neither a defense of the territory of northern Phrygia nor of the river itself, but rather a vantage point chosen to give their own attacking forces the best possible chance of killing Alexander. They nearly succeeded.

The Granicus River flows northward from Mount Ida. Its lower course has many places where the east bank is considerably higher than the west. The Persians chose one such spot, which had the added advantage of a small lake a short distance west of the river to keep Alexander's troops from flanking their position from the south. Taking advantage of the high banks and rocky river bed, which would disrupt the enemy, the Persians massed their cavalry on the higher east side with the mercenary infantry in the rear.

The Persian cavalry was some 12,000 strong; the infantry cannot have been more than 8,000, despite traditional claims to the contrary. Macedonian infantry superiority meant that the Persians could not camp close to the river, for they could not long defend it against any sort of well-planned attack by superior numbers.

Even though they were stationed atop the higher east bank, the Persian cavalry was only temporarily protected by the river. If Alexander could get his phalanx across the stream without breaking formation, the long *sarissa* would do its work, and the enemy cavalry would break formation.

The Persians were counting on the river: the phalanx would either be delayed or would break its formation to present a long and vulnerable flank as the men came across in a narrow column instead of a broad front. Either way, the Persians would have opportunity for the crux of their plan: an attack directly against the person of Alexander. Combat in this period of antiquity was still, in large measure, decided hand-to-hand in a field defined by the placement and efficiency of opposing phalanx troops. The general did not direct but led his troops, and his destruction ended their organized efforts. And whereas this was true enough for the Macedonians, it was doubly so for the Persians. Darius, their king, was himself the Persian state and government in many respects. Certainly this was true on the field. Without him the Persians would withdraw to their highlands. There they might choose another to take his place, but the military expedition of the moment would be forgotten and lost.

Alexander had re-formed his army at Abydus and now approached the river, his own troops in battle order. The Macedonian infantry was in the center, in two groups, flanked by the cavalry. Parmenion considered the situation and advised the King to wait for the morning, pointing out that their greater number of infantry would force the enemy to withdraw. He did not need to say that if the enemy withdrew they might be forced to fight on some other terrain not quite so dangerous to the few Macedonians leading the assault, for the point emerges clearly in the arrogance of the King's reply: he would stand ashamed before the Hellespont, which he had crossed so easily, if he were to be stopped by this little ditch. It was not the last time the general's advice was disregarded.

The Persian battle order forced Alexander to shift his weight slightly toward the wings. He then ordered the attack. It began with a cavalry charge, and then the King drove his mount forward, leading the Companions and secured by cavalry and infantry on the flanks. For a time confusion held the river. The Persians saw the opportunity for which they had planned and rushed the King, conspicuous under his white double plume. There were two waves in this Persian charge: the first engaged the Macedonian point in the river, the second was a cavalry wedge down from the crest led by Mithridates, son-in-law of the Persian king. Alexander drove for Mithridates, ran him through the face. The rest of the Persian nobility, not committed to action before this moment, rushed upon Alexander. His spear broke. He secured another. Then with helmet nearly sheared off and his back turned to finish one Persian noble, another, Spithridates, raised his arm to decapitate the King from behind. Persian victory was averted when Cleitus stopped the fatal stroke by severing Spithridates' arm at the shoulder. Only then was there a concerted Macedonian charge up the bank to break into the Persian center. Where once the center might have withdrawn deliberately to surround the King, it broke, and with that the wings disintegrated. The King's forces rushed the mercenaries, who stood still and found themselves surrounded. They asked for quarter, showing their willingness to serve Alexander, yet all but about 2,000 were slaughtered. Only at great peril to themselves could Greeks serving for Persian pay oppose Alexander.

It is difficult to place much confidence in the traditional statements of losses on both sides, except that the Macedonian figure probably was lower than the Persian since the satraps lost the battle. More interesting is the fact that although suspiciously low,

Macedonian figures show greater casualties among the cavalry than the infantry, evidence that this was essentially a cavalry battle. The losses among the foot must have occurred substantially in the opening moments of the fight. The Persians lost the flower of their western leadership, though Memnon escaped. The 2,000 mercenaries spared from slaughter went off in chains to Macedonia, to forced labor. Alexander may have rationalized this act by appealing to his position as hegemon of the Corinthian League, against which these mercenary countrymen had been fighting. Yet, they were not turned over to the league itself for judgment. The King also sent 300 full sets of the armor seized from the Persians to Athens with orders to announce the dedication as having come "from Alexander and the Greeks, save Sparta." The theme of Greek liberation was still being sounded, but now the King had ignored two opportunities for directly involving the League of Corinth: the prisoners were sent to Macedonia and the armor to Athens. And soon he was to begin a completely independent policy for the Greeks of Asia Minor.

Appointing Calas, the relative of Harpalus, as satrap of Hellespontine Phrygia, Alexander and the army moved out to the south, well inland. This part of Phrygia was extremely important to the success of the expedition as the area through which all communications and supply by land would have to go, and the King could ill afford to secure only its coastal regions. Obviously enjoying special treatment, Chalcedon, Cyzicus, Pergamum, and some other cities of the area continued under Alexander—though perhaps after several months' break—to mint the autonomous Greek coinage they had struck under Persian rule.

As the army approached Sardis, the garrison commander surrendered the city. Alexander visited the acropolis as soon as he entered the walls and while there was persuaded by a thunderstorm to erect a temple to Zeus. When he departed from Sardis he left behind the kind of divided authority that the Persians had learned to exercise: a Macedonian satrap, a second Macedonian as general of the garrison, and a Greek to collect the tribute.

From Sardis, the King sent Calas and Alexander the Lyncestian, Calas' successor to the command of the Thessalian cavalry, into Memnon's territory.[4] They took with them the allied troops including those from the Peloponnesus, but excluding the Argives. Calas was the relative of the ill-destined Harpalus; Alexander, son of Aeropus the Lyncestian, who had saved himself by hailing Alexander king after Philip's death, and even so was later to be executed for treason, was the one possible rival for the throne. The Peloponnesians were Alexander's least reliable allied troops, or at least their homeland was the most likely to rebel against the Macedonians; yet the Argives were among his staunchest allies in the south, and Argos itself had long pursued policies that were favorable to northern and central Greece. In short, Alexander was using expendables for a hazardous reconnaissance in force.

Next came Ionia. At Ephesus, the King removed from office the Persian-supported oligarchs and restored the democratic faction to power. The people immediately went on a vengeful spree, cutting down those who had been responsible for the destruction of Philip's statue. Alexander waited until the ringleaders of the oligarchical faction were eliminated; then he halted the purge, much to his greater popularity among Ionian Greeks. With Ephesus stabilized, the King dispatched Parmenion on a tour of the remaining cities of Ionia north of Miletus. Everywhere, he restored democracies and canceled the tribute payable to the Persians.

After deputizing the acquisition of Priene to Parmenion, the Macedonian king moved on to Miletus, the outskirts of which he easily took. Meantime, some 160 ships of his Greek allies had moved southward to take up positions covering the harbor. Then a part of the fleet moved in to blockade the entrance to the harbor itself, effectively keeping out the Persian fleet when it came, despite its superiority in numbers. To break the blockade, the Persian fleet continuously offered to give battle. Parmenion began to weaken. When he spied an eagle sitting on shore, he insisted that this was the favorable sign for a naval engagement. He even volunteered to command it himself, arguing that a victory would have great value in destroying Persian naval communications and end their ability to raise an insurrection in Greece. Conversely, a Macedonian loss would not greatly profit the enemy because the Persians already had superiority at sea. Alexander's reply, however, illuminated another aspect of the problem: though they were few, the King ran the danger of losing his naval allies only to find them later fighting on the Persian side. He refused to make his enemies this present of allied valor and talent. As Alexander said, Parmenion had misread the sign of the eagle: the bird was sitting on the land, and on the land they would win their struggle against the Persians.

Miletus fell to the siege machinery of the Macedonians while the Greek fleet held the Persian at bay. During the closing moments of the fight, some Persians fled; most were killed; the remainder went into slavery. Milesians who appealed to Alexander's mercy were accepted as his allies. This special treatment was due to the city's long-standing importance.

Once Miletus was taken, the Persian ships gone, and the need for the naval screen at the harbor's mouth had passed, Alexander determined to abandon his fleet. Arrian offers a detailed explanation. The King had insufficient funds to maintain a fleet of such large proportions, which in any case was not equal to the Persian fleet and so was far more expensive than effective. Besides, now that the army was master of Asia, there was no need for ships. Seizure of the coastal cities would limit the effectiveness of the enemy's navy. Alexander must already have noticed the way in which Ionian contingents in Persian service returned to their cities once they fell. Tarn mentions Diodorus' statement as an added comment on the King's reasoning.[5] According to Diodorus, Alexander retained a small number of ships to serve as transport, primarily for his siege equipment. Among these was a contingent of twenty Athenian ships. We have already seen the importance of the city of Athens for the control of northern and southern Greece. Continued presence of Athenian ships would serve as hostages for the behavior and cooperation of this key city. The decision was justified, for in the period of the Persian counteroffensive, when Memnon was making every effort to stir up revolt in Greece against Alexander, he received little encouragement from Athens.

There are, however, other considerations. Asia, won with land troops, would be held with the same forces, though the issue was still not entirely settled. Halicarnassus was to give Alexander genuine difficulties. Moreover, a winter campaign in Lycia, Pamphylia, and Pisidia was yet to come. Without it, southern Asia Minor might never be secure. Also, many of the Persian ships were not actually based in Asia but in Phoenicia. If Alexander meant seriously to erase the fleet, he would have to take these cities, too, with his land troops. But immediately important was the fact that the geography of the interior presented sufficient threat to make any commander nervous. If the Macedonian hold on the Ionian cities was not to be maintained by sea, the mountains behind them and the easy valleys leading to the interior would have to be secured. A campaign into central Asia Minor was as necessary as leaving garrisons along the coast.

Departing from Miletus, Alexander moved on to the south to Halicarnassus, where he met serious resistance. After a difficult siege of several weeks the city fell, opening Caria to the Macedonians. During the time of Philip, Pixodarus had deposed Ada, widow of a former dynast, to seize the Carian throne for himself. In this position Pixodarus had sought a marriage alliance with the Macedonian royal house. Later, he had secured Persian support for his son to succeed him. Now the elderly suppliant, Ada, adopted Alexander as her son and sought his aid. In espousing her cause, Alexander was far from supporting democracy, but he was consistent in his policy of helping the party out of power to insure loyalty in his absence. He entrusted Ada with the duties of a satrap.

These arrangements at Halicarnassus ended the campaigning season for 334 B.C. Alexander endeared himself all the more to his Macedonians by sending the newly married men home to spend a few months with their wives before rejoining him in the spring. They were to bring as many recruits as possible when they returned. Cleander went to recruit new troops in the Peloponnesus. Alexander's frequent establishment of garrisons was beginning to tell against his forces. After these missions departed, Parmenion went back to Sardis with the Thessalian cavalry, the allies, and the baggage train. All were instructed to meet the King in Phrygia in the spring. Alexander, with a small but highly mobile force, would spend the winter campaigning against the rugged hill tribes of the southwestern corner of Asia Minor.

3. Conquest of the Interior

Once the situation at Halicarnassus was under control and dispositions made for the winter, Alexander with a small force began to push eastward on a campaign that would take him into Lycia, Pamphylia, and Pisidia. While at Phaselis in eastern Lycia, Alexander received an accusation of treachery against Alexander, son of Aeropus the Lyncestian. Evidently, the man had been the object of some suspicion when he was included with the Peloponnesians on the King's first long-range scouting mission. The accusation against him came from Parmenion, whose capture of a Persian messenger had disclosed the whole plot. According to the story, the Macedonian deserter Amyntas had appeared before the Persian king and offered Darius the name of the Lyncestian Alexander as the man most likely to agree to an assassination attempt. The Persian messenger then went off to meet the Lyncestian with the promise of great reward if he would kill the young King of Macedon. Alexander of Lyncestis was in Phrygia at the time; hence the messenger's capture by Parmenion. He revealed Darius' offer of 1,000 talents of gold and the throne of Macedonia for the murder of the King. Parmenion sent the messenger under guard to Alexander. It is not disclosed whether the message ever got to its intended recipient, or if he had in fact agreed to participate in the plan. Certainly, he never got the chance. Alexander ordered an immediate trial *in absentia* and endured a chiding for having appointed so doubtful a man to command the Thessalians. The Lyncestian was condemned. Alexander then dispatched a messenger of his own, with native dress and guides, to take a verbal message to Parmenion. Some scholars have considered the disguise evidence of Macedonian weakness in southwestern Asia Minor. Actually, Alexander probably employed the ruse more for fear of the Macedonians than of the enemy. The trial had called attention to the possibility of rebellion among the Thessalians, and there is little doubt that those close to the King believed a strong show of force under a claimant to the Macedonian throne had, with Persian help, a chance of creating general rebellion. But revolt, if a real threat, was ended before it began. Parmenion seized and imprisoned the Lyncestian.

From Phaselis Alexander moved along the coast in the direction of Pamphylia. Using his engineers to cut steps in the rock, Alexander sent a large portion of the infantry up the face of Mount Climax and across the heights to level ground. The King himself made his way with a small party along the narrow ledges and beaches far below. Since the mountain face drops almost straight into the sea, there are many points where water comes up to the face of the cliffs and passage usually is impossible. When a strong north wind blows, however, the level of the sea falls as the wind shifts the water outward. Thus, under optimum conditions of wind and timing in antiquity when the shoreline probably was higher than it is at present, it was possible to make one's way along the water's edge, wading where necessary. The wind, which had been blowing from the south, shifted at the right moment, and Alexander made his way along the bottom of the cliffs without mishap. Some said that divine intervention had changed the wind. Callisthenes, the official historian, made much of it in his dispatches to Greece. Propaganda aside, the King need only have known the relative shallowness of the coastal shelf and that the difference in water level due to north- and south-wind conditions was sufficient to offer safe passage. It is even possible that the normal day's variation in inward and outward breeze would be sufficient; the King had ample time to wait since the bulk of his forces had to climb across the face of the mountain.

Once again on level land, after passing Mount Climax, Alexander received the submission of Perga, first of the three cities that controlled Pamphylia. Next was Aspendus, like Perga away from the sea. Once past Aspendus on his way back to the shore at Side, the King learned that the second city had changed its mind about its easy submission. Returning to it, he doubled the terms for submission; Alexander was particularly anxious to receive more of the horses for which Aspendus was famous. The second visit completed, he marched to Side. It is worth noting that when the King left Pamphylia, he placed a garrison at Side on the shore, rather than at Aspendus, despite its temporary rebellion.

The beautiful and isolated coastal plain of Pamphylia is still one of the most pleasant locations in the Turkish Riviera, and at the time of Alexander's visit it must have been a true garden spot. Nearly sixty miles from east to west, the plain widens to a breadth of about eighteen miles at the eastern end. A series of mountain streams, in which even today clear and cold water abounds through the summer months, feed the valley. The name Pamphylia attests its favorable impression upon all comers. The area is formed by a coastal alluvium that straightens an inverse bend in the Taurus Mountains; the mountains in turn separate Pamphylia from the arid plains of the interior. There is only one good pass system leading north out of the valley, the one used today by the road to Burdur. Modern road engineers still have not challenged Mount Climax. For the most part, even yet the way to the east is only a dirt road that tops ridges thousands of feet above the sea as it makes its torturous way between one secluded cove and the next. Pamphylia was the only settled area between Lycia and Cilicia; its possession gave Alexander the southern coast of Asia Minor west of Cilicia.

From this and from Alexander's previous decision to go north, a clear pattern of conquest for Asia Minor had begun to emerge. The eastern portion of the southern coast was sealed between Side and the city later to be refounded and called Seleucia, modern Silifke. West of Silifke the road led away from the coast to Konya, ancient Iconium. Even in the days of Babylonian conquest, which got as far to the west as did the efforts of any pre-Persian empire, the Chaldean forces report nothing farther west than Pirindu, which must have been somewhere in the mountainous region about Silifke.[7] And the Persians, though they had an important settlement a few miles from Silifke, left the central southern coast alone. Pamphylia may have been questionably Greek (though usually regarded as under Rhodian influence, it was linguistically distinct as late as the writing of the second chapter of the Book of Acts); it was Persian even less.

Alexander must have been aware of these geographical considerations, for even before leaving Halicarnassus he had arranged to meet Parmenion in Phrygia to the north in the spring. There was no intention of going directly east from Pamphylia to Cilicia and Phoenicia; a lonely medieval fortress improbably located on the beach at modern Anamur controls the one small coastal valley in the entire region, and in the process shows the true nature of problems of defense for this region. The garrison at Side was for purposes of defense and had nothing to do with penalizing a recalcitrant ally. Otherwise, Aspendus would have received the troops. Side, like Anamur right on the beach, received the forces whose chief task it was to repel invasion from the area. The foresight of this coastal tour that preceded the rendezvous in Phrygia makes it clear that Alexander's campaign intended to blanket important military and economic areas of Asia Minor. He had begun by coming inland to secure Hellespontine Phrygia in the north. The cities of Ionia on the coast came next, and then the southwest corner of Asia Minor was crossed and Pamphylia secured. Then the King was ready to head for the inland plateau.

The road from the plain to the north passes a turn leading through a side canyon to the west even before it has passed the upper reaches of the plain itself. The way through this canyon proceeds in the general direction of Halicarnassus, and therefore was not at this stage a natural route for the army. Still, it was blocked at its Pamphylian end by the city of Termessus, some six miles up canyon from the plain. The city lies at the upper end of a mountain bowl, high on the southern flank of the narrow valley. Just below the city the valley narrows as it makes a sharp turn, and the road leads up over a ridge between two sharply rising humps. The people of Termessus had fortified these two points and thus could effectively block the road. Fortifications from the Roman period still stand here three miles below the city to show how well the fortifications worked; the barrier was the chief source of revenue for the earliest city, as travelers no doubt paid for the privilege of going west this way to avoid the extra eighty or so miles of the closest detour. The city of Termessus therefore had a two-stage defense. The first was the gate across the road below the city, and the second was the wall behind which the city perched in the steep upper canyon. Alexander was able to force passage through the lower defenses and so to free the road to traffic, but lacking siege machinery on this winter campaign, he decided that the effort to take the upper town was not worth its prospective results. That he was satisfied with having breached the road fortifications indicates a primary interest in communications. By going north to Celaenae he could control the more northerly route west into the upper Maeander Valley and so dominate the whole southwestern corner of Asia Minor.

Moving from Celaenae where he appointed Antigonus satrap of Phrygia, Alexander needed only to go straight north along the valley to arrive at the upper end of the marshy plain that would lead his army around east and north to the upper reaches of the Sangarius River. Then the march could proceed in easy stages down the river following its bend to the north and come out on the central plateau area to which he had sent Parmenion and the others to wait for spring.

The route led directly to Gordium. As the King approached the city, he undoubtedly could see a number of the large tumuli hiding dead Phrygian kings of some three centuries earlier. The city once had been the capital of the large state we follow Greeks in calling Phrygia. It probably had known itself by a name something like Mushku, for so it appears in Assyrian annals. We are told that Alexander was immediately seized with a desire to visit the upper city.

Up in this higher town stood a wagon, probably two-wheeled, whose yoke was fastened to the tongue with a large, elaborate

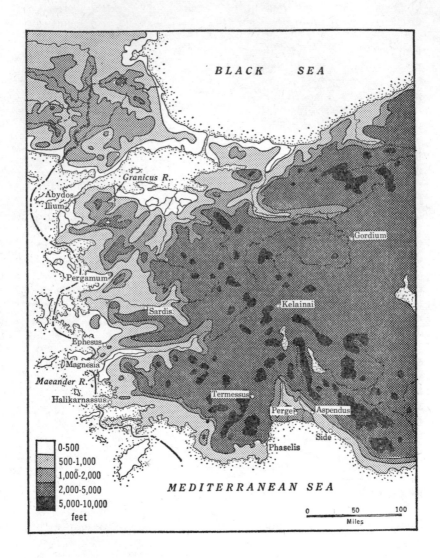

knot that no one had been able to untie. According to legend, the man who loosed this knot would rule Asia. Alexander promptly undid the knot. There are two versions. In one, he sought in vain for a loose end with which to begin, drew his sword, and slashed the knot. The other story is that he withdrew the dowel holding the knot in position on the tongue, and then unraveled the knot, which was of cornel bark that clung tightly together. The two stories offer antiquity's comment on Alexander's character: he was clever enough to solve a problem that had baffled all others, or he was direct enough to attack with force an otherwise insoluble problem.

Alexander had gained too much in his training from his father, from his own settlement of affairs in Greece and the north, and now in the conquest of Asia Minor, for him not to have intended some meaning for this episode at Gordium. To the north and west of Gordium lay Hellespontine Phrygia, that part of Asia Minor closest to Macedonia. The lowest-level route eastward from Byzantium proceeds directly to the lower Sangarius. The way upriver turns first south, then east, and south again, until it reaches Gordium. The city therefore lay directly across Alexander's best line of transport and occupied a favorable position from which to move toward the Hellespont from the interior. The city lies at a place where the river crosses a rolling and now quite arid plain. It is roughly at the center of the level plateau area, which gives access west and south to the upper valley systems leading directly to the Ionian coast. A strong military establishment at Gordium dominated the western plateau, and with it access to the coastal cities. Further, there are no effective natural boundaries between Gordium and the southeast until the Taurus Mountains are reached. Earlier Phrygian interest in the east is well attested by the appearance of Mita of Mushku in Assyrian annals down to the time of Mita's accommodation with Sargon of Assyria (722-705 B.C.). This orientation toward Mesopotamia receives further support from the excavations at Gordium, which have uncovered various artifacts showing eastern influences. Finally, Alexander himself had just come from the south. Firm possession of Gordium gave him control of western Asia Minor. In this sense, the legend of the Gordian Knot was true, yet in reality by taking Gordium Alexander had tied a knot rather than loosed one since both the northwest and the southwest had now been enclosed—and with them, all Ionia.

At Gordium the campaign for Ionia ended, but the war had only begun. It was quite clear that a fleet was indeed needed and that the bases of the Persian fleet in Phoenicia would have to be taken, for by now the Persian counteroffensive was well under way. Memnon had been active since Alexander had departed Halicarnassus for Lycia. Now, positions had been reversed: Alexander was in command in the interior, but the seaboard again was open to Persian attack. Memnon began by taking Chios after the previously dispossessed oligarchic faction betrayed it to him. He was able to seize all of Lesbos except the city of Mitylene, and against this he laid siege. In this siege, Alexander enjoyed his greatest luck of the campaign so far, for Memnon died. Yet, the admiral's plans for the counteroffensive extended beyond his own death; he had appointed his nephew Pharnabazus as his successor, subject to confirmation by the Great King, and Pharnabazus was prepared to continue the effort. He took Mitylene by agreement. There would be no destruction if the citizens would dismiss the mercenaries Alexander had left behind, drop their alliance with the Macedonian King, and accept Persian-appointed tyrants and Persian tribute levies. Pharnabazus then moved north with his fleet. Tenedus was disposed to honor its agreement with Alexander and its position in the League of Corinth, but when Macedonian relief appeared to be nowhere in sight, the island surrendered.

The situation was serious. Alexander had ordered Hegelochus to the coast to raise a new fleet, but the general had accomplished little outside the Hellespont, where he was more or less fixed by Alexander's need for secure communications. Then when Pharnabazus sent Datames to operate among the Cyclades with some ten Phoenician warships, rumor in Greece had it that a full-scale Persian invasion was soon to come. Antipater began to organize Greek naval defenses, and the two forces met at the island of Siphnus. Datames was defeated by Antipater's fleet, but he was able to escape, and the Persian fleet continued to operate without any further opposition from Macedon through the entire year 333. The chief effects of these operations were felt among the islands. Alexander retained the land masses and maintained his communications, but it was not until early 332 that the Macedonian fleet could report headway. As Alexander came away from the loosened chariot at Gordium, Asia may have appeared secure, but there were some things to ponder concerning Greece itself.

Curtius tells us that Alexander had not yet learned of the death of Memnon.

East and north of Gordium lay Ancyra, the largest remaining city of the central plateau area. While there, Alexander received an embassy of the Paphlagonians from the Pontic Mountains to the north, between the plateau and Black Sea. They offered submission and requested that the Macedonian army not come through their territory. Since it lay outside of his line of march, the King agreed. Though serious fighting in this direction occurred after his death, Alexander never controlled either these mountains or Armenia to the east. Moving southeast of Ancyra, the army next entered Cappadocia, which was left under the control of its satrap Sabictas, who may have been a Persian. If so, the King may have been taking advantage of the isolation of the area, kept from the west by his own strength and from the east by the Armenian mountains, to test the device of relieving his already overtaxed administrative staff by adding Persians to Greeks and Macedonians in the command structure.

Now only the Cilician Gates stood between the Macedonians and the plains beyond. Ever since the days of the Hittite Empire, this narrow defile had funneled through itself armies moving between the central highlands and the rich coastal plains of Cilicia. It led in part among awesome shadows between massive cliffs as it gave access through the Taurus Mountains from plateau to plain. The modern railroad line follows the torturous line of the canyon itself, but twice it must tunnel through the side to negotiate the narrow chasm. In pre-Assyrian days, forgotten engineers had provided a detour by cutting a tight shortcut into a parallel canyon on the lower, Cicilian, side of the main ridge. Here the way was narrowest; at this point are the Cilician Gates proper. In and near it a handful could stand off an army by rolling down stones or by taking advantage of countless opportunities for devastating enfilade fire from side canyons against the flank of a column slimmed to four abreast by the gorge. Alexander was quite properly concerned about the effect of even a small force of defenders.

As the army moved off the plateau and into the mountains, the King went ahead with a scouting force to view the situation at the lower end of the cut. He apparently left the main body of his troops back where the gorge was still wide, probably at the point where the track left the original canyon. Alexander and his small force entered the narrows under cover of darkness, all weapons at the ready including drawn bows. Upon learning that Alexander was present in person, the defending force fled. Another reason for their flight may have been that they had just learned that the Persian commander at Tarsus was withdrawing and would leave them isolated if they remained. In any case, Alexander seems to have learned at this point that Tarsus was to be abandoned after being laid waste. He immediately sent back for the rest of his army, and an all-night march brought them all out on the upper foothills at dawn. From there they could see Tarsus and much of Cilicia.

4. *Cilicia*

Descent from the foothills above Tarsus was rapid. Parmenion raced ahead to halt destruction of the city. For the most part, the effort succeeded. The Persians withdrew, having lost again the opportunity to pursue the scorched-earth policy Memnon had advocated. Within a few hours Alexander, too, was in the city.

Of all the many rivers and streams that crossed this comparatively lush coastal plain, the one that went directly through the city of Tarsus was said to be the most clear and cold. This was the Cydnus. Alexander was tired, hot, and possibly suffering from an upper respiratory infection now greatly irritated by the rapid ride through the dusty middle of a summer's day. He plunged in. The water was cold enough to precipitate a chill. Shock, combined with exhaustion and infection, caused the King to faint. He was taken from the stream looking half-dead.

This time the situation was more than serious, not only because of the King's seizure, the extent of which was not yet known, but also because of the continued state of Alexander's affairs. Little time had elapsed since his decision to reorganize a fleet in the Aegean. Although his intent was to use Ionian ships, saving time over what would have been necessary to secure a fleet from the Greek mainland, the plan was recent and had not yet had time for great effect. Alexander may not yet have known of the death of Memnon. Greece was increasingly restive, especially Sparta, whose rebelliousness was to grow into open revolt. Rumors in Athens had the troubled young King delaying in Tarsus, in want of everything, fearful of Darius who was on his way west. Indeed, news of the Great King's massive preparations may have arrived in Cilicia, for within a short time the Persian king himself was to appear.

After various unsuccessful efforts to alleviate Alexander's raging fever and insomnia, the physician Philip stepped forward. He was an old friend of the King's family, as much concerned for the well-being of his beloved young charge as for the fate of army and mission. He offered a potion, which he said would work where others had failed. The King was about to drink from the cup when a letter from Parmenion was thrust into his hand. The general had just learned that Philip was in Persian pay, that he had accepted an offer of 1,000 talents and the promise of one of the Great King's daughters in return for poisoning the Macedonian leader. The young King simply gave the letter to Philip without comment as he drained the cup, his eyes searching Philip's face for reaction. But there came only calm advice that if the remainder of his orders were also followed, the patient would recover. He did, but slowly. The King had been seriously ill, and he still was. At least he was not dead. His protestations of recovery threw the badly shaken army into elated demonstrations of their regard for the physician. Alexander settled back to recuperate. The length of his stay in Cilicia is not known precisely. It may have been a month or two; at least it was several weeks before the army began again to move.

The first item of business as Alexander returned to his duties was an order for Parmenion to proceed with a strong force of allies and Greek mercenaries to the Syrian Gates. This is the steep pass that provides an outlet near the southern tip of Cilicia, where the plain has narrowed to a mile or so in width at modern Iskanderun (ancient Alexandria). The pass gives access to the 'Amq Valley. Because this valley offers a low-level route along the Orontes River into Syria and easy access to the great Mesopotamian plain, the pass leading to it bore the name Syrian Gates. With its southern approach flanked by guards on the canyon sides, the pass would be closed to Darius. Apparently, Alexander did not realize that there was another route into Cilicia from the east: the Amanus Pass, due east of Tarsus.

Alexander then proceeded west to the city of Anchialus where he found remains of a large city and the "tomb of Sardanapalus." Either on or near the tomb the Assyrian king was depicted on a relief. An accompanying inscription offered advice from Sardanapalus, son of Anakundaraxes, "who had built the cities of Ancialus and Tarsus together in one day and had learned that there was nothing more to life than food, drink, and women." The passerby should busy himself with these things alone; all else was worth only a snap of the fingers. In illustration of this, the relief showed the King in the act of snapping his fingers. Arrian says that "Assyrians" at Anchialus explained the inscription to Alexander.

There are many problems. The most obvious is that nothing could be more out of character for Ashurbanipal, who usually is considered to be the king known to the Greeks as Sardanapalus, or for any other Assyrian king likely to have placed his tomb in Cilicia. There is an interesting possible solution in the reliefs of Esarhaddon at Nahr el-Kalb and Zendshirli (ancient Sam'al), where the King is shown holding his right hand up before his chest, fist clenched, thumb up. This might suggest that he had just snapped his fingers except that from his clenched fist drop two ropes, the other ends of which run through the lips of two suppliants who are pleading for mercy. Such a relief, with ropes and suppliants obliterated, might have existed at Anchialus. Thus Alexander's "Assyrians" may only have remembered the tradition of the name, itself interestingly garbled, and used it along with what they thought they saw on the relief to pretend to read a nearly defaced inscription. Unreliable details aside, Alexander at least now had evidence that he had entered territory over which once Assyrians had ruled.

The Macedonian forces then moved to Soloi. The King fined the city 200 talents of silver because of its still pro-Persian sentiments. He also left a garrison there, and Arrian believes this too was because of Soloi's hostility, but it may have resulted from its location on the coast. This is the city the Romans under Pompey later rebuilt and called Pompeiopolis. Still unexcavated, it offers a tattered row of columns leading down to the harbor and bits and pieces of buildings in the tough grass and bush.

An interesting pattern appears here with the cities of Cilicia and southern Asia Minor. Soloi, along with the towns of Pamphylia and Phaselis, through which Alexander had passed late in the preceding year, were founded by Rhodes during the period of Assyrian interest in Cilicia. Rhodian pottery, found in all these places, attests continued contact over a long period of time. The inland cities of Cilicia may have been founded in a much earlier period by mainland Greeks. Arrian says that Mallus, east of Tarsus, was founded by Argos and that Alexander knew of this and respected the tradition by remitting the tribute owed Darius, since the Macedonian king also claimed descent from the Heracleidae of Argos. Yet, if these cities had originally been Greek, they had long since forgotten details of origin and language.[6] The earlier and actually less Greek cities were apparently more favorably disposed to Alexander than the later and perhaps consciously Rhodian ones, which may have reflected the hostility toward Macedonia of the Persians' Greek mercenaries.

There was more trouble for the King from the people of the hills to the northwest of Soloi. Alexander spent seven days on a military demonstration in these hills, which had also offered resistance to the Babylonian invasions of the early sixth century.[7]

Upon returning to Soloi from this minor hill campaign, Alexander learned that the Persian counteroffensive had been blunted at Halicarnassus. His generals on the west coast were beginning to move ahead. It was the first break in what for months had been a difficult problem, and the news was greeted with general celebration. The King sacrificed to Asclepius, the god of healing, and held games with competition in both athletic and poetic events. The army marched in review. The episode smacks of an effort to tone up and put back on its feet the expedition, which had nearly faltered at Tarsus. When the Macedonians left Soloi, the King gave the city a democratic constitution, a further illustration that the institution of a garrison was more a military expedient than punishment for the city.

Upon returning to Tarsus, Alexander was ready to enter the final phase of the conquest of Asia Minor: the establishment of permanent administrative arrangements. The delay in Cilicia was long enough for the King completely to recuperate from his illness; perhaps he also had deliberately awaited news of generals and fleet on the west coast. But during this time he and his subordinates were working out administrative and financial details.[8]

Both the nature of Cilicia itself and the prospect of leaving it for further operations demanded the settlement of a number of issues. As Alexander must have realized, Cilicia was an important crossroads. To the north, through the Cilician Gates, lay the route along which Alexander's vital line of communications extended, and along which he had lately come. The security of this route, where it narrowed to go through the gates and beyond them where it widened into Cappadocia, Galatia, and Phrygia, was a matter of supreme importance. A few very brief hints indicate that the King entrusted the control of these areas to some of his most capable people. To the west lay the comparatively difficult but nevertheless possible route through modern Silifke. There the way turns north to make the climb up the Taurus passes to cross over to Konya on the plain. This is the area Alexander had bracketed but not visited with his campaign in Pamphylia and his later approach through the Cilician Gates. South lay the road through the Syrian Gates, Alexander's next line of march, access to which he had already established by sending Parmenion to take and hold the Gates. It is likely that the King knew most about the routes to north, west, and south, but the road east presented a problem for the Macedonian expedition. This way leads through the Amanus Pass to modern Islahiye, three miles distant from Zendschirli, or ancient Sam'al. From Sam'al, as from the southern outlet of the Syrian Gates, easy and nearly direct access may be gained to the Syrian and Mesopotamian plains. What is more, the way is quite easy behind the Amanus from this pass to the outlet of the Syrian Gates. It is difficult to imagine that Alexander could have spent so long a time in Cilicia and not have been aware of the Amanus Pass. There was hint of its existence in the line of settlements and the road leading east towards the mountains, not to mention the possibility of local intelligence concerning the pass.

In addition to being a crossroads, Cilicia was and had been greatly important for its own sake as well. As Alexander was at least dimly aware, it had been under Assyrian domination between about 730 and 630 B.C. Kue, as the Assyrians knew Cilicia, was important both in its own right, and because it was the key to further efforts to the northwest. For them, the question was not so much a matter of further expansion in that direction as defense against the northwest. Also important were the "silver mountain," which Assyrian annals place just north of Kue, and the sources of iron, spread through the Taurus and into Cappadocia and Armenia. The reasons for Assyrian presence in the past may not have been known to Alexander, but the fact of it was clear. Cilicians had enjoyed virtual independence during the final years of the tottering Assyrian Empire, but this autonomy was first limited by the Medes after 600 and then ended about 586 when the Babylonians appeared and remained in control until 539. Thereafter, the area was Persian. Alexander's only hint of Assyrian in-

terest in Cilicia may have been the "Sardanapalus" relief at Anchialus, revealing little of the Babylonian interlude. But he could
have known the tradition from Herodotus that one Syennesis of
Cilicia had, along with Labynetus of Babylon, helped to arrange
the famous peace between the Lydians and the Medes at the
Halys River in eastern Phrygia at the time of the eclipse in 585
B.C. And he could have pondered this story of a Cilician political
structure sufficiently important to be an interested party in the
division of all Asia Minor between Lydians and Medes.

Moreover, the King had not far to look for local explanation of
this past importance in the natural characteristics of Cilicia itself.
The area is a triangular pocket, the sides of which are the Taurus
Mountains to the north, Amanus Range to the east, and the coast
to the south and west. It is accessible by land only through three
easily held passes or an arduous march from the west. To the
south, it is shielded by the sea. Within the rough right triangle
thus formed, the land is rich and agriculturally self-sustaining; it
is still some of the best land in modern Turkey. In Roman times
it was the center of an active textile industry, when its capital
Tarsus could also boast a school of philosophy; the reference to
Tarsus as "no mean city" by Paul, the apostle, is well known.
Finally, although nicely protected by mountains, the sea offered
easy communication, attested by the frequency of Cypriote materials in the eastern portion of the area, and by Rhodian in the
west, both of which came in by sea. Alexander's recognition of the
fact may explain his garrison at coastal Soloi, as noted previously.

It is therefore not surprising to discover Alexander completing
arrangements here that had much to do with the control and security of Asia Minor as a whole. Unfortunately, precise information is not available for the supply route. Antigonus, who had
been made satrap of Greater Phrygia, was soon to have his hands
full with Persian survivors of the Battle of Issus and with problems of securing actual control of some of the peripheral areas
along Alexander's march through Asia Minor, as in the case of
Lycaonia to the southwest. More immediately in Cilicia, Alexander appointed Balacrus satrap.[9] The three years to elapse before
Menes appeared in Cilicia as military commander would indicate
that Balacrus was unusually entrusted with a combined military
and civil command, testimony of the importance the King attached to this area. And here Alexander began a new coinage, his
first within the conquered territories. Many of the Greek cities of

Asia Minor had been allowed to continue their own coinage, which in fact had for some time circulated within the Persian Empire as the chief currency aside from shekels and the purely Persian gold darics.[10] Supplemented in varying degrees by satrapal issues, these coins probably formed a substantial part of the taxes from the satrapies, which Persians once, and Alexander now, collected. Tarsus and Soloi together contributed heavily to the satrapal issues; the coinage of Tarsus was particularly large, doubtless for the same reasons that persuaded Alexander of the area's importance. Alexander ended the coinage of Soloi but increased the activity of the mint at Tarsus by beginning there an imperial Macedonian issue, the first since that of his father, Philip.[11] Now, the King would have Tarsus as a base from which to pay his troops. Its mint quickly came to rank with those at Pella and Amphipolis, which for a time had continued Philip's coins posthumously.

As Alexander left Tarsus to go across the Cilician plain still green in autumn, his progress was virtually a triumphal procession. There were frequent sacrifices to the gods along the way. While at Mallus, Alexander received news of Darius. The Persian Great King, with an army that beggared description, was camped at Sochoi, just two days' march from the Syrian Gates.

CHAPTER III

Issus to Egypt

1. The Battle of Issus

UPON RECEIVING INFORMATION THAT DARIUS WAS ENCAMPED AT Sochoi, Alexander moved southward from Mallus toward Issus and the Syrian Gates. News of Persians was not unexpected, for Darius had been long in coming. Now the issue between the King of Macedon and the Great King would be decided by action on the field. Whatever its complications, the Battle of Issus was less than four days away.

Few battles of antiquity have had greater literary attention than the one fought on the narrow plain at Issus. The ancient sources are confusing: Diodorus misplaces important items in the terrain and fails to notice that Darius fought from Alexander's rear. Curtius appears to have visited the site, which in part led Tarn to suppose Curtius wrote from a special "mercenaries source," an account left by one of the Greeks serving with Darius. This, however, now has been challenged by Pearson,[1] and certainly Curtius beclouds otherwise interesting and perhaps accurate statements by predicating impossibilities by the Persians and naiveté to Alexander. What we have of Callisthenes reports only the battle order and the course of the conflict, repeating or perhaps initiating the hopelessly exaggerated numbers for the Persian troops, for which he was severely taken to task by the practical Polybius.[2] Arrian alone presents a rational picture, though he appears mistaken about some aspects of the terrain. His mistakes have been repeated in many modern accounts.

A second reason for difficulties with the battle appears after consideration of the ground on which it was fought. The area consists entirely of an alluvial plain north of modern Iskanderun and just past the point where oil tanks now perch on the rounded hill that approaches the sea to form the Jonah Pass. The plain doubtless is wider now than in antiquity. Very likely, the rate of increase in width has been greater at the mouths of the streams that cross it. There are many such streams, and all dry in the fall now, as in Alexander's time. The two main draws, the Deli and the Payas, are simply the largest ones to have cut haphazardly through the sandy gravel. Their positions inspire little confidence as a means of locating the battle.

Still, points of strategy based on fixed land forms, considerable reliance upon Arrian's narrative, and close attention to problems of time offer a reasonable approach. First, the land forms. The plain at Issus is a southern extension of Cilicia. It lies beyond low hills through which cuts a nearly level pass where large sections of a Roman aqueduct still flank the modern road. These low hills would not be suitable ground for holding a phalanx in formation during a battle, but also they would not have stopped an army before the erection of the imposing late medieval fortress that still looks down from the sharpest rise to the east of the shallow pass. The hills define the base of an elongated triangle that lies between the Amanus and the sea and turns slightly as it points south toward Iskanderun. The triangle is about eight miles wide at its base and stretches nearly twenty-five miles as it curves gently from east to south. It is squeezed to nothing by the low hills of the Jonah Pass, which again offer a poor site for an infantry battle but no real obstacle to the passage of an army. The western side of the triangle, the coast, may have moved farther out since Alexander's day, but except for about a mile on either side of the mouth of the Payas, the present coastline is probably parallel to the ancient. The triangle has grown wider since antiquity, but its general configuration cannot have greatly changed. South of the Jonah Pass, the coastal plain spreads out again for another twenty miles. At the north end of this strip lies Iskanderun, whose name attests Alexander's passing.

Above Iskanderun a defile leading to the Beilan Pass, antiquity's Syrian Gates, rises sharply enough to present a genuine threat to an army coming south if the top were adequately held. Alexander's men had held the top for some time since his orders to Parmenion to take it, issued upon the King's recovery from his illness at Tarsus. The other side of the gates is a more gentle canyon. Arrian's "Myriandrus" [3] could more easily be located here than at modern Beilan, which clings desperately to the steep side of the abrupt northern approach. Like the Cilician Gates, there is here no real alternative route for turning its defenders' position, although unlike the northern approach to Tarsus, it requires serious climbing from either direction.

Back beyond Issus and the low hills marking its plain, it is possible to turn eastward to the Amanican Gates, the Amanus Pass, which we have noted before. The western approach to the pass can be gained by a busy but not difficult climb; the east is a dizzying drop little different from the rest of the Amanus face except for its lower height. The natural advantage this offers for defense against an eastern approach, however, is marred by the fact that there are alternative routes, about three miles apart. The modern railroad from Konya to Damascus takes one, the automobile road the other.

East of the Amanus the land is open and flat, offering easy travel between the eastern approaches of the Syrian and Amanican Gates. The two passes are about sixty miles apart, a three- or four-day march. Sochoi, where Darius had been staying, doubtless lay at the edge of the mountains—there are no foothills—in the vicinity of modern Hassa. There, it would be midway on a virtually straight line between the two passes.

Darius' preparations appear in great detail in Curtius, more briefly in Diodorus. Assyrian campaign experience concerning the amount of time required for such a march would show that the Persian king must have left Babylon around midsummer, when it was clear to him that Alexander was coming east from Gordium. He called to arms the troops that regularly formed the Persian army. These would be primarily his household guard and personal support troops. Although the Persians had used the western satrapal levies along with Greek mercenaries at the Granicus, and they were to rely largly upon eastern levies later at Gaugamela, at Issus Alexander fought Darius' own army.

It is difficult to determine the precise nature of Darius' forces. However, several types are mentioned; these may serve as a general indicator of their composition. Foremost in Persian eyes were the cavalry under Nabarzanes. These mounted troops, protected by a coat of light mail and armed with javelins, were the core of Darius' bodyguard and his household defense. Their numbers were undoubtedly considerable, due to the nature of Persian government, which always had to be ready to deal with marauding tribes inside the boundaries of the empire and pressures from without. They were the elite backbone of the Persian striking force in an empire to whose vast distances the time between the

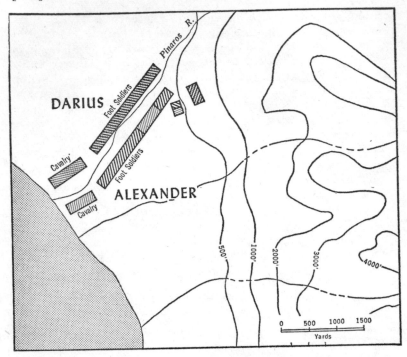

battle of the Granicus River and that at Issus is ample testimony. News of the defeat of the satraps; the decision to meet the threat with imperial troops; the organization of the army; and the march west may be assumed to have filled the fifteen or so months between these two events.

The Persian infantry consisted primarily of the Cardaces, about whom scholars have been much in doubt. In all probability, they were light-armed foot soldiers, possibly entirely made up of younger men. The fact that Darius' battle order placed them behind a screen of archers, which no phalanx would require and which he did not use to protect the Greek mercenaries, would indicate that they were not hoplites. The body of infantry upon which the Persians mostly relied, however, were the Greek mercenaries, functioning as a phalanx more than 10,000 in number. They were not the 30,000 given in our sources, but about 10,000 are known to have escaped.

The total number of Persian troops cannot have been the 600,-

ooo Macedonian propaganda claimed for them. Between 40,000 and 50,000 would be more likely. The size of ancient armies was a function of the logistics by which they could be supplied and the ability of subordinate commanders to control their troops and remain responsive to general direction. As techniques in both areas were perfected throughout antiquity, the size of field armies steadily grew, but it did not surpass the 60,000 mark until the end of the fourth century B.C. If Darius' army actually was larger than Alexander's, which Macedonian strategy would indicate was the case, it was only slightly so. Whatever advantage Darius might have had in quantity was probably offset by a lack of efficiency in controlling troops beyond the optimum number for his command structure. In fact, Alexander's army of some 47,000 at the time of the start of the expedition probably represents something very close to that optimum figure, since he had opportunity of increasing its size but did not, and more than once showed a willingness to allow those who wished to return home. Nevertheless, it should be noted that he was careful to receive enough to keep his strength close to that number.

Taking Alexander's information at Mallus that Darius was at Sochoi, two days away from the Syrian Gates as a starting point, the movements of the two armies can be fairly well established by geographical considerations. Alexander may have thought the Amanus Pass could not be held. An enemy with superior numbers scattered through the surrounding hills could not be controlled, and no phalanx could function well in the narrow canyons. There was one important side pass and too many smaller ones.

Moreover, the haste with which the Macedonians made for the Syrian Gates shows he may have thought he could catch Darius at Sochoi. He left his sick and wounded in camp at Issus in order to hasten the march. Two days later he was through the Gates. Arrian mistakenly says Alexander went through the Gates to Myriandrus, because he has confused the Syrian Gates with the Jonah Pass. Once through the pass on the second evening, Alexander was held down by a storm that lasted through the night and seems to have kept him at the spot through most of the third day as he awaited opportunity to proceed to Sochoi, probably unaware that the Amanus Pass was every bit as accessible as the Syrian Gates from Sochoi. This storm, which did not hinder Darius, was local and is thus further evidence for Alexander's position in the pass rather than down on the coast at Myriandrus.

During the first two days, Darius made his way to the Amanus Pass, probably near modern Bahce. Passing through it, he came down into Cilicia and turned south to Issus on the third day. There he massacred some of the sick and wounded Alexander had left behind. He made sure the ambulatory would not fight again by having their hands cut off and the stumps seared. He then sent them ahead along Alexander's line of departure to make sure that word of his mighty presence would come to the rest of the Macedonians.

When Alexander learned that Darius had slipped in behind him, he hurried back through the gates in the late afternoon of this third day. He then sent some ships along the coast to see if the report was true. He had taken up position at Jonah Pass when the ships returned to report that Darius was indeed at Issus. Curtius accurately states that by this time the King could see the situation for himself, for in the dusk thousands of Persian camp-fires began to appear at the other end of the coastal triangle.

Alexander addressed his men as they stood atop the low hill looking at the myriad tiny lights in the distance. The extent of the enemy forces was perhaps unknown, but they would be fighting in defiles that could be used to keep Darius from full deployment. If they won, they should have defeated the Great King himself, not just his underlings as had been the case at the Granicus. After so great an accomplishment at the expense of the Persian king—now with greater enthusiasm than accuracy—nothing would be left but to rule all Asia and to put an end to their many labors. And here their battle- and travel-hardened abilities would be ranged against Asiatic softness; moreover, they had an Alexander matching strategy with a Darius. There may be something to this last. At this point, Alexander did have precise knowledge of the terrain that lay between them; he had just been over it. His forces would be going north into an opening triangle. They could proceed far enough for full deployment, but not too far lest they offer unlimited field for Persian cavalry. The high ground to the right would be crucial if a flanking movement should develop from the Persian left. But the level ground between, sharply defined at either side by hills and sea and steadily narrowing to the Macedonians' rear, was nearly ideal. The phalanx could operate efficiently, and if pushed back would be concentrated instead of broken by the terrain itself.

At dawn, Alexander marched north, his troops in column.

Moving slowly, he called one after another of his units up on line as the space widened, keeping the plain filled. Perhaps he could entice Darius into the wedge.

The distance covered by the army moving north depends upon the location of the point at which Alexander's front was spread to his liking. There is general agreement in the literary sources that this point was just a few hundred yards south of the Pinarus River, for there Alexander halted in the hope that the Persians would charge. The river, however, had already been chosen by Darius, who sat tight. The Persians intended to use the river as a defense behind which to withstand a Macedonian charge. Darius' selection of the spot is a good indication that here his own troops were spread to his liking. Once Alexander's troops were on line, he continued to move slowly forward, using hand signals to halt progress in order to allow his front to redress itself evenly after passing various obstacles. The location of the meeting, that is, the precise location of the Pinarus River, is much debated. It cannot be as some have urged, a matter of the time required to march north from the Jonah Pass, for Alexander was moving slowly with frequent pauses. Polybius' comments on the spacing of such troops[4] would indicate that Alexander required approximately a three-mile front to bring his army up on line with 5,000 horse eight deep and 35,000 foot sixteen deep.[5] The exact number of his forces is not known, except that he had used a number of men for garrison duties and had lost a few. At the present day, this requirement of a three-mile front is more than met at the Payas stream bed, some nine miles north of the Jonah Pass. The Macedonians could easily have come this far by midafternoon, moving in slow stages. If the two armies were roughly the same size, Darius would have come to about the same location.

As the gap narrowed, the two armies were drawn up in similar fashion. Darius had been at the river most of the day in a fixed position. Nabarzanes and the cavalry were on the right, next to the sea. If they could outflank the Macedonian phalanx, they would be able to drive it into the hills, where it would lose formation and the men could be ridden down. The Persian center was held by the something over 10,000 Greek mercenaries. Between them and the cavalry on the right, were the Cardaces; in front of them, the archers. A detachment of infantry had taken up position in the hills on the Persian left, in advance of the river. The Persian rear was occupied by the Asiatic levies, whose number is doubtful. All modern streams in the Issus plain considered, the banks of the river were at best about five feet high, though very likely they were for the most part nearly vertical. Where they were low or broken, the Persians had erected palisades. Under horses' hooves, the packed sand and gravel that formed the banks was sure to crumble; the advantage was only temporary.

Alexander worked out his battle order as he proceeded north. His care in filling the plain as it widened was a security measure against an early Persian skirmish. First the phalanx spread from sea to hills with cavalry at the rear. Then the cavalry Companions took the wings, ultimately coming up even with the front on the right; beyond them were lancers and archers. As soon as the young King was close enough to perceive the Persian cavalry next to the sea, he ordered the Thessalian and allied cavalry to sweep around behind the line to take up position on his left opposite the Persian horse. More lancers and light horse were kept to the rear on the right, facing the hills, to meet Darius' foot detachment there. Alexander placed himself with the Companions, commanding the whole right wing. The phalanx on the left was under Craterus, but Parmenion commanded the entire left wing.

On the Persian side, once his order was set, Darius recalled the cavalry screen he previously had placed in front of the river. Alexander had space sufficient for full battle formation in the last thousand yards south of the river. At this place, the line of hills turns west and briefly runs parallel to the coast. There was a preliminary skirmish with the Persian detachment in the hills, who fled to higher ground. Alexander was then content simply to hold them in the hills with a few light horse, as he continued slowly to advance.

While still well away from the enemy, the King called for a last halt. Ptolemy reports (through Arrian) that the Macedonians considered Darius a man of little spirit when the Persians had not charged by this time. Actually Ptolemy must have known that the Great King's generals were well aware of the narrowing field behind Alexander and wished to have the full thousand yards in which to fight. Alexander used the brief respite to rest his men and to pass along the front in the quietly ominous air of the hot November afternoon. He called upon all the leaders by name, even down to the rank of captain, exhorting them to do their best. Those among the mercenaries who had already distinguished themselves in one way or another also received royal attention.

This done, the slow progress forward resumed. As the phalanx approached within archery range, Alexander ordered his right into a headlong charge that swept them through the rain of arrows, into the ravine, and up among the Cardaces. The suddenness of the charge caught the enemy by surprise, and both Cardaces and the archers trying to scurry back through their ranks were overwhelmed. Not so with Darius' Greek mercenaries, however, who now moved to take advantage of the precipitous charge that had separated the sections of Alexander's phalanx toward the center. They were pressing hard and, among other things, venting Greek ill will against Macedonian conquerors of their homeland. Confused action boiled in and out of the rapidly crumbling gravel draw. Order appeared only when the Macedonians became aware of Alexander's success against the Cardaces and with some help from the right began to push back onto the northern bank.

Yet, it was the Great King who lost the battle for the Persians. As soon as he saw his left crumbling, Darius wheeled his chariot about and fled. When the Persian cavalry, which had gravely discomfited the Thessalian and allied Greek cavalry on Alexander's left, perceived the flight of their king, they also withdrew. In more ordered flight, they headed for the Taurus Mountains and, ultimately, Cappadocia. This allowed the Macedonians then to press heavily against the Cardaces and Asiatics to the rear in a general massacre. Much, however, if not most of the Persian cavalry had made its escape. Moreover, most of the Greek mercenaries were able to exploit the disorder of Alexander's phalanx to break through. They kept on going south. Two thousand of them later rejoined Darius; 8,000 went on to Tripolis, then to Egypt, and finally back to Greece where they participated in the Spartans' unsuccessful revolt against Antipater. Although it is not possible to estimate the actual enemy dead—100,000 is an impossible figure—it is not likely that Persian losses were terribly severe. Arrian mentions only five commanders who lost their lives.

Meanwhile, Darius had continued his flight. First in his chariot, then, when the ground became broken, on a horse. As he made the change he cast aside not only his armor but also the robe that was his badge of office. The brief description of his flight makes it evident that he made no attempt to go by way of

Issus and the Amanus Pass at Bahce, but rather made directly for the mountains along the line of the broken modern track that leads from Dörtyol to Hassa. If he did, he must have come out on the other side quite close to Sochoi. Ignoring a thigh wound, Alexander pursued Darius, but succeeded only in recovering chariot and robe. Darkness prohibited further efforts. Great King, cavalry, and Greek mercenaries hurried off in three different directions into the night.

After returning from fruitless pursuit of Darius, Alexander refreshed himself and allowed some attention to his wound. Chariot and accouterments were not all Darius had lost. The Macedonians had captured the royal pavillion in which Darius lived while on campaign. Alexander immediately visited it and was enough impressed with its splendor to exclaim at what it was to be a king. He then attended a banquet with some of his personal friends to celebrate the victory. The sound of anguished wailing from nearby soon interrupted conversation, and Alexander learned that the noise came from the captured mother, wife, and daughters of Darius. His return with Darius' armor, chariot, and robe had convinced them the King was dead. Touched by their grief, Alexander dispatched Leonnatus to inform them that Darius was still alive, that he had got away after only abandoning the things with which Alexander had returned. Curtius and Diodorus paint a dramatic picture of their receipt of this news after first assuming Leonnatus had come to take them to their own spoiling and death. Overjoyed, their wailing stopped; the silence can only have disclosed an answering echo off in the distance as women court attendants were herded off shrieking to treatment of a more usual sort.

The next morning Alexander and Hephaestion visited the women's quarters. Sisigambis, mother of Darius, mistook Hephaestion, taller and more handsome, for Alexander. After having made obeisance to the wrong person, she was devastated when she learned her mistake. It could have led to a troublesome situation at the Persian court. Alexander dispelled her—and perhaps Hephaestion's—discomfiture by smilingly stating that there had been no mistake: Hephaestion also was Alexander. Arrian has his doubts about the whole episode, but it is clear that Alexander gave these Persian women every consideration. He so impressed them by his magnanimity that they never ceased to praise him as the one man to whom it would be right to lose an empire. Much later, he married one of Darius' daughters, but perhaps never so much as looked at the Great King's wife, Statira,[6] who was reputed to be the most beautiful woman in Asia.

Some final arrangements remained before Alexander could proceed with the next part of the plan for closing the Phoenician ports. Arrian says that it was at this point that he appointed Balacrus satrap of Cilicia. There are reasons for thinking the decision might have been taken earlier, although the camp for casualties at Issus indicates the King intended to return before moving south, and may not yet have completed his dispositions for Cilicia. He had other things to consider as well. Alexander can hardly have known their destinations yet, but he did know the Persian cavalry had gone north to the Taurus. Their potential threat to his supply lines in central Asia Minor was obvious. In time, the threat was realized as the problem of keeping communications free ultimately led to three battles between them and Antigonus. Further, the Greek mercenaries who had successfully broken past the Macedonian phalanx were somewhere ahead of him to the south. They could mean trouble. It was time for Alexander to organize his thoughts, if not to regroup his forces and plans. The coastal and island cities of Asia Minor were now under the threat or in the possession of the essentially naval Persian counteroffensive. He needed the Phoenician cities to implement the decision taken at Miletus, to destroy the enemy fleet in a land campaign. Threats could come from either side. And the interior areas of Syria and eastern Asia Minor were something to consider as well as the Aegean coast. After Issus, Alexander probably began to be aware that just to conquer Phoenician cities would not be enough to terminate Persian countermeasures.

2. *Phoenicia*

Passing through the Syrian Gates in the late fall of 333, Alexander came down into the 'Amq Valley. Some of the geographical characteristics of this lowland area have already been mentioned. From its narrow westward end through which the Orontes River approaches the coast, the valley widens before dividing into three well-defined prongs to the north, east, and south. The northern prong leading to Sam'al has already been mentioned as the possible location of Sochoi. Due east, a series of gentle rises leads to the vast plain of the middle Euphrates, Darius' route to Issus. South, following the Orontes, the way is nearly level into Coele-Syria. Near modern Homs, it offers a choice between Damascus east of the Antilebanon, or the Beqaa Valley and its southern gorge where the Litani River (the ancient Leontes) comes out from behind the Lebanon to empty into the Mediterranean near Tyre. Alexander recognized this gateway to the Syrian and Mesopotamian plains by appointing Menon as satrap of Coele-Syria.

The King took none of these inland routes but continued along the coast toward the Phoenician cities whose naval contingents were so important to Persian control of the Aegean. Approaching Marathus, he was met by Straton, son of Gerostratus, king of the island city Aradus, its mainland counterpart Marathus, and the small cities of the triangular plain that now forms the boundary between Syria and Lebanon at the coast. Gerostratus had left the city to his son while he himself joined the satraps Pharnabazus and Autophradates, now the key figures in the Persian counteroffensive. Despite some Macedonian success they had successfully garrisoned Chios, from which they had seized Kos and the city of Halicarnassus on the mainland. With this position of strength, they put to sea and met Agis of Sparta at the island of Siphnus in the Aegean. Agis was applying for money, men, and ships with which to conduct open war against Antipater and the Macedonians. The negotiations were upset by news of Alexander's success at Issus. Pharnabazus returned immediately to Chios to see to the island's security. Autophradates left Agis with ten ships and some thirty talents of silver, and sailed for Halicarnassus. Agis sent the ships and money to his brother Agesilaus with instructions to seize the island of Crete and later made his own way to join Autophradates at Halicarnassus. The party at this city which once Alexander had conquered now ominously included the Spartan king, the Persian satrap, the king of Aradus, and several other Phoenician and Cypriote kings who had sailed with Gerostratus.

Straton, in the absence of his father and what must have been the bulk of Aradus' naval strength, freely surrendered the city and its possessions. He placed a golden crown on Alexander's head, and with it gave the Macedonian king possession of the plain leading to the first easy pass into the interior to join the southern prong of the 'Amq Valley. Later, crusaders realized the importance of this pass and on its northern flank constructed their best-known fortress, the Crac des Chevaliers. From here, Alexander dispatched Parmenion to Damascus, where the Persian king had left his noncombatants and his war chest.

Parmenion took with him the Thessalian cavalry and seized Persians and money alike with ease. Alexander soon learned that envoys from Athens, Thebes, and Sparta had also been taken. The King ordered Parmenion to remain in Damascus to guard the money, but to send the Greek envoys to him. When they arrived, he released the Thebans out of pity for their state. The Athenian was cordially treated and kept with the King with full honors until his death by disease. Alexander would give only personal considerations as his reasons for this clemency. He kept the Spartan, from a city openly hostile to the Macedonians, under open arrest for a time. Arrian says the detention lasted until the King had come upon great success; it may have ended when Spartan rebellion had been put down.

At Marathus, Alexander also received Persian envoys bearing a letter from Darius. It accused the Macedonians of having violated the tenor of Philip's agreements with Artaxerxes. In fact, upon the death of that King, Philip had attacked his successor Arses, and Alexander in turn had sent no representatives to affirm the former friendship between the two kingdoms. Instead, he had engaged in unprovoked attack greatly to the cost of the Persians. Only because of this had Darius taken the field in defense of his holdings. Now the battle between them had come out as the gods had decided, and he was asking the return of his captured mother, wife, and children as king from king. He would be Alexander's friend and ally and asked for envoys to accompany his own on their return to exchange guarantees of cordial relations.

Alexander responded with a letter of his own, to be carried by the hand of his own envoy who was, however, instructed to discuss nothing with the Great King. Alexander's letter has often been called the manifesto by which he rationalized his aggression against the Persians. The Persians, he said, were the first ones guilty of unprovoked attack, and he had been charged by the Greeks to take revenge. Moreover, Persians had recently given further cause by their aid for Perinthus when it was under siege by Philip. Artaxerxes had even invaded Thrace. Philip was murdered by conspirators sent by Darius who then had boasted about it in his letters. Furthermore, Darius was himself a usurper, having conspired with Bogoas to kill Arses and seize the throne, contrary to Persian law.[7] The Persian king had consistently sought to undermine Alexander with lies to the Greeks, money to Sparta, and clandestine overtures to his friends; in short, he had made every possible effort to ruin the peace Macedon had given to Greece. Only then had Alexander taken the field. He had first defeated Darius' generals and satraps, and then Darius himself. He now held the territory the gods had given to him. Those Persian troops and allies who had not fallen in battle but had fled to Alexander were now with him of their own free will. Under his care, they would fight with him against the Persian king.

Alexander followed this survey of their relations with advice: "Come to me now as to the lord of all Asia; if you fear ill treatment, send some friends to receive pledges first. When you come, ask me for mother, wife, and children, and anything else you want, and you will receive them. For whatever you persuade me to give, you shall have. And hereafter when you send to me, send as to the king of Asia, not as to an equal, but as the lord of all your possessions if you need anything. If not, I intend to deal with you as with a criminal. If you have any counter claims against this kingdom, run no longer but stand and fight, for I shall come wherever you might be." Most modern scholars find it difficult to take this advice seriously, preferring to consider it a calculated boast for the purpose of challenging Darius to a final conflict in the western end of the empire. How the last phrase is to be interpreted rests with discovering just when Alexander actually reached his decision to go on into the Persian empire from Phoenicia. As we have seen, there has already been cause for his consideration of the thought in the threat of Persian reprisals from the mountains of eastern Asia Minor.

From Marathus the way led toward Byblus. Its envoys advanced to meet Alexander, accompanied by representatives from Sidon to the south, from some of the kings of Cyprus, and from Tyre. All promised submission. The decision to remove the threat posed by the Phoenician fleet in the hands of the Persians was beginning to bear fruit.

Moving along the narrow shelf between the mountains of the Lebanon and the sea, the Macedonians could see still more of the beautiful coastline flanked by snow-covered mountains as they rounded each new point. It is difficult to determine how much of the original timber cover remained in Alexander's time; cer-

tainly, the ridges and upland valleys were not as barren as they
now are. But this area had been the source of the Cedars of Lebanon for Solomon and the dynasts of Mesopotamia and Egypt for a
thousand years.

Some miles south of Byblus, the ancient road squeezed into a
narrow trail that clung to a tangled rock face as it zigzagged up
over a bluff protruding out into the sea. Here, there was only one
choice of the way to go, and the armies of centuries have followed
in single file this same narrow trail. Almost no invaders, including those in modern times, have been able to resist the temptation to commemorate their passing by an inscription. The place is
Nahr el-Kalb, named from the small river that issues from the
impressive caverns a few miles up the canyon immediately before
the bluff. As Alexander's men made their way across the canyon
mouth and up the steep trail, they passed inscriptions placed
there by Assyrians, Neo-Babylonians, and Egyptians. The inscriptions now are nearly obliterated by the weather, though it was
possible substantially to read them eighty years ago. In Alexander's time, they must have been in nearly perfect condition.

Although no mention is made of this site in the sources for
Alexander, here was clear evidence that he could identify for the
widespread interest of Near Eastern kings in this coastal area of
Phoenicia. Nahr el-Kalb had a near duplicate of the Assyrian inscription of Esarhaddon at Sam'al, which Alexander had not
seen, but which must have been closely similar to the one at
Anchialus. There are also clearly recognizable Egyptian inscriptions. It is not possible to guess how apparent general Egyptian
influences in this area were to Alexander; much if not most of the
artifacts, sarcophaguses, and inscriptions excavators have un-
earthed at every site southward from Ugarit must have lain
buried in his time. Yet, Alexander was very much entering the
Egyptian sphere of influence, and here at Nahr el-Kalb was
tangible evidence of the fact. Alexander may, like Napoleon, already have known that a secure hold on Syria and Palestine was
necessary to the defense of Egypt. Now he could begin to ponder
the opposite proposition: that control of Egypt was necessary to
the security of the Phoenician cities that had been the object of
his campaign.

The King had received promise of submission from the anti-
Persian faction at Sidon. Arriving at the city, he replaced the current king by one of its citizens. Alexander seems to have had some

reservations concerning the offer of the Tyrians also to submit. Perhaps doubts were planted by the Sidonians, who had their own reasons for hostility to Tyre, which had greatly profited by Artaxerxes' destruction of Sidon. He told the Tyrians that he wished to sacrifice to their god Melkart in the city. Their reply was that whereas they were happy to offer exchanges of friendship and alliance, they could not admit him within the walls. There was, they said, a temple of Melkart in the old city on the mainland, where Alexander could sacrifice if he wished.

The subsequent long and difficult siege of the city, followed by its complete destruction and the sale of its surviving populace into slavery has focused much attention on this unfortunate—for the Tyrians—refusal to permit the King to sacrifice in the city. Tyre's illustrious history may be traced back a thousand years before this time, and a brief consideration of it helps to explain this refusal. For it can be shown that the Tyrians thought they must for the time refuse Alexander permission to enter the city.

Tyre was an important center as early as the fourteenth century B.C. It is mentioned in the Amarna letters from the time of Ikhnaton in Egypt, and it probably enjoyed peaceful relations with Thutmose III before that time. Tyre continued to play a leading role in the ninth century B.C. when Phoenicians first began to open the West with trading outposts at Utica in North Africa and Gades beyond the Straits of Gibraltar in Spain, and perhaps even in the British Isles. The city ultimately was the source of the important western colony Qart Hadasht, whose name the Romans have passed on to us as Carthage. Certainly, for the next two hundred years, Tyre predominated in Mediterranean trade and colonization, and matched this with commercial enterprises on the mainland in the Near East. By the seventh century, the city had outposts nearly everywhere where trade was of importance. The catalogue of places, people, and goods involved in this vast trade empire provides one of the most fascinating chapters in the Old Testament: *Ezekiel* xxvii. Unfortunately, the passage is almost mysterious because of its use of so many words that appear nowhere else in Hebrew literature and so defy accurate translation. But the picture is clear of a bustling metropolis, full of the sounds and smells of the world at large.

During the period of Neo-Babylonian predominance in the sixth century, Tyrian trade underwent something of an eclipse due to the strong hand Nebuchadrezzar exercised in Syria and

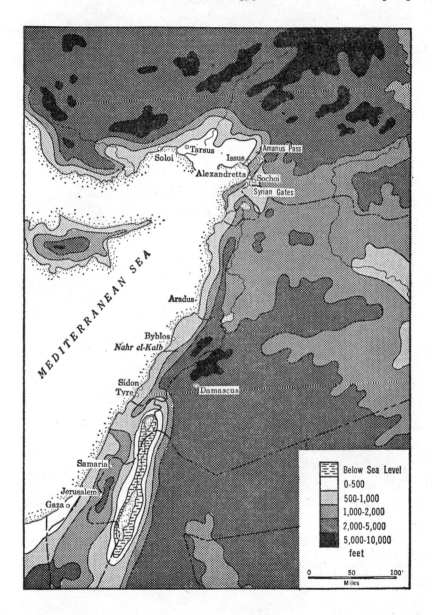

Babylonia. Under this aggressive leadership, the center of gravity of eastern trade shifted temporarily in the direction of Babylon itself. Nebuchadrezzar's unsuccessful siege of the city for thirteen years offers a hint of Tyre's reaction and the resulting struggle. Tyrian trade ground to a standstill, plunging the city into a depression. Sidon was able to capitalize on Tyrian difficulties by taking the lead in Phoenician trade for a time. However, with the advent of the Persian Empire and the more lenient policies of a government whose attention initially, at least, was centered in Asia Minor and the East, Tyre again emerged strong and wealthy. Little wonder that Tyrian policy was inclined to favor the Persians and found this reciprocated when Artaxerxes devastated Sidon, giving former Sidonian possessions to Tyre.

Furthermore, Tyre's physical circumstances gave every indication that Alexander's siege would be as unsuccessful as that of Nebuchadrezzar. At least a thousand years before, two small islands had been joined by a mole, the connection broadened, and a fairly large city laid out on the resulting elongated space parallel to the shore and about half a mile away from it. On the inland side there were two harbors, the larger one to the north called the Sidonian Harbor, and a smaller one to the south, the Egyptian Harbor. The entire circumference of the island, about two and one-half miles, was fortified. On the mainland side between the two harbors, the fortification wall rose to a reputed height of one hundred and fifty feet. There was every reason to believe this sufficient to meet any threat from the land. Alexander had no navy. Even if he had a fleet, it would be impossible to mount siege machinery of sufficient strength and height to batter down such imposing walls. The course of the actual siege gives clear testimony to the validity of this reasoning had the Macedonian king used any normal approach to the problem.

Finally, Tyre could not well receive Alexander unconditionally until the city knew more of his chances of success in his expedition against the Great King. For centuries, Phoenicia, along with Syrian and Palestinian states, had attempted to steer its way carefully between the two centers of power in Mesopotamia and Egypt. The "Harbor of the Egyptians" at Tyre testifies to the importance of relations in that direction. Alexander might weaken Persia sufficiently for a resurgence of Egyptian nationalism, or the Persians might still launch an even greater counteroffensive from Egypt. The city would have to take both possibilities into account. And beyond this was the still unresolved question of what Alexander would be able to accomplish in the face of a full eastern levy under Darius.

Upon the Tyrian refusal to permit him within the city walls while at the same time offering an alliance, Alexander angrily dismissed the envoys. He then called together troops and companions and reviewed the situation.[8]

Men, friends and allies, it is clear to me that we cannot safely proceed to Egypt so long as the Persians control the sea. Nor can we pursue Darius, leaving behind us this city of Tyre, which cannot make up its mind, and both Egypt and Cyprus still in Persian hands. Not safe because of these reasons, but particularly not safe because of the situation in Greece. For, while we chase off to Babylon against Darius with our army, the Persians can seize coastal establishments and then carry the war into Greece with much larger forces, since Sparta already is fighting us and Athens remains loyal to us rather more from fear than from good will.

But with Tyre destroyed, we would have all Phoenicia. The best part of the Persian navy, its Phoenician contingents, would come with us willingly, for neither Phoenician rowers nor marines would take the chance of sailing for others if we had their cities. And Cyprus would not find it hard to come over to us, or at least it could be taken easily with a naval expedition. With ships from Macedonia and Phoenicia sailing the seas for us and Cyprus also on our side, we could control the sea and our campaign to Egypt would be greatly aided. Then with Egypt, we will have no worry concerning either Greece or our homeland, and can march to Babylon, secure at home and armed with even greater prestige. For we will have removed Persia from all the sea and the land this side of the Euphrates.

The speech gives forceful indication of the King's thinking. The Persian counteroffensive had retaken Halicarnassus and Kos, and though set back by news of Issus it was reforming for more serious efforts of which joining forces with Sparta and other disaffected areas in Greece were a large part. The Persian cavalry escaping from Issus had moved north to threaten from the east Alexander's line of communications. If they should break across that line, they could add their own strength to the naval units at the coast. The Greek mercenary survivors were even now on their way back to swell Spartan strength on the mainland, though at this point the King may only have known that they had sailed to Egypt from Tripolis. Alexander's determination to confine the war to a land campaign had now reached its point of decision.

Without Tyre, they could not take Cyprus and Egypt. Particularly without Egypt, they could not pursue Darius into Mesopotamia, for the Macedonian position in Greece and at home would not be secure. Finishing touches were applied to the argument the next day when the King announced he had dreamed that Heracles took him by the hand and led him into the city. The army was persuaded. The difficult siege began in January of 332 B.C.

By now, Alexander must have learned of the Neo-Babylonian failure to take the city by conventional means. From the start, he determined to destroy Tyre's island advantage by constructing a mole out from the shore. Work on this causeway began immediately, using stone gained by dismantling Old Tyre and timber from forests in the vicinity. Initially, the work was easy in the shallow water just off shore, where the main problem was anchoring the fill in the shallow mud. Closer to the city, the bottom dropped to about twenty feet and construction slowed, doubtless halted more than once by the fierce late winter storms that can arise to lash the Phoenician coast. Furthermore, the closer the end of the mole came to the city, the more its workmen were subjected to fire from atop the high wall facing the work. Tyrian ingenuity added to this discomfort by attacking various sections of the mole from small boats. To meet these problems, Alexander ordered construction of palisades along the sides of the mole and two huge towers at its end. The towers are alleged to have been 150 feet high, reputedly the highest built in antiquity, and shielded from fire arrows with rawhides. Once constructed, the mole began to accumulate sand deposits, and now has changed the island into the tip of a broad-based isthmus whose modern height, about twenty feet, would indicate that the mole was fairly high. If the towers actually were 150 feet high, they may have topped the wall by several feet.

The Tyrians constructed towers of their own in order to rise above Alexander's constructions. But an even greater surprise was in store for the attackers. The islanders raised the sides of a cavalry barge and filled it with wood, brush, and everything combustible they could find. They constructed two yardarms twice normal length out from the forward mast, and from the ends of them suspended cauldrons filled with some highly inflammable material, probably naphtha. Loading the stern to raise the bow, they waited until the wind was blowing in towards the mole.

Then they fastened hawsers to the stern of the barge and used their triremes to tow it into the wind until it was in place, pointing towards the mole. Quickly reversing direction, they rushed it onto the mole, setting fire to the material on board. A skeleton crew remained with it until the last minute, then swam off. The barge ran up on the mole, its prow close to the towers, which immediately caught fire. The triremes hove to just off the mole so their men could shoot at anyone attempting to put out the fire. With towers and ship afire, the yardarms quickly burned through and dumped their naphtha on the blaze with what must have been nearly explosive effect. The two towers and the men trapped in them quickly disappeared. The horror of this spectacle was still fresh when the Tyrians led up some captives to the top of the city wall in full view of the Macedonians before slitting their throats and casting them into the sea.

The hostile literary tradition reported in Curtius and Diodorus has the King's resolve weakening after this setback. According to their view, he thought of raising the siege and pressing on to Egypt. The story is doubtful, however restive he may have been at the delay. Instead, Alexander ordered his men to begin from the base of the mole and broaden it, while directing the construction of more towers.

The King employed the lull for a side expedition. Parmenion had long since taken Damascus, but the interior of Syria all the way from the Euphrates to Palestine was one area where Persian presence clearly amounted to more than military occupation. There is evidence of the ownership of land in Syria by at least one Persian who later became satrap of Egypt,[9] and local loyalties may have had a chance of stronger establishment there than along the coast with its tradition of rebellion against the Persians. Furthermore, Arab pressures were increasing, particularly in the hills away from urban centers. Arab hillmen in the vicinity of Damascus and in the mountains just west of it, the Antilebanon, would require some attention if the hold on Damascus were to remain secure.

Leaving Craterus and Perdiccas in charge of the siege, Alexander took a small but representative force and moved up the Litani gorge into the lower Beqaa Valley and on into the Antilebanon. Plutarch[10] attaches an anecdote to this expedition. Alexander's old tutor, Lysimachus, insisted upon accompanying the King, protesting that he was just as strong and courageous as

Achilles' tutor, Phoenix, had been. The allusion to the old game these two had played when Alexander was a boyish Achilles was persuasive, and Lysimachus was taken along. Later in the high country when they had dismounted to proceed on foot, Alexander dropped behind with a few soldiers to help the old man. The small party soon found itself completely outdistanced and alone on an extremely cold night. They huddled together until enemy campfires began to appear in the darkness. Then the King dashed to one, slew two of the men sitting beside it, and ran back with a lighted brand. They then kindled so great a fire that most of the enemy fled and the remainder were easily routed. After Alexander rejoined the main group, the Macedonians spent some ten days in the area. Part was reduced by fighting, but more by negotiation. The party then returned to the coast at Sidon.

The King's return marked the turning point in the siege of Tyre, already some months in progress. Previous difficulties had shown the necessity of increasing his naval establishment if the mole was to be protected sufficiently to proceed close to the city walls, and Alexander's lieutenant, Craterus, had already begun to collect what ships he could at Sidon. Returning there now, Alexander learned that Gerostratus of Aradus and Enylus of Byblus had discovered his seizure of their cities while waiting at Halicarnassus with Autophradates, whereupon they left the Persians and returned to Phoenicia with their contingents. With them had come the ships of Sidon. About this time, too, one ship from Rhodes, three from Cilicia, ten from Lycia, and a large galley from Macedonia had also appeared. Furthermore, news of Alexander's success had reached Cyprus, and some 120 ships from there increased the company to a total strength far in excess of the Tyrian navy. Added to this was the arrival, from the Peloponnesus, of Cleander with about 4,000 Greek mercenaries.

The siege of Tyre now entered its second phase. Alexander organized the fleet, which had lately come to him, and launched a naval attack against the city. The Tyrians apparently had determined to meet such an attack if it should come and sallied forth in full force, only to learn much to their surprise that Macedonian strength was greater than they had supposed, not knowing of the Cypriote additions. They thereupon wheeled about and made for the two harbors, giving up control of the sea to Alexander. They then closed the harbors with a line of triremes across the entrance of each. Some of Alexander's Phoenician ships attacked this line at the Sidonian harbor and sank three of the enemy. However, the crews were able easily to swim to safety, and the King shifted his tactics to a simple outer blockade of both the Sidonian and the Egyptian harbors, placing the remainder of his fleet at anchorage close to the mole where they would find shelter from the wind.

Now, work at the mole proceeded with renewed effort, aided by the arrival of technicians and laborers from Cyprus and elsewhere in Phoenicia. The King's problem is easily stated. As he turned to the procurement of rams with which to batter the city walls, he needed to broaden the base for their operation over a wider area than the 200 feet, which Diodorus, possibly exaggerating, gives as the width of the mole. To do this, Alexander determined to use ships as bases for the operation of rams in addition to those brought into play on the mole itself. At least two ships would have to be lashed together to afford an adequate base for the operation of a ram. How this was done we are not told, but a beam of sufficient weight to batter Tyre's walls might well capsize a trireme. Furthermore, the ships would have to be firmly anchored close to the walls, and this would mean each needed a roof for protection from missiles. When Alexander attempted to secure anchorage for his ships close to the wall near the mole, he discovered that the defenders had thrown large rocks into the sea to keep the ships away. This problem was solved finally by throwing ropes with slip knots about the rocks and winching them up onto the mole. The next move was to anchor the ram-ships. Tyrian defense against this was a quick sally with triremes to cut the anchor cables. Then Alexander placed a line of his own triremes behind the rams to keep this from happening, and the Tyrians responded with divers who cut the cables below the water line; finally, the King ordered them anchored with chains.

Tyre was in trouble. Desperately, her people attempted one last sally. The King's ships blockading the harbor had been in position for some time without action, and the crews had taken to leaving them with skeleton crews only as they disembarked at noon for lunch and errands on shore. Noting this, the Tyrians put up a curtain of sails across the entrance to the northern harbor to hide their preparations. Suddenly, thirteen of the largest Tyrian ships came out from behind the screen at midday. The crews rowed in silence without calling the count. It was a moment before the Cypriotes guarding the north harbor saw them. When they did, there were hurried efforts to man the defenses by the few still with the vessels, while the Tyrians bore down on them with shouts and cheers.

The result was chaos. Three ships were rammed, and they promptly sank; the rest were driven ashore and broken up. It might have changed the course of the siege had Alexander not decided to forego his usual rest after lunch that day and instead returned to the Phoenician ships on the south side of the city. Upon learning of the attack on the other side of the mole, he ordered the Phoenicians to seal the southern harbor in order to confine any similar attack from that quarter, and taking those ships whose crews had been quickest to man them, made around the city for the battle scene in the northern inlet. The defenders on the wall saw him coming and attempted to signal their comrades, but to no avail. Most of the Tyrians were rammed and sunk and two were captured at the harbor entrance, though the crews made their escape by swimming off.

The Macedonians now began to employ the artillery and rams they had so laboriously worked into position. The wall was too strong to be breached near the mole and in the northern half of the city, but soon the rams in the southern quarter began to make some headway. Alexander attempted to use the first small breach that occurred by throwing a bridge across it, but this was easily thrown back. Three days later with more favorable weather, a wider section was broken down. The Macedonian forces moved in for the kill. All along the walls, but particularly at the harbors, the units of the fleet were instructed to attack while Alexander moved up catapult ships, boarding bridges, and troop carriers. The first wave of the assault began under the lead of Admetus, who fell almost immediately. Alexander commanded the second wave, secured the breach and some of the flanking towers on the wall, then moved into the city.

Meantime, the harbor defenses had been stripped to man the walls, and both Phoenicians and Cypriotes began to invade the southern and northern harbors, respectively. The Phoenicians had to charge booms thrown across the harbor entrance, but when they broke through these, they made short work of the vessels they found inside. The Cypriotes had an even easier time in the north. With the enemy pouring in from three directions, the Tyrians decided to abandon the walls and make their stand in the inner city at the shrine of Agenor. A bloody scene followed, with the Macedonians cutting down every man they found save those who fled into the temple of Melkart for sanctuary. The soldiers did not stop until fatigue had begun to replace anger over the length of the siege and Tyrian atrocities.

The King of Tyre, Azimilik, had returned to the city during the course of the siege and at its close had taken refuge with the city dignitaries and some envoys from Carthage in the temple of Melkart. These received a free pardon from Alexander, although he promptly declared a war he was never to prosecute against Carthage. All the rest alive within the city were sold into slavery. According to Arrian, some 8,000 had been killed and now 30,000 were sold. The time was July, 332 B.C.

3.   *Decision at Tyre*

Nothing like the prodigious efforts of besieger and defender alike had been seen in all of antiquity. During seven months, Alexander had raised enough structures to fill a small city. He had used ships to carry rams possibly weighing as much as twenty tons.[11] Sand quickly began to build up against the sides of his mole, permanently changing the coastline.

With Tyre, Alexander gained nothing, for he left the city in ruins as he had Thebes and as his father before him had left Olynthus; but without the city, every difficulty he had mentioned in his preliminary speech to the troops was potentially true. It would have been a focal point, immune to attack, for the organization of every rebellion that might come along. As it turned out, the Phoenician naval contingents had returned home as Alexander took their bases. Most of them had arrived during the siege of Tyre. With its fall, they all were in. Alexander's land campaign had succeeded. The possibility of spreading revolt to all of Greece was gone, though Sparta remained actively hostile. Furthermore, the threat to Asia Minor from the east was still as real as ever.

Alexander's subsequent sacrifice to the god Melkart has been the subject of nearly endless discussion since the day on which it occurred. Melkart was identified by the Greeks with their own Heracles, and Arrian says that the shrine of Heracles at Tyre was the oldest in the world. We know it had been seen by Herodotus, which would make it at least a century old, but we also know that the Greeks tended to see Heracles in every local legend of a hero whose physical abilities enabled him to accomplish unusual exploits. In Greek legend, Heracles' personal ability and strength had enabled him to do what no other man could. For this he had grown into a god. The Macedonian king, whose expedition had begun with the emulation of Achilles in a new Trojan War, now turned to Heracles. A new note was struck, for which the most positive evidence comes from Alexander's coins, so often showing Heracles with the skin of the Nemean lion over his head.

Much more important for the course of Alexander's campaigns, and for the direction of world history, however, was a second exchange between Alexander and Darius. Sometime during the siege of Tyre, in all probability after the arrival of the Phoenician fleets and the widening of the mole showed that the fall of the city was inevitable, envoys appeared from Darius with a new offer. By this time, it was clear that Tyre would not stem the Macedonian advance and that the Persians had lost their supremacy at sea. Scholars have greatly debated the validity of these letters between Darius and Alexander, and whether there were two or three. The most accurate literary tradition, however, in Arrian and based upon the work of Ptolemy, seems to make it clear that there were only two and that the exchanges occurred at Marathus and Tyre. This second, and therefore final, offer from Darius proposed to give Alexander 10,000 talents for the return of his mother, wife, and children, all the territory west of the Euphrates River to the Greek Sea, and the daughter of Darius in marriage as security for treaties of friendship and alliance. The provisions reduce to three main points: ransom for the Great King's family equivalent to nearly ten years of the Macedonian national income; security from attack by Persians still in Ionian ports and the much more worrisome Persian cavalry in the mountains of eastern Asia Minor; the pledge of the King's own daughter to secure his compliance with the agreements.

Alexander called a council of the Companions. The King presented the Persian offer, which was followed by the renowned exchange between Alexander and Parmenion, who had rejoined the main force during the siege of Tyre. The general's opinion was that he would accept the offer if he were Alexander. The King promptly replied that he would accept it, too—if he were Parmenion.

The old general's viewpoint seems fairly clear. Before becoming the ranking officer with Alexander, he had matured under the

policies of Philip. These policies had been to continue Macedonian control over Thrace and the Greek mainland by means of
an expedition to free Ionian Greeks from Persian domination.
This aim had given point to the formation of the Corinthian
League, and that point had been realized with the conquest of
Asia Minor. At least since acquiring Damascus, the expedition
had become financially sound, and now the Persians were offering
even more money. Furthermore, since the troops had been out for
more than two years, it was time to take a realistic view of the
situation. The area west of the Euphrates was precisely the territory that was most Hellenized and most likely to prove governa-
ble; all bounds of moderation had now been reached, and it was
time not only to enjoy the fruits of victory, but to turn to the
genuinely serious task of administering them. There is almost
unanimous agreement among modern scholars that Parmenion's
advice represents what Philip's view would have been.

The point was a good one, especially with troops who had had
small leisure to enjoy the fruits of victory. To get behind Alexander's reply to his reasoning is more difficult. The young man who
had insisted that he would make no decision until the actual occasion arose, must have placed great reliance upon the information
he had gathered when now, as king, he was making a decision on
the circumstances obtaining at Tyre. Some things may be noted
as strong possibilities.

At this point, Alexander had information from several sources.
Those available to him before the campaign were the written materials with which we are familiar and undoubtedly more of
which we have no knowledge. The first to note is the work of
Herodotus. This epic account of the great war between Greeks
and Persians has been hotly debated among modern critics, both
as to the accuracy of its information concerning the Near East and
its actual use by Alexander. Despite the fact that Herodotus visited Egypt and possibly Babylon, his information about the
politics of each is poor. The modern research that has shown the
possibility of a visit by him to Babylon has also shown that his
stay was so brief he was unable to arrange the major buildings
and quarters of the city in their proper order. If Alexander did
read Herodotus,[12] he was to discover his inaccuracy when he himself visited Babylon. It is difficult to imagine that, for what it was
worth, Alexander did not avail himself of one of the few accounts
by an eye witness of the territories that lay ahead of him on his

plan of conquest. We are never told that Alexander read anything, save the *Iliad*. On one occasion, Alexander already had
reason for interest in Herodotus' account of earlier affairs in Cilicia, as noted above.

The well-known *Anabasis* of Xenophon, the story of the 10,000
Greek mercenaries who took service with Cyrus the Younger and
later were surprised to learn they were marching against the
Greek King himself, is another pertinent work not cited by the
historians of Alexander. Still, if the Macedonian king did read it,
he would have learned something of the extent of the Persian
Empire, and that the one ineffective battle for empire was fought
on the upper Mesopotamian plain at Cunaxa, to which Alexander had not yet come.

The case for Greek literary figures who were closer contemporaries of Alexander is clearer. Isocrates had long been urging
Philip to invade the Persian Empire, as we have frequently noted.
In the course of making these recommendations he had discussed
at length the revolts of Phoenicia and Cyprus,[13] and until these
were retaken by Artaxerxes, he had used them as a major part of
his argument that the seizure of Asia Minor was militarily feasible. We have a clue to the source and accuracy of his information
in the reference to his friend Diodotus, who often had served on
sensitive missions for various Asian leaders.[14] An incidental argument used by Aristotle shows that there was an appreciation
among the Greeks of the relationship between Egypt and Persia
and the bearing it might have upon Persian efforts to interfere in
Greek affairs. He has the speaker asserting that "it is necessary to
make military preparations against the [Persian] king to keep
him from taking Egypt. In the first place, Darius did not come
over [into Greece] until after he had taken Egypt; likewise
Xerxes first took Egypt and then moved against [Greece]. Therefore, the king must not be allowed to take Egypt." [15] Despite
problems connected with the actual time of writing and whether
or not it was before or after Alexander's expedition, the argument must be set against the background of Artaxerxes' efforts to
reinstate Persian control over Egypt. The thought is nearly a par-
aphrase of Alexander's own speech before Tyre.

The fortunate instances where direct sources of information
about the Near East can be cited, as in the case of Isocrates'
friend Diodotus, are rare. Yet, such private intelligence must
have been fairly common, for there were many occasions for send-

ing trade and political legations to the Great King. Such, from Athens, Sparta, and the remnants of the Theban population, were found by Parmenion at Damascus. Moreover, a great deal of information concerning Greek artistic influences at the Persian court has recently come to light.[16] Alexander himself was to find a party of Greeks near Persepolis when he arrived there. These, to be sure, had been grievously mutilated by the Persians to keep them there, and this may cast some doubt on the cordiality of recent Greek relations with the Persians, but the fact is that many Greeks were indeed present and active among the Persians. Persian references to Greek materials and workmanship in their palace construction have recently been collected by Cameron and Kent.[17] Further evidence of this contact by way of trade comes to us from the many finds of Greek, particularly Attic, pottery at Al-Mina,[18] in Syria,[19] and in Palestine.[20] Finally, the presence of Greek coins in the western portions of the Persian Empire has already been mentioned, and their penetration in the eastern Mediterranean littoral and on into Arabia may be noted here.[21] Greeks enjoyed many opportunities for discovering the nature and extent of Persian control within the empire, and Alexander may be assumed to have provided himself with as much of this information as possible even before the expedition began.

By the time the Macedonians had reached Tyre, several chances for augmenting this intelligence had occurred. At Anchialus in Cilicia, the King had had opportunity to note the former presence there of Assyrians. Despite problems of identification, the monument was evidence of actual military presence in Cilicia from Mesopotamia. Alexander's march across the 'Amq Valley gave him occasion to notice this highway to the east, uncluttered by natural obstacles. That he came to appreciate at least some aspects of this geography appears when he dispatched Parmenion to Damascus from Marathus, where the general could take advantage of the low-level route leading from the coast into the interior and then south by easy stages to the city to which Persian noncombatants and gold had been sent. And Alexander's own minor campaign from Tyre into the Beqaa Valley and on to the Antilebanon along with Parmenion's knowledge of Coele-Syria enabled him to acquire considerable understanding of the valley systems behind the Lebanon. Whether or not the King became aware, at this time, of the tradition of Persian landholding in this area, he must have begun to realize that these valleys are natural highways leading from Mesopotamia toward Egypt. By the time he had come as far south as Tyre, he had three times crossed points of access to them from the coast: the 'Amq Plain, the gap at Marathus, and the defile of the Litani.

And at Nahr el-Kalb, just north of modern Beirut, he had passed first Neo-Babylonian inscriptions on the north bank of the stream, then Assyrian and Egyptian panels cut into the rock along the narrow trail up the ridge above the southern bank. He very likely saw no difference between Babylonian and Assyrian writing, but the fact of Egyptian and Assyrian presence was inescapable. Alexander probably did not see the Assyrian inscription at Sam'al, but he had seen similar ones in Cilicia and at Nahr el-Kalb. Here was evidence of Mesopotamian interest and control along the northeastern corner of the Mediterranean in the period before the Persian Empire. And at Nahr el-Kalb, where Assyrian and Egyptian inscriptions are within a few feet of each other, these two influences clearly had met. Perhaps here was concrete evidence in part as to why, for Persians, the conquest of Egypt seemed to precede active interest in Greece: Mesopotamians had frequently been interested in Phoenicia and the Persians had specifically used Phoenican navies, but Egypt and Phoenicia were mutually vulnerable, and one could not long be held without the other.

Although such circumstantial evidence permits us only to guess at Alexander's line of thought, the fact is that he had already begun to draw some conclusions before the arrival of Darius' second communication during the siege of Tyre. The Battle of Issus marks the point at which the Macedonian king began to claim lordship of all Asia. He did so in his statement of what would be accomplished by the battle as he addressed his troops before it began, and he made the claim part of his manifesto to Darius afterwards. To the extent the claim referred to Asia Minor, it stood on the solid ground of his campaign through the area, even though the country continued to be under Persian threat from East and West alike. Furthermore, he had twice defeated a Persian army and once the Great King himself and could now speak as a champion offering a challenge to settle the military issue once and for all.

At Tyre, two more factors appear in Alexander's statement before the siege began. These were the necessity of securing Egypt in order to hold Phoenicia, and the fact, later demonstrated when

Phoenician contingents joined him during the siege, that the possession of Phoenicia would clear the seas of Persian strength. The progression of thought stands out clearly: Tyre was necessary to secure Egypt; Egypt was necessary to retain all Phoenicia; with them both the seas belonged to Macedon; and then the expedition could enjoy security in Greece, at home, and in Asia Minor. So much Alexander had said in his speech before Tyre. He would possess what Darius pretended to give in offering of all the territory west of the Euphrates to the Aegean Sea. As the end of the siege of Tyre came into sight, this potential was close to realization. An isolated Egypt would be easy to take; it was already amply restive.

Thus, before replying to Darius' second message, Alexander decided to attempt the conquest of the whole Persian Empire rather than just its western end, which had originally been his objective. His success so far, the potential acquisition of Egypt and the control this offered for his rear areas, and easy routes to the east all put the attempt within the range of necessity. There were no natural boundaries between Syria and Mesopotamia. Eastern interest and influence in Syria and Palestine were obvious for the past and possible again in the future. What would keep the military resources of the East, with which Persians once had conquered Asia Minor and threatened Greece, from coming again when they were regrouped under Darius or a successor? The intelligence of the occasion itself showed Alexander what he must do, had he the grit for it. There is no real reason for supposing that his father, Philip, would not have reached the same conclusion had he been able to come so far. Parmenion may not have been so clearly speaking for Philip's policies, as often has been supposed, when he said he would accept Darius' offer if he were Alexander.

The reply to Darius was brisk. The offer of money was meaningless, for he had no need of it. He had Darius' daughter in his possession, and he would marry her if he chose with or without the King's permission. There was no necessity to accept a part of the King's territory, which he already had, instead of the whole, which he could take.

It is possible that the meeting with the Companions and the reply to Darius actually occurred after the city of Tyre had fallen. If so, the treatment Alexander gave the King and city leaders who had taken refuge in the temple of Melkart is interesting. They, after all, were the real instigators of the city's resistance that had caused him so much delay. Yet, while the city was depopulated by slaughter and the sale of captives, the oligarchy in command of the city was pardoned and released.

Part of the reason for this no doubt was Alexander's new interest in and emulation of Heracles, with whom Greeks identified Melkart. But we also may observe that few in Phoenicia would have had better information than the leaders of Tyre about the interest, influence, and control of Persian power; about roads and trade and local arrangements; or about the relative strengths of Egypt and Mesopotamia. We need only recall the prophet Ezekiel's description of the Tyrian market with its goods from unnumbered places and merchants who combed the seas and land alike. If Alexander received no suggestion from these Tyrians that more extensive military action was necessary and possible before he replied to Darius, he surely must have learned something about how the action could be taken afterward.

With Tyre behind him, Alexander moved south past Mount Carmel toward Egypt. Although he received the nominal and short-lived submission of Samaria, he did not visit Jerusalem. Now the coastal plain had widened, and his progress southward evidently was unimpeded until he neared Gaza, the last outpost before the desert regions that separate Palestine from Egypt. Batis, the eunuch general in command of Gaza, decided to rely upon the city's location on a high mound some two and a half miles from the sea. The location was a good one, and its defense was aided by the deep sand that surrounded it and the offshore shoals that would make naval support difficult. There is no evidence that Batis' resistance was part of any large Persian plan; his troops largely were Arab mercenaries, and once before Gaza had resisted Persian troops during Artaxerxes' reconquest of the area.[22]

Again, the King was faced with a difficult siege. The height of the city walls atop its mound necessitated the construction of a large ramp on which to bring rams into play. Once this was done, Alexander prepared to begin the attack by sacrificing to the gods. During the sacrifice, Arrian tells us a hawk, wheeling above the altar, dropped a stone on the King's head. The seer Aristander assured the King that the sign indicated the fall of the city, but also that Alexander should take particular care of himself that day. When the siege engines were brought up, the Arab defenders sallied forth to attempt to set fire to them and managed so to harass the Macedonians that the machines were even pushed from the top of the ramp. The King jumped into the fray to keep his men from fleeing, and, although he was successful in holding the position, he was hit by a catapult missile from the walls. The bolt came with such force its point went through shield and corselet and inflicted a severe shoulder wound. The Macedonians regrouped for a change in tactics.

The King brought up more engines from Tyre by sea, surmounting difficulties of shoals and treacherous terrain. He then attempted to construct a circumvallation around the entire city, hampered no doubt by the soft, dry sand. Still the rams and catapults could not breach the defenses, so Alexander finally resorted to the use of sappers who dug under the walls. Once undermined, the walls began to crumble, and the city finally was taken. But it had been done the hard way. Gaza joined the rank of the devastated, but with an apparent difference: neighboring tribes were used to replace the slaughtered and dispersed populace, and the town was retained as a fortress by the Macedonians. The story that Batis was dragged alive around the city by a maniacal Alexander imitating Achilles' treatment of Hector is of value only for what it shows the hostile literary tradition is willing to believe of the King. It has been demolished by Tarn.[23] Alexander by this time had become more interested in Heracles than Achilles, whose exploits he had left far behind.

4. *Egypt*

With Gaza fallen, Alexander turned his back on the problems of Asia Minor and Greece. It took seven days to move through the desert terrain between Gaza and Pelusium, where Assyrian armies so often had met difficulty. Ahead of him had gone the 8,000 mercenaries who had escaped from Issus, the Macedonian deserter Amyntas in command. The renegade, however, had failed to rouse Egypt against Alexander, and had gone off to Crete with his men, ready for trouble in Greece. In place of resistance, therefore, Alexander received the welcome of the Persian satrap of Egypt, his people glad to be rid of Achaemenid oppression. [24]

Although for centuries Egyptians had meddled in the affairs of Syria and Palestine, by 525 B.C. the Persians had conquered

Egypt, which now found itself part of the Achaemenid Empire. However, as Persian control faltered a century later, Egyptian leaders again used every indication of trouble in the West as an opportunity to assert their independence and to further their Syrian interests. The rebellion of Evagoras (389-380 B.C.) on Cyprus received aid from the pharaoh, Hakoris, which in time amounted to an effort to put together a coalition of Cypriotes, peoples of southern Asia Minor, and Athenians. Athens contributed the general Chabrias with a number of troops.

Persia was in serious difficulties, and the Great King's response was to arrange with the Greeks the King's Peace of 387 B.C. The Spartans used the peace and Persian support in attempting to secure control over all Greece, but they failed their Persian masters when they could not prevent Chabrias from leaving Athens again with a large force of mercenaries to go to Egypt. The death of Hakoris in 380 resulted in a series of dynastic disputes in Egypt, which were ended only when Chabrias lent his support to Nektanebos, sufficient to help him secure the throne. Further efforts abroad, however, were ended when the Persians finally succeeded in getting Athens to recall Chabrias, and even to send the general Iphicrates to command Greek mercenaries under the Persian king.

Despite the recall of Chabrias, relations between Greece and the Nile underwent a rather steady development during the succeeding period. Nektanebos had devoted his attention to building up his power inside Egypt, but by 365 he had been able to re-establish relations with Greeks. After the never cordial friendship between Sparta and Persia turned to open hostility, relations between Egypt and Greece grew stronger. In 362, the Crown Prince Tachos came to the Egyptian throne, and soon he was extending financial support to the Spartan king, Agesilaus, on campaign in Asia Minor.[25] By this time, Spartan activities in Asia Minor had embarrassed the Persians, and the western satraps were restive. In fact, the empire west of the Euphrates seemed to be falling apart. Tachos determined to seize this advantage to revive the Saite policy of Syrian conquest. His preparations began immediately with great reliance upon Greek mercenaries. The Athenian Chabrias was back, and late in 362 Agesilaus himself appeared with 1,000 hoplites. Chabrias helped the Pharaoh increase his financial resources by suggesting a tax on temple lands. Early in 360, the Syrian campaign began with Tachos himself in command. Agesilaus led the Greek mercenaries, and Chabrias the naval support, while Egypt was left under a local governor. The expedition went well for a time as Persian satraps fought each other and the Great King. It was ironically typical of Egyptian history that the effort was ended by the rebellion of the man left in charge of Egypt, aided by priests disaffected by Tachos' tax efforts. The campaign failed as the rebellious governor put his son on the throne as Nektanebos II.

All Egypt and the Egyptian troops in the army went over to the new Pharaoh, but the Greek mercenaries were the strongest element in the armed forces, and their two commanders were courted by both sides. Chabrias wanted to remain with Tachos and tried to persuade Agesilaus, but when the Spartan king received permission from home to do as he wished, he went over to Nektanebos. Tachos then fled to the Persian court where he was welcomed; Chabrias returned to Athens.

Tachos' failure ended Egypt's last serious attempt to control Syria until after Alexander. In that failure Greek generals and mercenaries had played the deciding role. But Agesilaus' career in Egypt was not yet finished, for the new Pharaoh soon found himself under attack by Mendesian competitors for the throne, and he had to turn to the Spartan for further help. For a time, both the Pharaoh and his Greek troops were shut up in one of the cities of the delta until Agesilaus was able to turn tables with a delayed attack. Thus, Nektanebos secured his throne. Declining offers for further service, Agesilaus, now eighty-four, returned home to Sparta loaded with honors and rewards.

Despite the rebellion of Artabazus against the Persian king from 355 to 352, Nektanebos did not renew Egyptian meddling in Syria, but confined his attention to Egypt. Athenian fear of provoking the Great King, which ruled out any coalition with Egypt, is probably the major reason for this quiescence. Later, around 345, Phoenicia, Cyprus, the Jews, and perhaps Cilicia were all again in rebellion, over which Isocrates chortled while urging Philip to attack the empire. Nektanebos joined to the extent of sending 4,000 mercenaries under Mentor of Rhodes to Tennes, King of Sidon. Phoenicians and their Greek mercenaries defeated both the satraps of Syria and Cilicia, even while the new Great King, Artaxerxes Ochus, was preparing to lead his army west from Babylon.

Artaxerxes, determined to rebuild the Persian Empire to its

former strength, planned a campaign in Phoenicia to end this chronic rebellion. The ultimate objective, however, was the major enemy, Egypt. His representatives went to Athens to recruit mercenaries. These Persians happened to be in the city when Philip's envoys to discuss the peace between Athens and Macedonia appeared, an opportunity for Philip to learn of the Egyptian situation. In Athens and Sparta, the Persian request for troops was put off, but they received large numbers from Thebes, Argos, and Greeks in Asia Minor.

Meanwhile, Artaxerxes was enjoying some success in Cyprus, and soon the Phoenician revolt began to lose momentum. Tennes finished the rebellion by betraying Sidon. He was executed, but Mentor, the Rhodian mercenary commander, took service with the Persians. Artaxerxes proceeded through the desert south of Gaza with great difficulty and reached Pelusium, which he placed under siege. Egyptian defenses were hampered by Nektanebos' insistence upon personal command of his troops, greatly irritating his Greek commanders. Further, Mentor's defection had revealed Egyptian defense plans to the Persians. After the fall of Pelusium, Nektanebos fled to the Nubians in Ethiopia, and Artaxerxes Ochus received all of Egypt with little further opposition.

The Great King determined finally to end Egyptian resistance and interference. Persian troops and their Greek mercenaries plundered everywhere, even to the point of removing documents from temple precincts. The treatment was harsh, but it succeeded in halting further rebellion. Success in Egypt gained recognition of superiority everywhere for the Persian king. Even Philip of Macedon entered into negotiations with him. Artaxerxes Ochus is listed in Egyptian sources as pharaoh from 340 until the time of his death from poison in 338.

In Greece, the result of Artaxerxes' death was Philip's ability to move into central Greece after the battle of Chaeronea without interference from Persia, while in Egypt the Nubian prince, Khabash, perhaps incited by Nektanebos, managed to pry Egypt away from the Persians during the reign of Arses, Artaxerxes' successor. However, just before or during the first year of Darius III's reign the Persians reinstated their control. But harsh rule and depredation had left their mark, and by and large the Egyptians were ready to welcome Alexander when he came.

During this tangled period from the fifth to the late fourth century, it had become apparent that the key to military success for Persians and Egyptians alike was the use of Greek mercenary troops. Asiatic contingents were inferior to hoplites, and Greeks were recruited with enthusiasm. High rates of compensation aroused equal enthusiasm among the Greeks. From the time of Necho's attempted aid to the Assyrians, Greek mercenaries, traders, and generals had increasing contact with the land of the Nile. Initially, Greek mercenaries had been paid in land and allowed to settle in various places in Egypt, but by the time of Amasis, after 565, native reaction had more or less confined them to specific military garrisons and to the Greek trading city in Egypt, Naucratis. With this, the use of money for rewards became more common. In order to have acceptable means with which to make such payments, the pharaohs had turned to minting their own coins, often in imitation of Greek, particularly Attic, coinage.[26] With this change, the importance of mercenary commanders also increased, not only as military experts, but also as intermediaries between Pharaoh and troops.

Greeks were not alone in coming to the military aid of the Egyptians for pay; Carians, Libyans, Phoenicians, Syrians, and Jews also participated. But particularly as those soldiers who lived through military campaigns returned home wealthy from Egyptian pay and rewards, opportunities abounded for Greeks to learn of Egyptian affairs. The frequent use of these people not only against enemies outside Egypt, but also against the enemies of the Pharaoh within the country, increased the extent to which they were able to comment on dynastic affairs.

It is not surprising, then, that there should be much evidence of a material nature for the mutual influences of Egypt and Greece upon each other. Work on the subject of Greek artifacts in Egypt reveals their presence at Thebes, Memphis, Buto, Abydos, and the desert oasis of el-Khargeh,[27] where Darius I built a temple. There is also evidence from Greece. The Athenian statesman Solon had visited Egypt at the end of the sixth century, and Alexander may well have seen his statement concerning Nile tributaries.[28] All Greeks were aware of Athens' intended help to the Libyan rebel Inaros in 450. Herodotus includes a lengthy discussion of Egypt, though we have before noticed the question of his value for Alexander's campaign. Aside from literary and inscriptional evidence, there are also evidences of Egyptian cults and artifacts in Greece.[29] For a time, the evidence seems to show that Athens enjoyed a near-monopoly in trade with Egypt after the decline of Naucratis.[30] Taken all together, previous Greek information about Syria, Phoenicia, and Egypt make it nearly impossible to suppose that Alexander lacked detailed information when at Tyre he pointed out the necessity of coupling Phoenicia with Egypt. To have turned his back on the south while pursuing Darius would have been potentially disastrous.

After receiving the submission of Egypt at the hands of the Persian satrap, Mazakes, Alexander went down the east bank of the Nile and then crossed over to Memphis, where he observed proper courtesies by offering sacrifice to the Apis bull as well as to other gods. After this and athletic and literary contests, he determined to make a journey west to the desert oasis of Siwah. He went down river to the coast and then proceeded west toward Libya for a distance of several hundred miles before turning south across the desert. The Persian king, Cambyses, allegedly had tried to visit the oasis but had lost his army in a sandstorm. Alexander's party had almost the same difficulty. But a sudden rain saved them when suffering from lack of water, and later they managed to get their directions from the flight of birds making for the oasis. Arrian cites Ptolemy in saying that talking snakes guided the King. In time, the oasis, with its temple of Ammon, was reached.

The size of this undertaking, a trip across largely desert terrain over a distance approximately equal to that between Issus and Gaza, has led many modern scholars to discuss Alexander's reasons for making it. Arrian (Ptolemy) says that he was seized by a desire to do so, also that he wished to enquire about his own descent from the gods. To this we may add the suspicion that he intended to succeed where Cambyses had failed. It has long been recognized that the word "desire" in Greek accounts to explain Alexander's acts is merely an indication that he did not wish to reveal his real reasons. Some reasons for this journey, made despite the urgency of securing the administration of Egypt and getting about the pursuit of Darius, may be suggested.

Alexander's propensity for seeing himself as especially favored by the gods must be taken seriously. Just as he had crossed the Danube successfully where Persian attempts to do so had failed, and had taken Tyre where Nebuchadrezzar had not succeeded, the young King no doubt had been enticed by Egyptian accounts of the intense difficulties of getting to Siwah, difficulties Cambyses had not been able to surmount.[31] Furthermore, the desert Ammonium had been important to Greeks since the sixth century. Berve[32] has shown that the god Ammon was not the same as the Egyptian Amun, of such importance in the period of the Egyptian Empire in the second millennium B.C. The Ammonium at Siwah is mentioned by Pindar, by Aristophanes, by Plato, and in various inscriptions. Although Ammon was the desert god of Cyrene, and his worship had been adopted by Greeks, in Alexander's time he was not considered identical with Zeus.[33] Yet, the importance of his shrine had come to surpass that of Thebes. Even Athens had a temple to him and named a sacred trireme "Ammonis" in his honor.[34] Consequently, Alexander determined to apply to Ammon, the god associated with Egyptian wisdom and Greek religion, for information concerning his own destiny and position.

Diodorus[35] offers a further hint that Ptolemy omits. While the King was on his way to Siwah, he was met by some envoys from Cyrene. They brought gifts and asked for friendly relations, which Alexander granted. Cyrene's relations with Egypt in the past had frequently involved contact with Greeks.[36] Moreover, Alexander could hardly have come through Palestine and Egypt without becoming aware of the fact that trade routes, primarily for incense, led westward through Egypt into the North African desert. After Alexander's conquest of Siwah, these traders could make their way to Carthage by the line of oases through the interior.[37]

Finally, Alexander set out to consult Ammon concerning the foundation of the city he intended to leave behind him in Egypt.[38] This god, in whom Egyptian and Greek elements are inextricably woven, was ideal for the necessary divine consultations before laying out a city whose chief purpose it would be to mingle Greeks with Egyptians.

Arrian describes the oasis:

The territory where the temple of Ammon is situated is desert all about, all in the grip of sand and without water. The site itself is small, hardly more than forty stades across at its widest. Nevertheless it is crowded with garden trees, olives, and palms, and alone of the land round about catches the dew. There is a fountain there, quite unlike fountains in other parts of the world, for even at noon the water is cold to taste, colder still to touch. When the sun sinks at evening it becomes steadily warmer until the middle of the night. Then again it begins to cool. Already cold at dawn, it is chilled the most again at noon. So it goes by day and night. Also the region offers natural salts, which may be excavated and which are used by the priests of Ammon in trade with Egypt. For, when going to Egypt they take the salts in palm baskets as presents to the king or someone else. The crystals of this salt are large, some reaching nearly four centimeters in breadth, and are clear as glass. These salts are considered purer than sea salts, hence they are used in sacrifices by Egyptians and others especially concerned for religious matters.[39]

What happened when Alexander reached Siwah? The debate began in the year 331 when he was there and has never been settled. Diodorus and Plutarch say that the first greeting he received was as the son of the god, and immediately the hostile literary tradition turned to explaining this away as having stemmed from the priests' faulty Greek, *O pais dios,* "divine son," being somewhat close to *O paidion,* "young man." He entered the precinct of the god upon his arrival, leaving outside the members of his own party. One thing he heard inside is beyond dispute: he was told to what gods he must sacrifice. It is possible that he asked whether the murderers of his father had been truly dealt with and was assured they had. Less likely was the question of whether he would conquer the world.

The serious problem in this regard is the question of the King's divinity. As newly crowned Pharaoh of Egypt, he could expect to receive some formal greeting as son of a god, since pharaohs all were so regarded, but not as son of Ammon. That Alexander recognized the difference is shown by his subsequent refusal to allow flatterers to call him the son of Ammon. Being called the son of Zeus was another matter, which we shall consider later. However, this is a close enough brush with divinity to consider the developments so far. Twice, occasions for asserting that outright divine intervention had occurred in his behalf had already arisen. At Mount Climax, the court historian Callisthenes said that the seas had retired before him as before a god; and Arrian, while noting changes in the wind, admits that he might have received special consideration from heaven. The second occasion was on the way to Siwah, when a rain relieved the party's dehydration. The birds do not count, for Alexander surely was aware of the technique of finding oases by the flight of birds.

Alexander's military success against the Persians is much more important than doubtful signs and portents. The ancient world could scarcely believe that anyone could do what Alexander had done unless the gods were with him, and Darius' first letter had already made the point. This idea of charisma, divinely given power to an individual so that his acts are superior to all others, uniquely fitting him to be king, is as old as monarchy itself. Success as king was proof enough that he had charisma. Furthermore, the purported ancestors whom Alexander both venerated and emulated had possessed a shade of divinity, and Heracles for one had become a god as a result of his labors.

Perhaps most important is that Callisthenes and others had by this time come to flatter Alexander with hints of special blessing. Later, they were to raise the question of outright deification. The result is that from the time of Siwah on, the suggestion of deification is superimposed in our sources on the accounts of everything else Alexander did. Justification, for those willing to accept it (Alexander himself was not), was the way in which natural forces had appeared to obey his desires. To the extent Greeks generally were willing to believe that a king who was able to act entirely above the law was a god among men,[40] the young King's growing autocratic tendencies added fuel and motive for the flatterers. There can be little doubt that, by this time, Alexander had come to regard himself as set apart from his fellow men. And the greater the gulf between him and other mortals, the more able he would be to cross cultural lines in fusing together Greek and Eastern ideas. He needed the willing acceptance of both sides, for the size of his army and the demands of his campaign against Darius would not permit him to dictate their cooperation. He already had trouble enough in Greece.

Leaving Siwah, the King returned to the coast and proceeded to the spot near the Canopic mouth of the Nile, where in January 331 he laid out the foundation lines for the greatest of the many cities to bear his name, Alexandria. Arrian's account of the selection of the site and its major centers is very brief. Clearly, Alexander intended a spot suited for maritime trade, for henceforth Egypt would be freely open to those who plied the eastern Mediterranean. The character of the Egyptian coastline, with its many lagoons and marshes and problems of annual flooding, limited the number of suitable locations. The subsequent commercial success of the city is more likely to have come from Egypt's new and wider outlook than the specific location of its foundation, once the requirements of harbor facilities and building space had been met. However, the almost immediate blossoming of Alexandria is in itself a good indication of Alexander's perception that Greeks and Egyptians were indeed ready for expanded contact.

In this connection, the problem of the sources requires some thought. Arrian, repeating Ptolemy, is almost alone in stating that Alexander founded Alexandria before going to Siwah, though he could easily have visited the spot and indeed must have had some idea of the nature of the coastline before leaving for the desert. Since Arrian is far and away our best source, most moderns have accepted his statement until the study by Welles mentioned above. The question is why Ptolemy, who clearly could have known better, reverses the order of events, hints that Alexander sought information about his divine descent, abbreviates both accounts, ignores the possibilities of connections with Libya and the West, and attempts to force two talking snakes upon us.

The answer must be sought in the complications resulting from Ptolemy Lagus' seizure of Egypt after the death of Alexander, for it was after a career as king of Egypt that he wrote the memoirs on which Arrian depended. At that time, he had claimed deification for himself as his coins show and, while he perhaps needed some reference to Alexander's deification that could be directly associated with Egypt as a precedent for his own, he may have been jealous of his commander's claim as founder of Alexandria. A reason for jealousy may have come from the difficulty the Ptolemies faced in maintaining direct control of the city. By the Roman period the city had become *Alexandria ad Aegyptum,* stressing its claim that it was attached to Egypt, but not part of it.[41] Those who use Arrian's report of Ptolemy must keep in mind that he wished to run Egypt for himself at the time of its writing.

Apparently, while Alexander was busy with the founding of his city in Egypt, his admiral from Ionian waters, Hegelochus, arrived with news that the Persian counteroffensive in the islands of the Aegean had come to a stop. The capture of Phoenicia had borne final fruit. But two problems remained. Antigonus, Alexander's commander in Phrygia, was under attack by Persian survivors of Issus who were in the process of forming the state of Cappadocia, which was to offer Alexander's successors so much difficulty. Further, in Greece uprisings were increasing in frequency, with Sparta the chief center of trouble. This was soon to grow into Antipater's Spartan War.

Nevertheless, Hegelochus's news was good, and when Alexander returned to Memphis, he celebrated magnificent games for the occasion. He also sacrificed to Zeus, the King, throwing some light on the events at Siwah, since Ammon was not mentioned. During this interval, embassies from Greece waited upon him, and Antipater sent him 1,100 mercenary infantry and cavalry reinforcements.

Unfortunately, our sources say almost nothing about what Alexander saw of Persian presence in Egypt. But one item that surely would have caught his interest if still in evidence was the canal the first Darius had dug between the Nile and the Red Sea. Although the evidence for the canal in Darius' time is quite clear, and it is mentioned by Herodotus,[42] it is equally obvious that the Hellenistic period after Alexander knew nothing of it. Persian neglect and changed policies may have allowed the canal to disappear without a trace. But if Alexander knew of it, he had direct evidence for Persian contact with Egypt, by sea around Arabia.

He then turned his attention to the special problems of Egyptian administration. For centuries, few natives had served with the pharaohs' armies of foreign mercenaries, leaving Egyptians unaccustomed to military activity. This gave Alexander an opportunity to put into political practice the suggestion of ideological fusion inherent in his observance of Egyptian religious practice and his visit to Siwah. He left no satrap, but instead turned the country over to an Egyptian, Doloaspis. Garrison commanders and someone to shepherd Persian mercenaries were also appointed. Cleomenes from Naucratis was left in charge of "Arabia," that is, the territory east of Memphis toward the Sinai Peninsula. Later, we hear only of Cleomenes among all these officials, and he seems quite easily to have moved ahead of Doloaspis into superior if not sole charge. All this while Alexander was in the east. In time, the King would become irritated by news of Cleomenes' harsh exactions and insolent injustice.

In the spring of 331, the Macedonian army left Egypt to retrace their steps toward Tyre. Sometime in late 332, the people of Samaria had revolted against Alexander and murdered his garrison commander in the city by burning him alive. The city was retaken and converted to a colony. The rebels were pursued into the ridges east and south of the city to be slaughtered in the many caves where they had taken refuge.[43] Going on to Tyre, Alexander again received Greek envoys from Athens and from some of the recently returned cities of Ionia. Final dispositions, including the release of Athenians captured at the Granicus, were made with them in preparation for his direct assault against Darius. Since the envoys also brought news that there were revolts against the Spartans in the Peloponnesus, he dispatched a good part of the fleet he would no longer need on his overland campaign to help them. Finally, Alexander made some changes among the commanders in Phoenicia, Cilicia, and Lydia. Once these arrangements had been completed, the army moved from Tyre up along the Litani, through the Beqaa Valley, and out onto the plain of north Syria. Ahead lay the Euphrates River.

CHAPTER IV

The Fall of the Persian Empire

1. Gaugamela

THE DEPARTURE FROM TYRE BEGAN A NEW PHASE OF ALEXANDER'S mission, the result of decisions taken and announced at Tyre, and secured by the seizure of Egypt. Prior to this time, his conquest had been Greek-centered, and had been so proclaimed. Asia Minor and the Greek cities of Ionia had been the earlier goal, which in turn had led to Phoenicia and finally to Egypt. Consequently, the Macedonians already had an empire west of the Euphrates, to some degree logical in its outlines and offering hope of permanence. The area long had felt the influence of Greeks. Its military unity was strong enough to have been the main subject of the King's speech at Tyre. With Egypt and Phoenicia under control, Asia Minor was secure, the broad Euphrates a natural boundary separating it from the centers of the Persian Empire. And, generally speaking, this was the area that Rome later incorporated into her empire. Parmenion's position had been that the weary Macedonians should settle for this much and leave the rest to Darius. He might have added that no Greek army had penetrated farther east than the Euphrates, where Xenophon's 10,000 had been stopped at Cunaxa. On the other hand, Darius was in flight, however much he might later return to renew the conflict.

Alexander had stressed this last point in his speech to the assembled troops: the security of the coast was essential to preparations for any attack against Darius in his home territory. The combined presence in centuries past of Egyptians and Mesopotamians in Phoenicia and Palestine showed what might be expected from the East if at any time Macedonian control in Egypt grew lax. Indeed the Romans, though they held to the line of the Euphrates for the most part, found themselves under nearly constant pressure from Parthians and Persians. The alternatives of resting at the Euphrates and going on were both arguable. A deliberate decision by Alexander settled the matter in favor of further campaigns. To signal the change, the King began to stress a propaganda line he had used before, but which henceforth would receive special attention. As he had stated in his first letter to Darius, the Persians were to pay for their depredations in Greece and their tyranny over Greeks. The idea was not new; Pericles had urged it upon the Athenians after the Persian Wars. Now the chance—and perhaps the necessity—had come to carry the war of revenge into the Persian heartland. Thus, vengeance began to supersede liberation as a theme while Alexander moved to open up a new world to Macedonian political control.

Before leaving Tyre, Alexander saw to administrative arrangements for his now sizeable empire. Cleomenes in Egypt, Coeranus in Phoenicia, and Philoxenus in Asia Minor were entrusted with supervision over local garrisons and rulers. Harpalus acquired the more important and widespread problems of financial administration and probably general political oversight. The situation in central Asia Minor was still the major military problem of the West, and Antigonus earned special favor with the King by his efforts to hold back the Persians in this area.

Parmenion had gone ahead of the army with orders to secure the west bank of the Euphrates at Thapsacus. He was to build a bridge and to have it ready when the rest arrived. He found Mazaeus holding the opposite side with Darius' remaining 2,000 Greek mercenaries. He built the bridge as ordered but left the far end unfinished, lest the mercenaries seize it for use in an attack of their own.

As the Macedonians moved past the numerous villages of northern Syria, they were approaching the land of the two rivers, fraught with mystery and natural dangers from sun and storm. Its vast distances and arid wastes would require careful planning for the line of march. Its culture, whose antiquity rivaled that of Egypt, was dimly understood by the best of Greek information, and must have seemed odd and wonderful to most of Alexander's troops. Indeed, a strange mixture of fact and fancy concerning Mesopotamia had filtered to the West. To most people in the Greek sphere, it was a land of mighty kings who were sadistically cruel and addicted to sensual pleasures. These orientals had long shown an ominous interest in the West, as Persian threats and Phoenician monuments both testified. And the despotic tyranny, which was its heritage, had been prolonged by the Persians, who like the rest had become effete and sadistic under the enervations of an exotic land. What was worse, somewhere ahead lay an army threatening with perhaps the full might that once had gained the Near East for Achaemenid kings. Against this army, Alexander, the new Heracles, was leading his forces in order to right centuries of wrong in the conflict between East and West.

Alexander approached the Euphrates as Mazaeus retired from the other side. The crossing was unopposed. After reaching the other bank, the King withstood the temptation to march directly along the Euphrates toward Babylon, an impossible route in summer. That way led along the river banks through desert and quicksands, which made access to water difficult. In cooler weather it was adequate for traders' safaris, but insufficient for an army. Here, Assyrian kings long before had traveled only with hardships until they learned that the best way led along the foothills to the east. In the hot and dry late summer of 331, Alexander avoided even the Persian royal road and took this better route, which would provide forage in the relatively cool altitudes at the edge of the steppe. The way curved south as it went east and would bring the Macedonians to a place where they could strike out across the lowlands for Babylon.

After a little more than 200 miles, the army reached the Tigris, which it had some difficulty in crossing; the Persians could have inflicted severe damage had they been there. Anticipating Alexander's route along the foothills, however, they had waited in Babylon, making final military arrangements until news of the Macedonians' departure from Tyre came to the Persian high command. This gave them enough time to reach the region of Arbela with sufficient margin to choose and prepare the battlefield before Alexander's arrival.

The Macedonian king continued to have worries of his own as his army moved down the Tigris. The situation in Greece had come to a boiling point. In the summer of 331, Agis of Sparta declared open war against Macedon. How much Alexander actually knew of this is debatable; final word on the outcome of the conflict between the Spartans and Antipater was delayed until he was entering eastern Iran. But he may have known that Agis had received the support of the 8,000 mercenaries escaped from Issus, had completed his naval preparations, and seized Crete in readiness for a deciding battle with the Macedonians. Also at this time, Darius' wife died while in the custody of Alexander. She apparently was worn out by the hot and weary miles, for which life as Darius' queen had been poor preparation. She succumbed despite the consideration she had received from the Macedonians. A eunuch reportedly escaped to Darius that same night with the sad news. The Persian king was only with difficulty persuaded that Alexander had indeed extended every courtesy to his women captives. When finally convinced, he launched into a eulogy of Alexander's enigmatic treatment of the royal family.[1]

Alexander proceeded down the Tigris for four days after his crossing in late September. Then, scouts reported the presence of a thousand Persian cavalry ahead. The King gave chase for about eleven miles and managed to take some captives. These revealed the extent of Darius' preparations. The Persians were at Gaugamela seventeen miles away, in a broad but well-defined plain between low hills on the south and a sharper rise to the north. They had leveled the field by removing all rises and obstacles of every sort. Alexander went on another ten miles before establishing an intrenched camp where the army remained another four days, secure in the knowledge that Darius would be reluctant to leave his carefully prepared battle site. During this time, the moon went into eclipse. Alexander ordered sacrifices to Moon, Sun, and Earth, and the phenomenon was reported as a favorable sign; it also permits us precise dating for the ensuing battle. On the fourth day, the King set out at dusk for Darius' position, leaving his supply train and noncombatants in camp. Halfway there, the Macedonians came down off the hills. Persian campfires stretched as far as the eye could see. There was a hurried council with the generals. Most were in favor of immediate attack; Parmenion suggested that it might be best to reconnoiter first. He and the King then rode forward with a small cavalry guard to inspect the field lying before them. That Parmenion then urged the King to order a night attack and that Alexander replied that he would not steal a victory is doubtful. Both were aware of the dangers.

Instead, the King very likely delivered his usual address to all the commanders. This was Darius' last stand; he had done them a favor in making his fight here instead of retiring before them. He could have left them only scorched earth while using his superiority in cavalry to harass the Macedonians and wear them down. After this battle, the rest of Asia would be theirs. Alexander then ordered absolute silence as they approached the enemy. He did not know the Persian battle order and would have to adjust his own as he learned it. The troops must be able to hear last-minute commands. Until that time, his own disposition would rest upon one major fact: the Persian superiority in cavalry. The Macedonians could best protect themselves by forming a defensive square with strong support on the sides to withstand the inevitable cavalry flanking attack. When it came, the enemy horsemen would very likely open gaps through which the invaders must be ready to dash.[2]

He then proceeded to arrange his own lines. In order to utilize the inherent strength of the phalanx to the right, he would attack from that side. Therefore, the phalanx was placed in right-center, two battalions to the left under Parmenion and four to the right under Alexander himself. The heavy right wing consisted primarily of the Companion Cavalry. To their left, between cavalry and phalanx were the hypaspists. In front were archers and javelins. The mercenary and allied cavalry formed the right side of the square, inclined to the rear at an angle of forty-five degrees until such time as they might need to pull in to close the square. These were backed by the Agrianian spearmen, archers, and mercenary foot who were assigned to defend the right side against a flanking attack by the superior Persian cavalry. On the left, proceeding from the center phalanx battalions, were the allied Greek and Thessalian cavalry with a battalion of allied Greek infantry, screened by Cretan archers. More of the allied and mercenary cavalry formed the left-flank guard, also inclined at forty-five degrees. The remainder of the infantry phalanx was spread along the rear, ready to form an enclosed square if the wings came in. The intrenched camp, seven miles to the rear, was defended by a small group of Thracian infantry. Once the battle order was set, Alexander and his army bivouacked for the night.

After the battle was over, the Macedonians found a document giving the Persian order.[3] Their days spent in preparation must have reached fever pitch when news came of Alexander's approach. The field was cleared of all obstacles, and its most obvious lines of entry were strewn with caltrops,[4] in order to spike the hooves of the Macedonian horses. Persian dispositions, too, rested upon the realization of one major fact: Darius had insufficient infantry. Now only 2,000 Greek mercenaries remained with which to engage in the pitched battle for empire demanded by the Great King's prestige. His cavalry would provide attack and mobility, but without infantry he had little staying power.

Still, as at the Granicus and unlike Issus, the Persians were not concerned with holding their immediate position beyond the effort to keep the battle within the confines of the leveled field. Their plan was to attack in order to decimate the enemy and get Alexander, for which the Persians had a special weapon, the scythe chariots. Precise construction of these chariots is not clear. A long, sharp pole is reported to have protruded between the horses in front, and blades were attached to the wheels on the sides, though they cannot have been placed to rise in the air without digging into the ground. One thinks of Roman racing chariots, and Darius' vehicles might have been formidable indeed if they had been constructed to run in front of the horses like a buck rake. The device had not worked against the Greeks with Xenophon at Cunaxa,[5] but once it had succeeded against Spartan hoplites.[6]

The main body of Darius' army consisted almost entirely of the eastern levies, with a few Syrians, Mesopotamians, and the 2,000 Greek mercenaries. The full front line, except for two battalions of Greek infantry and one of archers, was made up of cavalry. The superior numbers of Persian horse permitted doubling on the wings, which were commanded by Mazaeus on the right and Bessus on the left. The numbers given for Darius' forces in our sources are not credible, but it is worth noting that he had sufficient troops to fill a space twice as wide as Alexander's front. The Great King was in the center line, and the scythe chariots were placed in advance of the center, even with the front ranks of the horse on the wings. With Alexander in position on the low hills after dusk, the Persians were forced to remain under arms fearing attack. Darius and his relatives spent most of their time riding among the troops to rouse and encourage them.

The Achaemenid king may have had some time for thought, listening to shouts in the night and the thump of horses' hooves on the sandy ground between the campfires. Artaxerxes Ochus' success in the West had put an end to the Phoenician revolt and had recaptured Egypt. It also had halted Macedonian designs for encroachment upon the Persian Empire, and he and Philip had entered into negotiations that would leave each a free hand to attend to his own affairs. Philip had used this respite to work out his acquisition of Greece. He continued to do so without Persian opposition, for just as he was at Chaeronea, Artaxerxes was poisoned by the eunuch kingmaker, Bogoas. The murder, ending the life of the strongest King since Darius I, had a profound effect on Persian history. With Arses on the throne, the Nubians took away Egypt, and Philip soon found himself able to send Parmenion and Attalus into Asia Minor. Arses too was poisoned after a two-year reign. This in June of 336, one month before the assassination of Philip. All of Arses' family were also murdered by the bloodthirsty Bogoas, who then placed a distant cousin on the throne as Darius III Kodomanos.

The new King, however, was not of the same mold as Arses. Personal prowess in battle during his younger days had earned him appointment to the difficult satrapy of Armenia, where he must have done well, considering his later elevation to the throne. His sojourn in the mountains of eastern Asia Minor may throw incidental light on Persian successes based on Armenia against Antigonus in Phrygia. Darius apparently continued to show some strength as king, for soon Bogoas determined to put him aside in the usual fashion, only to find himself poisoned instead. Rid of this disturbing influence, Darius was secure on the throne he had taken at almost the same time Alexander became king of Macedon. Some twenty-five years older than the Macedonian king, he began immediately to put the Persian Empire back together. His Greek general Memnon stopped Philip's push by defeating Parmenion at Magnesia. Ionia was regained, and Macedon pushed back to a bridgehead on the Propontis. By 334, Persia again had Egypt.

Darius was attempting to recreate a proud empire. The Achaemenids had dictated Greek peace for a century and a half with such success that Persian absences had become as eloquent as their presence in the course of Greek history preceding the rise of Philip. The lists of attendants on the stairways and throne at Persepolis offer the names of subject peoples by the dozens. A pair of gold plates claim submission all the way from Northern Scyths beyond Sogdiana to Ethiopia in the south, and from Sind to Sardis, east and west.[7] The royal line from which Darius sprang could be traced back even further than the empire itself, to three centuries before the meeting of the Great King with Alexander. Again and again, these kings had fought out of the high valleys of Persia at the head of their free citizen cavalry troops. And again and again, they had lost their impetus in the quagmire of Near

Eastern politics and societies, especially that of Babylon, where heat and pleasures more than once forced a Persian king to retire to the cool mountains with his army.

The administration of this empire had been forced to concern itself with the trade centers of Mesopotamia and the West. There was always competition from Egypt, and there were often revolts in Phoenicia. Equally often, the western satrapies showed a tendency to split away to join the mainstream of the Mediterranean, of which, economically, they were increasingly a part. But always the real power lay in the self-sustaining centers of Persia itself.[8] There, the King could retire to put together another force. His superior armies then could take advantage of open routes to the west and competitive interests there, to put down rebellion and glue the pieces of the fragile empire back in place. In later years, the Achaemenids had placed increasing reliance upon mercenaries recruited from the West, upsetting the old way of doing things. Yet, this was in large measure a matter of substituting money for Persian manpower. Actual superiority of the mercenary phalanx over the fast-riding and armored troops from the eastern highlands had been little tested. Perhaps Gaugamela would do that.

Especially in later years the empire also had become conservative in the extreme. It seemed to exist only by and for tribute, collected with trickery and rapacity, adding to the centrifugal tendencies of the western satrapies. Often this conservatism was destructive of trade and the very wealth it sought, as in the case of Xerxes' spoiling of Babylon. And always, success brought more wealth to be cached away in the imperial treasuries at Persepolis, Ecbatana, and Susa, isolated from the commerce its circulation would have benefited. Darius was undoubtedly the world's richest man in his day. Yet, this government was tough and real; it constantly reasserted itself, as we have just seen. Herodotus speaks of couriers along the royal roads and the "eyes and ears of the king," the imperial police. Alexander thought enough of Persian administration to retain its satrapal organization, though he exercised more care than the Persians in separating military, financial, and political offices. One notices that long after the Persians were to be known as particularly adept at bookkeeping.[9]

In all this, the chief factor holding the state together was the person of the King[10] and his ability to raise troops. But Babylonia, not Persia, was the center of gravity for the empire. It lay athwart Persian lines of contact with the West which, if it was to be administered at all, would have to be directed from Babylonia. The city on the Euphrates also was the center of much of the trade from which Persia drew its wealth, at least until the time when Xerxes destroyed its temples, pulled down sections of its fortifications, and interfered with its trade to the south. This doubtless occurred because Babylon was the center too of potential and actual resistance to Persis when not under strong control. Darius was now defending this Babylon at Gaugamela, and its defense meant that there was little territory on which to fall back.

Three times, Alexander met three different Persian armies: at the Granicus, at Issus, and at Gaugamela. Capacity for recruiting had been strained to the limit. Besides his cavalry, Darius had only a limited number of Greek mercenaries. These infantrymen had not been effective at the Granicus because of the satraps' insistence upon a cavalry charge. The escape of the 8,000 Greeks after Issus may indicate that they had been poorly used there too. They had played no real role in the battle, but neither had they suffered harm. At Issus, they were limited by the terrain, by Alexander's rush, and by Darius' flight from the field. But his departure from Issus cannot be laid solely to cowardice. Darius had not been a coward in the past, though now he was in middle age. Furthermore, the Great King in large measure was in himself the Persian state. The government was held together in his person and by his personal ties with troops and their generals. Alexander's later success was to show that without the person of the King, Persian centralized political structure vanished into thin air leaving major pockets of the nationalist resistance with which the Persians themselves had often had to contend. When the state was gone, the residue consisted only of the satraps Alexander appointed or retained.

On October 1, 331 B.C., Alexander slept late. Parmenion finally issued orders to bring the troops into the positions specified by the King the night before. The commanders stood nervously about the King's tent for a time, and then Parmenion diffidently entered to rouse him. Alexander explained his slumber as confidence in the outcome. The sun was well up when he led the army down onto the plain near the modern town of Keramlais six miles west of Tell Gomel, ancient Gaugamela.[10a]

When Alexander perceived the extent of the Persian line, and its cavalry massed in depth on the wings, he began to advance obliquely to the right. Oblique advance would tend to preserve the natural strength of the phalanx toward its own right, lessening the chance of a flanking movement by the enemy. But also, Alexander was making for the low hills off to the right, away from the cleared field and especially avoiding the caltrops. As he proceeded, he held in his sides for defense, anticipating the cavalry charge. If he could hold against its force, he would wait for the break in the enemy line which the charge might cause. All this was done in utter silence, save for the sound of footfalls in the rising dust. The drift to the right brought Parmenion's command (on Alexander's left) toward the Persian center. Once Darius became aware of the shift, he began to side-step his line to the left to keep the two forces as even as possible as he sent out his Scythian horse to stop Alexander's advance before it reached the low hills. When the Macedonians brushed this sally aside, he then sent Bessus, commander of his left wing, with the Bactrian cavalry around to outflank Alexander in order to stop him before it was too late to use the scythe chariots.

A furious cavalry engagement ensued, the opening of the battle. Alexander kept his right flank intact on its angle of inclination by feeding into the skirmish the troops next in line, waiting with his Companion Cavalry for a gap in the Persian line. Darius took advantage of this temporary stall to send in the scythe chariots from his left wing. They were almost completely ineffective under the shower of javelins raining down on them, and a number of the drivers were pulled off as they passed through the front ranks. Alexander had anticipated the scythes on information from his captives, and the phalanx simply opened lanes through which the chariots raced without damage. They were to get only one pass at the line. They were dangerous only when moving, and when they stopped to wheel about the rear ranks put them out of action. We hear nothing of chariots on the right wing; perhaps there were many less than the reported 200.

At this point, Darius made the one serious mistake of the engagement. Since Bessus' cavalry had passed the front of Alexander's line in its attack on his flank, the Macedonian king had sent his lancers to take the Bactrians in the rear. Darius, who could not see the actual engagement on the flank and knew only of the departure of the lancers raising full battle cry, was led to believe that Bessus was succeeding. The Persian king thus thought that the Macedonian line had begun to falter and ordered both cavalry wings into full commitment. The error consisted in the fact that all the remaining Persian cavalry on the left (Alexander's right) charged off to help Bessus finish things. This opened a gap in the Persian front, left of center. Into this opening, Alexander immediately drove his Companion Cavalry, formed as a wedge, heading straight for Darius; this charge was followed by the phalanx battalions of his own right. Darius saw the Macedonians storming through the confusion of the conflict and turned to flee into the cloud of dust that had risen to obscure most of the action. It was an effective screen. Alexander was left with nothing but the slap of reins and whip echoing back over the din of battle through the pall of dust. The young King turned to Bessus, who still seriously threatened the right.

Meanwhile on the left, Mazaeus had been pressing Parmenion's troops as much as Bessus was on the right. In fact, things had gone so well for the Persian general that he detached a portion of his cavalry and sent them toward Alexander's intrenched camp, seven miles to the rear, uncovered by the Macedonians' move to the right. When Parmenion learned of their departure, he sent a warning message to Alexander. The King, busy with Bessus and Darius, sent word back to let them go; the Macedonians would be able to recoup anything they might lose from Persian supplies when the battle was over. Mazaeus' detachment actually reached the camp and rifled the baggage before returning to the battle. Darius' mother is reputed to have rejected their attempts to rescue her. In the meantime, the drive by Alexander and the phalanx against Darius' chariot had left a gap in the Macedonian center, through which now Persian and Indian cavalry burst. They also broke through the rear phalanx and plundered the baggage that had been brought to the scene of battle; it apparently had been placed just behind the Macedonian position. Gathered with the baggage were the prisoners captured thus far in the battle. These were released. The result of all this was that Parmenion was in genuine trouble, outflanked by Mazaeus and cut off by the break in the center. He sent a second message to Alexander, who was in the process of forcing Bessus to withdraw. The King then turned to his left to aid Parmenion and burst out of the cloud of dust shrouding the right just in time to catch the Persians and Indians returning through the gap between the wings after plundering the baggage and releasing the prisoners behind the rear lines.

By now, the battle consisted of separate actions on right and left. On the right, Bessus had withdrawn without being really defeated and had to be contained to keep him from joining forces with Darius' right. On the Persian right—Alexander's left—Mazaeus' troops were cornered by the arrival of the Macedonian king and were fighting for their lives. There were serious losses on both sides before Mazaeus could disengage. When this happened, the battle was over because the Great King and the center were both gone. Bessus retired in an ugly mood with his troops toward eastern Iran, where Alexander would meet him again. Mazaeus skirted the field and made for Babylon, through with a king who had left him unprotected. By dusk, Alexander had won the day at Gaugamela. The young king next turned to the problem of the fleeing Darius. The chase went on for some thirty-five miles through the night. Midway, Alexander rested his men for a time. He then went on to Arbela, where the Persian king had met Bessus and a number of fugitives. There, the Macedonians gave up pursuit.

While pausing in Arbela, Darius had delivered a speech to his company of assembling fugitives and Bessus' cavalry.[11] The Macedonians, he said, would now go to the rich cities of the plain, where they would become glutted with spoils and burdened as well. He would use the delay to go to the eastern uplands whose remote areas would permit recruiting another army. The notion might have worked—though the sullen Bessus boded ill. The imperial treasuries might well delay Alexander. Indeed, they would have stopped him had the Macedonians been the barbarians Darius thought they were.

2. Babylon

After rejoining his troops at the field of battle, the King gave orders to move, as a stench from the dead began to rise with the shimmering heat. They marched directly south toward Babylon. Moving out over the plain away from the hills along which they had been traveling, the army crossed country more level than any to be found in Greece. Canals and date palms, settlements amid the lush growth, and always the stifling heat became increasingly the rule as they approached that almost mythical city, about which Greeks so often spoke but with little real knowledge.

If Herodotus visited Babylon sometime between 470 and 460 B.C., he saw only as much as was apparent from his ride down river, and perhaps the dock areas. He failed to notice most of the major buildings of the city as well as its general layout and, clearly, received little help from the inhabitants, perhaps because of the language barrier among a people who generally spoke Aramaic and had little familiarity with Greek.[12] Again, if Alexander used Herodotus at all, he here had another opportunity to see the historian's weaknesses. There is a better case for the King's use of Xenophon's *Cyropaedeia,* though its references to the Babylonians offer little information of value save the strength of Mesopotamian resistance to Cyrus' Persians.

Two ideas were prevalent in the Greek literature of Alexander's time concerning this city on the Euphrates. The first was that its people, though they were often confused with the Assyrians, were effeminate and debauched, as in Aristophanes' *The Babylonians.* Greek tradition frequently confused men with women rulers and had transformed the real Assyrian queen, Sammuramat, of apparently impressive but not miraculous talents, into the nonexistent Queen of Babylon, Semiramis, who allegedly built the city and traveled to India in conquest. The stamp of general weakness and frequent feminine rule was placed so firmly on the Babylonians by the Greeks, that the Neo-Babylonian period has only recently been rescued from the charge of being effete.[13] The second notion about Babylon among the Greeks was that it was the source of wonderful knowledge concerning astronomy, divination, astrology, and perhaps magic.[14] These things, with which Chaldean priests of the city were credited, are to some extent based on sound fact, for Mesopotamian astronomical observations and records accompanied by their explanation as omens have come down to us in large numbers. The first hints of this kind of knowledge had come to the Greeks in the time of the early Ionian philosopher, Thales.

Material indications of the presence of Greeks and Greek influences are not as rich in Babylon as they are for Phoenicia and Palestine, or even Persis. Aside from a few possibly Greek names on Neo-Babylonian cuneiform tablets, they are confined largely to numismatic evidence. Fifth-century coins from Athens, Aegina, Samos, and Lycia have been described as "probably" found at

Babylon.[15] One Athenian coin of about 450 B.C. was even found at Ur at the head of the Persian Gulf south of the city.[16] Coins, of course, often circulate much farther than the people who issue them; their occurrence is not sure evidence of Greek presence. Herodotus obviously felt uncomfortable when he found himself far away from things Greek during his visit to Babylon. There is, however, coincidental interest in the Lycian coin mentioned above and the Lycian guide Alexander was to employ to lead him into Persis.[17] Leon Legrain has recently published two seal impressions made from the obverse and reverse of a fifth-century Athenian tetradrachm.[17a]

As the Macedonian army approached the city, it was met by a procession of priests and people streaming through the gates. Mazaeus came out to present the city. His resistance was ended, and Alexander, mindful of the strength of the Persian's wing at Gaugamela, willingly accepted him with honors. Greek ideas about the Babylonians must have seemed confirmed, for the rest of the people, and especially the commander of the garrison within the city, not to be outdone by Mazaeus, chanted hymns and cast flowers in the young King's path. The Babylonian cavalry rode forth, not to battle, but to show its finery. Weapons and arms alike had been stylized to the point of being mere decorations to the eyes of the battle-hardened Macedonians, as proud dandies pranced to the wonderment of Alexander's weary men.

Babylon no longer was defensible after Xerxes finished with its walls and temples. The fortifications now had gaping holes. The ziggurat, the huge tower known locally as Esagila, had nearly been pulled down along with the destruction of other temples. Finally, the Persians, presumably at the time of Xerxes' sack of the city, had blocked the river channels to the south.[18] The city's economic superiority, as well as its military potential, were to be ended.

Still, the Macedonians found much at which to marvel once they got inside the walls. The Ishtar Gate, the great processional entrance to the city on the south side, was still intact with its massive portals and decorations showing hybrid mythical monsters on the glazed brick face. The soldiers must have wandered in awe along the way leading from the gate into the city, over paved streets with tar showing between the baked clay blocks. Not far from the gates were the hanging gardens. Curtius' accurate description of the substructure of the gardens with its heavy cross-walls, lends credence to what he says about the superstructure.[19] A forest on top of a building, which looked for all the world like a wooded mountain from a distance. Underneath, there were cool alcoves offering shelter from the heat of the day.

The Persians had had their troubles with Babylon, not only because of its resistance, but also because of enervation here in the verdant lowlands where, in between occasionally furious storms and floods, life was too easy. Tales of wholesale temple prostitution scandalized the Greeks when they learned that even wives of the wealthy were involved. This is doubtful, but prostitution for religious reasons is attested in the cuneiform sources of Mesopotamia. Alexander's troops rapidly came under the influence of this too-gay city, as the King was forced to remain there a month. During this time, the troops rested and wounds from Gaugamela mended.

When Alexander entered Babylon in October of 331, he had been king for six years. He had acquired the western end of the Persian Empire and now had penetrated to its center. It was again time for thought. Once in the city, with a chance to view its wonders, Alexander ordered the reconstruction of the temple Xerxes had destroyed. Work may have begun immediately on the ziggurat, which was cleared off and cut down nearly to ground level. The debris was removed to a location outside the Ishtar Gate, and ultimately a Greek theater was built on the mound, though it was completed long after Alexander's death, perhaps not even begun until after 311.[20] Work on the ziggurat lagged after the King left the city and had to be resumed when he returned from the conquest of India. Little is known concerning actual work on the temples.

The Mesopotamian tradition of the great New Year's celebration, the Akitu Festival, defined the reigning king's accession to, and later possession of, the throne. Each year the King would "take the hands of Bel" and lead the statue of the god out into the festive procession. This act, permitted only to the King, renewed his recognition as sovereign with the title of King of Babylon. The frequent willingness of Assyrian kings to participate in the festival had allowed the Babylonians to believe that they had a particular claim on Assyrian policies. Trouble between the two states was often signaled by the refusal, or inability, of the Assyrian king to "take the hands of Bel." However the Persians, perhaps from the time of Xerxes, refused to take the title, King of

Babylon, emphasizing instead the title, King of the Lands, in the oldest Mesopotamian traditions, going back to the Sumerians. In refusing, the Persians apparently wished to make it clear that, insofar as the official designation of the reigning king depended upon festival processions, those ceremonies would take place at Persepolis, not Babylon.

Alexander carefully followed Persian precedent in the matter of his own title. Although he undoubtedly permitted the Babylonian priesthoods to participate in new festivities, he took the title King of the Lands, not King of Babylon.[21] By so doing, at one of the centers of the Persian Empire, he was now tangibly proclaiming himself the new dynast of all Asia. And here, as in Phoenicia, there was reason to be aware that a large part of this empire, potentially a dangerous part, had yet to be conquered.

The Macedonian king clearly gave some thought to the East. Again, the evidence is only circumstantial, but his month in the city gave him ample time for probing. The presence in Babylon of information about its past at the time of Alexander's visit is shown by the continuation of cuneiform literature through this time and into the period after his death. Furthermore, the priests in charge of these documents were the very ones supported by the King's orders for reconstruction, and his careful attention to Persian example in his choice of titles indicates he used his information.

Babylonia had lived for centuries under what might be called its eastern problem. As early as the Sumerian period, troops from Elam in the mountains to the east had more than once descended to the plain leaving a trail of destruction and havoc. Later, in the Assyrian age, the growing union betweeen Babylonia and Assyria from the time of Tiglath Pileser III constituted a threat to the peoples of Elam. The threat was forestalled for a time when the Elamite king, Humbanigash, discerned that "it was preferable to fight the battles of Elam on the plains of Babylonia." [22]

To the end of the Assyrian Empire, the Elamites, and later other peoples of the mountains, plagued all efforts to exercise strong control over the plains. They participated in more than one major battle, and the declining years of Assyria were increasingly occupied with campaigns in the mountains to the east. The fall of Assyria between 612 and 605 B.C. came about under the combined efforts of Babylon and the hordes from the mountains who appear initially in Babylonian chronicles as the Umman-

Manda, but who later turn out to have been Medes.[23] The Persian invasion itself had come from these same eastern mountains. The Persians had first taken Babylon under Cyrus almost exactly 208 years to the day before Alexander's entry. Darius I had to retake the city again in 522 after a rebellion. Xerxes took it a third time in 482, when with Assyrian-like exasperation he destroyed temples and fortifications, laid a heavy tax on the inhabitants, and plunged the land into depression. Indeed, there were many reasons why the Babylonians should have called Alexander's attention to the cities of Persia beyond the mountains as the proper objective for the King's own propaganda of revenge.

The Macedonian king spent the remainder of his month in Babylon working out the direction of his new empire. Mazaeus, whose voluntary surrender after the trouble he had caused at Gaugamela was much appreciated, became satrap of Babylon. This was the second instance of what was soon to become a fixed policy with Alexander: the use of Persians alongside Macedonian officials. The first such appointment had been Sabictas, sent as satrap to Cappadocia as the Macedonians passed it by. Alexander had made a similar arrangement in Egypt, and his decision to try it again in Babylon might lead to the suspicion that the young King also regarded the threat of rebellion by the Babylonians as small. The city had few troops, and those whom it could boast had already impressed the Macedonians with their frivolous appearance. But again, the King was careful to divide the powers among the persons he left behind: Mazaeus would have one Macedonian as a garrison commander and another to supervise finances. It should also be noted that Mazaeus had shown much greater ability than is suspected of the Egyptian Doloaspis. Before the arrival of Alexander, this Persian had been satrap of Cilicia, where the King even now was issuing coins influenced by Mazaeus' own coinage at Tarsus. Furthermore, Mazaeus was allowed to coin at Babylon for local uses. Perhaps his chief qualification in the eyes of the Macedonian king had been his good sense to recognize the superiority of Alexander's position over Darius. In any case, the problem of finding able administrators was already becoming acute. The King had left officials to supervise every concentration of political power he had come across. And in this exotic area of Babylonia, new skills—and popular acceptance— were needed to provide a stable transition from Persian to Macedonian control. Two more Macedonians were entrusted with oversight of all the satrapies from Babylonia to Cilicia, but the 1,000 talents and orders they received to recruit additional troops would make it appear that gathering more soldiers rather than political oversight was their chief assignment.

Curtius is probably correct in saying that reinforcements reached Alexander in Babylon.[24] These were mercenaries and infantry from Antipater, who must have dispatched them before his trouble with Agis of Sparta. There may have been some further reorganization of the army as Antipater's reinforcements were worked into it. Alexander made at least minor changes in the assignments of his troops at almost every stop. Also, fifty nobly born young men arrived to serve as the King's pages. Their function was to attend Alexander personally, watch his tent at night, and accompany him on his hunts and general noncombat activities.

By now, the Macedonians had been in Babylon a full month, and the wounded had recovered. The soldiers were rested, perhaps too well, if reports of the diversions in Babylon are correct. There was danger of enervation and idleness, in any case. Near the first of December of 331, Alexander gave the order to move out to the east to Susa, and beyond that, toward the mountains of Persis.

3.   Western Iran

Alexander had sent Philoxenus on ahead to Susa to arrange the surrender of the city. Word came back as the King approached that all was in order. The Macedonians entered without difficulty. The first section of the imperial treasury was uncovered here, netting Alexander some 5,000 talents in silver, approximately $4.5 million at current value. The troops also found a number of treasures that had been captured by the Persians in their invasion of Greece. Among them were the sculptured figures of Harmodius and Aristogeiton, who lived in Athenian memory as the assassins of the tyrant Hipparchus at the end of the sixth century. These pieces were promptly shipped back to Athens as tangible evidence of the progress of Alexander's war of revenge. They were still standing near the Acropolis in Athens in Arrian's day, 450 years later. They also came across a large throne used by Darius, on which Alexander promptly sat.[25] He discovered that sitting on it left his feet a good yard off the floor, and ordered a nearby table placed as a footstool. The Macedonians had not yet realized that Persian thrones were deliberately raised so that the seated King would be over the heads of all his attendants.[26]

The usual games and sacrifices took place while the King remained in Susa. Abulites became satrap; Alexander, finding him in prison at Susa, concluded that he could take this as an indication of hostility toward Darius. It was the third Persian satrapal appointment. And again, Macedonian military commanders would accompany the new satrap. Menes went back to Cilicia, Phoenicia, and Syria as satrap. The King was beginning to think of his empire in terms of a regional organization. Now, Antigonus was in charge of Phrygia, where the military situation made him in effect the commander of all Asia Minor; Cleomenes was directing affairs in Egypt; Mazaeus, Babylonia; and Menes, the coastal provinces of the eastern Mediterranean. Since at the same time more reinforcements arrived from Macedonia, Alexander reorganized his cavalry by dividing them up into units of 100 each, the *lochoi*. One last arrangement involved the decision to leave the family of Darius behind in Susa.

Leaving Susa for the southeast, the Macedonians next entered the territory of the Uxians, from whom there was some resistance, as these wild tribesmen hoped for the continued monetary subsidies they had been receiving from Persian kings. They were tracked down instead. Darius' mother is alleged to have persuaded Alexander to spare them, so he let them off with a stiff assessment of horses and sheep. He apparently also ordered them to give up their nomadic existence and settle in villages, an effort to create some stability among them.[27]

The army met more serious fighting at the Persian Gates when they sought to enter the mountains separating Persis proper from the West. Ariobarzanes had stationed himself at the pass with a large number of troops. Alexander left Craterus in position before the Persians with orders to attack when he received the signal. Then, taking with him a Lycian prisoner who had been serving the Persians after being captured by them, the King made for a side pass about which the man had told him. Curtius has a graphic description of the extreme hardships undergone by Alexander's party as they fought their way through heavy snows and over rocky crags to get behind the position held by Ariobarzanes. The effort, however, was successful: they gained the Persians' rear, gave the signal to Craterus, caught the enemy in an assault on two fronts, and took the pass.

As they proceeded on through and down onto the plain of Persepolis itself, they were met by a group of Greeks, presumably artisans, all of whom had been mutilated by the Persians.[28] The Macedonians were horrified at this wretched array. Their story was that they had been maimed in a deliberate effort to keep them from running away. Their presence, if the episode is genuine, would seem to indicate that Darius had kept his Greek mercenaries away from this Persian capital and ignorant of the situation there. Out of pity, Alexander offered them a sizeable reward, but they insisted they were in too sad a state ever to return to families and homes. Finally, they were settled in a colony, each receiving 3,000 drachmas, almost ten years' pay at the going rate for mercenaries.

Shortly thereafter, the King arrived at Persepolis. Even Macedonians, who had seen Egypt's pyramids and the wonders of Babylon, must have been impressed by this city, which had received the special care and attention of Persian kings since its beginning. One may picture the troops wandering with echoing footsteps in the Hall of the Hundred Columns, through the magnificent portals of the apadana, up and down the grand processional staircase with its relief figures of the attendants and guards of the Great King. Then came the Treasury, where they found bullion, coins, jewels, and artifacts, the estimated value of which was equal to nearly a quarter billion dollars—more money than Macedonians had dreamed existed. When all this reached the markets of the Greek world, it was responsible for many of the changes that set the period after Alexander apart from what had gone before, that separate the Hellenic from the Hellenistic period of Greek history. It financed an explosion of political as well as economic activity, producing operations on a far grander scale than ever before.

The operation of the treasury at Persepolis still is little known. The clay tablets found there with cuneiform writing on them offer little information. Their contents concern only local arrangements: pay for workers, accounts of local supplies, and the like. There is some doubt that they even refer to the treasury the Macedonians found.[29] In the presence of all the valuables Alexander uncovered, some of the tablets indicate that workers occasionally were paid in goods rather than money,[30] though this may only reflect conditions of the local economy, still largely barter. The possibility has been suggested that the tablets found by the modern excavators of Persepolis refer to a purely local enterprise only incidentally associated with imperial affairs.[31]

The excavations in the Treasury throw other light on Alexander's stay in Persepolis, however. Macedonian soldiers mutilated some of the reliefs depicting the Persian king and his attendants. On one wall of the Treasury, the face of the king was hacked, and a duplicate relief on another wall shows that his attendant received the same treatment. The scene is an interesting one. A Mede stands respectfully before the king, bowing slightly, with his right hand raised to his mouth. Between the two reliefs, both the hand and face of the Mede and the face of the king are mutilated, leaving us to speculate whether it was the act of obeisance or the person of the Mede that, along with the King, had aroused the wrath of the troops.[32]

Alexander remained at Persepolis until the spring of 330. He learned that Agis of Sparta had been defeated by Antipater at Megalopolis in the Peloponnesus, good news indeed. Also, the King made a thirty-day foray into the surrounding countryside.

But the event to arouse the greatest interest was the burning of the great palace. The results of this conflagration have not failed to shock all who have seen its remains. According to one story, Thais, an Athenian courtesan, suggested to the King during a drunken orgy that they set fire to the palace; this is not likely, for Athenaeus says that Thais was not present at the time.[33] Arrian tells us Parmenion advised against it, that burning the headquarters of the Great King would be irresponsible and hardly conducive to confidence among the Asians. Alexander is alleged to have replied that it would be fitting vengeance for Xerxes' destruction of Greece. Some modern writers have suggested it was revenge for Xerxes' destruction of Babylon; others, that it was an accident.

Several things must be considered in connection with the burning of Persepolis. Its excavators have found signs of transfer of the contents of the Treasury, leaving a trail of coins through the building, up a flight of stairs, and out over the roof.[34] This hurried looting would make the burning appear deliberate, as Arrian says it was. A possible reason for deliberate destruction may be found in the nature of Persepolis itself, for the city had a unique character among the capitals of the Persian Empire. It was outside the regular satrapal organization. It was never listed among the satrapies, a point of which Herodotus was aware.[35] Surprisingly enough, the isolated city was rarely used. It served as a burial place for the kings, and it housed the major section of the imperial treasury. Many things point to its existence almost solely as a ritual city for the Persians. It was the center of the festive ceremonies that occasioned the crowning of a new king, in what was perhaps a deliberate transfer of the notion of the Babylonian Akitu Festival to Persian home territory. As such, it symbolized the empire itself, as is borne out by many of the decorations excavators have found in its ruins. Among them are things symbolic of Life, of the Sacred Mountain in which the kings were buried, of Water without which Life could not exist, of the Great King's claim to the four quarters of the earth, and of the enormous power resident in the Persian throne. If such be the case, Alexander's act in destroying Persepolis could have been symbolic of the destruction of the Persian Empire.[36]

Beyond this, he destroyed the one center to which Darius, or a pretender to the throne, could repair and most easily send out a call for Persians once more to rally to the defense of the empire. The reasons are clear. It was the center of the Persian heartland, and the place from which Great Kings before had moved out with their cavalry to conquer and reconquer. Because it was economically self-sufficient,[37] it possibly could serve again in the same manner. One may note that in recent years, an increased dependence upon Greek mercenaries had tended to change this previous reliance upon the free Persian cavalry.[38] This brought about a change from dependence upon levies of free subjects and allies, to the reliance upon monetary resources instead. But Persian funds at Persepolis and elsewhere were far from exhausted, and though Alexander may have thought there hardly could be much more after seeing what had been left at Persepolis, he had no way of knowing the actual extent of Persian funds. However, the most important consideration is the fact that, even without his treasury, the Great King could quite possibly still appeal for cavalry levies. This central point of Persian strength must have appeared ominously threatening to Alexander, since he had not really defeated the cavalry contingents of Darius either at Issus or at Gaugamela. So, if it was no accident, Persepolis was burned as a center of strength both symbolic and actual, around which further resistance could have been organized. Just as Olynthus, Thebes, and Tyre had paid the price of being centers of actual and potential resistance to the Macedonian juggernaut, Persepolis' smoking ruins now joined their ranks.

When spring of 330 was well along, Alexander left Persepolis for Pasargadae, where he found the tomb of Cyrus the Great. Perhaps out of veneration for Cyrus, engendered by reading Xenophon's *Cyropaedeia,* he ordered the tomb cleaned and redecorated before going on to Media, where he had heard Darius was staying. Alexander's information was that the Persian king intended to remain in Media while the Macedonians went south to Persepolis. He would stay so long as Alexander kept to the lowlands. If the young King moved to follow him, he would retire to the east, to Parthia, Hyrcania, and ultimately to Bactria, ravaging the countryside to make Macedonian progress as difficult as possible. He had sent what remained of his women and baggage on north to the Caspian Gates while he waited in Ecbatana. Learning all or part of this, Alexander moved north toward Ecbatana, subduing the Paraetacae along the way, and leaving in charge Oxathres the son of Abulites as his Persian satrap of Susa. Now another rumor came: Darius had acquired some Cadusian and Scythian allies and had resolved to fight. Leaving orders for the baggage train to follow at its normal speed, he hurried toward Ecbatana. Three days away from the city, modern Hamadan, he was met by Bistanes, son of Artaxerxes Ochus. Darius was five days gone from the city, and he had taken 6,000 foot soldiers and 3,000 cavalry along with 7,000 talents for the purpose of acquiring more recruits. Unable to overtake the Persian king immediately, Alexander had time for a short stay at Ecbatana.

While in the capital of Media, Alexander discharged the Thessalian cavalry and the rest of the allies, with full pay and a combined bonus of 2,000 talents. He then gave to those who desired it an opportunity to enlist as mercenaries to accompany him farther. Opinion is nearly universal that this event, rather than the finding of Darius, marks the change in Alexander's official policy. Persepolis was destroyed; the Persian king was in full flight; the largest and most meaningful part of the empire had been seized. It was no longer a war of liberation and revenge for things done by Persians to Greeks. The aim henceforth was to be the acquisition and security of the full Persian Empire, which Alexander would administer as the new Great King.

Like all of Alexander's policies, this had grown through a period preceding its open acknowledgment. He had already faced the problem of administering this empire so foreign to things Greek and Macedonian by working Persians into its official structure. He could do this because men like Mazaeus were willing and able; he had to do it because his own managerial resources had long since been depleted by the multitude of satrapal and military appointments already made. Furthermore, he must adjust at least the outward manifestations of his reign somewhat to Persian usages, if they were to be able to understand him as the new Great King. This took the form of affecting Persian dress and mannerisms when dealing with matters of Persian state. It was also revealed in the King's changing attitude toward himself. Plutarch tells us that at this time he dropped the courtesy of beginning his communications with "Greeting" to all save Phocion and Antipater.[39]   Even if he had not been impressed with his own success, the very necessities of the situation would have tended to seal Alexander off from the Macedonians who did not understand his Persian ways because they had neither intended nor understood that the conquests now so long under way were to end in ruling the Persian Empire for its own sake. They had thought of conquest and of the fruits of victory, and they were jealous of the King's new manners. They were even more jealous of the favor he was showing the conquered Persians whom he placed in office. Tarn is correct when he points out that here begins the tragedy of Alexander,[40] separated from his wondering commanders by ideas and ideals alike. The King was not the man to show a great deal of patience with their lack of vision; indeed, it seems quite clear that he deliberately withheld from them a great deal of the information on which his actions were based.

There were also changes in appointments and commands at Ecbatana. The Thessalians and other allies who had indicated their wish to return home were allowed to depart, and the King sent Epillocus with them to lead them to the sea and to relay his orders to Menes in Phoenicia to find them transport to Greece. He ordered Parmenion to bring the treasury of Persepolis to Ecbatana and there to turn it over to Harpalus, who thus became the imperial treasurer. He would have 6,000 Macedonians as guards. Parmenion then went on ahead to Hyrcania in preparation for the King's departure in that direction. Ecbatana marks a change in the assignments of this general who so long had been the mainstay of the Macedonian army, for after this next move toward the Caspian, Parmenion was stationed in Media and put in charge of the King's communications. Of late, Craterus had been taking over the old general's military duties, and now the change was complete, though Craterus did not assume Parmenion's position as chief of staff.

Leaving Ecbatana, Alexander arrived at Rhagae, near modern Tehran, after eleven days of brutally rapid marching. It was midsummer of 330 as he reached this spot, just one day away from the Caspian Gates. Darius had already gone through the Gates, losing many deserters as he fled. The Macedonians rested five days, and the King appointed Oxodates satrap of the region. Two days later, Alexander was passing through the Caspian Gates, where he was met by Bagistanes and Mazaeus' son Antibelus, who told him that Darius was in trouble. Nabarzanes, Bessus, and Barsaentes the satrap of Arachosia and Drangia, had arrested the Persian king. At the time, Alexander had just dispatched a foraging party into the hills near the Gates, but he now departed hurriedly, leaving them behind and with orders for Craterus to follow with the main party at normal pace. The King, with a small number of troops, marched through the night until the next noon and all through the next night, until he arrived at the camp from which Bagistanes had come. There, he received confirmation that Darius was indeed under arrest. Moreover, Bessus had been hailed king by his Bactrian cavalry and the other Persians in his company. Artabazus and the Greek mercenaries had refused to accede to the change, and after some unavailing efforts to aid Darius, had left. Bessus, Alexander heard, planned to bargain with the person of the King if he were pursued. If not pursued, he intended to raise a new army with which to preserve the kingdom. Alexander pressed on despite flagging men and horses. Again, they marched all night through till noon the next day, now just one day behind the Persians. Finally, he ordered the cavalry to dismount and the infantrymen to take their horses to continue the chase. He was able to take a shortcut and came upon the party at dawn near modern Shahrud. Bessus had been dragging Darius along in a wagon, bound like a common criminal. At the last minute, most of the Persians fled, but not before Nebarazanes and Barsaentes had delivered a fatal wound to Darius. The King died before Alexander could reach him.

The young King sent the remains back to Persepolis for burial. There is a certain poignancy about this ruler who had been weak at the wrong moment. Whatever his youth had been, he was a poor fighter compared to the Macedonian genius against whom fate had ranged him. Almost nothing concerning harsh acts on his part has come down to us save the mutilation of the Greeks at Persepolis and the massacre and mutilations of the Macedonians at Issus. Whether conniving or caught in a trap not of his own making we probably will never be sure. What is clear is that his reign was a series of disasters once the Macedonian campaign began. His earlier victories against Bogoas and in Armenia and Egypt were not even remembered. Greek historians, who can hardly qualify as unprejudiced, have left us the impression of a man who was cowardly and inefficient, whose ignominious death was little more than could be expected.

The passing of Darius, however, is the point at which to take note of something new in the thinking of Alexander. For he now was discovering that Iran had two divisions: East and West. Persian inscriptions are always careful to make a distinction between western satrapies and those in the east, beyond the great salt desert.[41] The easiest way around this desert was in the north by the Caspian, the route Darius had hoped to follow in order to recruit a new army in the east. Some of the eastern levies, under Bessus, had fought at Gaugamela, but clearly Darius counted on being able to find more. The Iranian cavalry, the object of these efforts, with their tough, fast horses and personal armor, had not been defeated by Alexander. That he realized the importance of these troops, and that this was the major reason for his continuing eastward after finding Darius dead, is shown by two things. He delivered an address to his men in which he urged them to go on with him to the east. The empire was not yet secure; there were many possibilities of further rebellion. Bypassing Cappadocia had already proved that Persian provinces could not be held by a mere show of force at their borders. Curtius even has him saying that Bessus would be back knocking at the doors of the Greece if not stopped. The Persians all would submit when they saw by Alexander's deeds that he sought only to punish Bessus' crime against Darius, not to destroy them.[42] The other thing that makes Alexander's appreciation of the Iranian cavalry so clear is the fact that he incorporated a number of these armored cavalrymen, the cataphracts, with his own forces as soon as he was able.

But now Darius was dead, and the Macedonian king had determined to track down his murderers and to secure the east, for himself and for the safety of the empire. It was still summer, 330.

CHAPTER V

The East

1. Eastern Iran

ALTHOUGH BESSUS WAS AHEAD OF HIM, ALEXANDER TURNED BACK toward the Caspian and crossed the Elburz Mountains into the lowlands of Hyrcania bordering the sea. On the way, he split his forces, sending Craterus on a western swing to engage the Tapurian mountaineers. Erigyius was to lead the baggage train by the longer, good road of the mountains above Shahrud, while the King took a picked company and made directly over the top. They would meet in Zadracarta.

Alexander's objective was the tattered remainder of Darius' mercenaries, now only about 1,500 in number. After finishing his short campaign in Hyrcania, during which he confirmed at least one local Persian as satrap, he proceeded towards Zadracarta, modern Gorgān. On the way, the mercenaries began to join him, nervously willing to take their chances with the young King. Along with them appeared a number of Greeks, emissaries from the Black Sea regions to the dead Persian king. Alexander dismissed the envoys as having only been engaged in attendance upon their suzerain, the king of Persia. Those mercenaries who had served Darius before the signing of the peace and alliance at Corinth were also dismissed; the rest were enrolled among his troops. Alexander needed all the manpower he could get. A few Spartan envoys who had accompanied the East Greeks were detained.

After the meeting of Zadracarta, the Macedonians began their march eastward, through Parthia to Susia, a city of Areia, now profiting from the use of Persian itineraries and other documents, and Persian roads. At Susia, Alexander met Satibarzanes whom he promptly confirmed as satrap of Areia, and then sent the Persian towards the southeast with Anaxippus and forty mounted javelin men. News came to Susia that Bessus had proclaimed himself a new Artaxerxes, King of Asia, and wore the royal robe and upright cap of the Great King. He had Persian stragglers and Bactrians with him and was expecting Scythian allies. Alexander immediately left Susia for Bactria, joined on the way by Philip, bringing up from Media the mercenaries and Thessalian cavalry who had elected to remain with the King.

Just as the army was entering Bactria, however, a courier arrived with news that Satibarzanes was in revolt behind them. Anaxippus and the javelin men lay dead, and the Persian was arming all Areians who would assemble at Artacoana. Either the first flareup of Zoroastrian religious zeal against the foreign conqueror,[1] or a diversion instigated by Bessus to keep Alexander from the borders of Bactria, the rebellion presented severe problems. Not only was the effort to include Persians within a Macedonian government for eastern Iran at issue, but it was also impossible now for Alexander to go directly against Bessus.

Leaving the bulk of his forces with Craterus to return at a slower pace, Alexander took a picked force and raced back to Areia, covering the seventy miles to Artacoana in two days. Satibarzanes, much surprised, fled along with his Areians. Arsaces, a Persian probably from western Iran, replaced Satibarzanes as the King persisted in maintaining the principle of using Persian help. Quelling Satibarzanes' revolt, however, only revealed that Barsaentes was also in rebellion in Drangiana to the south. The strike against Bactria would be further put off as the Macedonians were forced instead to move southward. Craterus and the rest of the army joined the King as he entered the territory of the Drangaians. Barsaentes fled but was captured in India and returned later to Alexander.

When he arrived, Barsaentes was executed: according to Alexander, for his crime against Darius; according to Tarn, for rebellion.[2] Revolt in this area was a real problem, underscored by the possibility of collusion between Bessus, Artibarzanes, and Barsaentes. Alexander's propaganda was another matter. Earlier, Abulites had been rewarded because Alexander found him in a Persian prison, but Barsaentes was killed ostensibly for his crime against Darius. These instances would make Alexander seem both to reward and punish hostility towards Darius. By this time, however, Alexander intended to show that he had become the successor of Darius by punishing one of the conspirators against him. The determination to acquire and control this empire revenge had given him had now progressed through several steps: the appointment of Persians to official positions; the dismissal of the allies at Ecbatana; the decision to proceed against eastern Iran; and the propaganda claim to Darius' throne.

Alexander's efforts to place himself in the position of the Persian king, along with his increasing personal separation from the members of his command, had been a growing source of irritation to his generals for some time. In Drangiana, resentment boiled over in the conspiracy of Philotas, son of Parmenion. As noted before, Parmenion and his family formed a virtual dynasty among the higher ranks of the King's troops. Besides Parmenion himself, until lately the King's second in command, his oldest son Philotas had steadily risen in preference, and at Gaugamela commanded the Companion Cavalry. Nicanor had been an important officer until his death by disease only shortly before. A third son, Hector, although less known, had held high commands but apparently also was dead by this time. Finally, Coenus was Parmenion's son-in-law, still to give his greatest service and already high in the ranks. Yet, the family seems to have been in the forefront of those who resented Alexander's parade of Persian dress and manners. And these occasions became more frequent in the heart of the Persian Empire.

Parmenion had grown increasingly out of step with the King's strategy as well as his political policies. As he showed at Tyre, he saw little reason for crossing every succeeding mountain range or river, and had long since begun to wish for a more circumscribed empire. More than a few times, specific advice from the general had been rejected, as at the Granicus and Gaugamela, as well as at Tyre. Some would believe Alexander resented Parmenion's failure to hold the left at Gaugamela without help, which had cost the King his chance to capture Darius. This is not likely, for the course of the battle shows that it was Bessus' cavalry, not Parmenion's misfortune in facing Mazaeus, that delayed the pursuit. But in any case, relief from his command duties had come more often of late, though in effect it began as early as Tyre when Parmenion arrived from Damascus to find Craterus and Perdiccas in command during Alexander's absence in the Antilebanon. Moreover, he may have been left behind in Memphis while the King visited Siwah.[3] The crucial point came at Ecbatana, however, when Alexander dismissed the allied cavalry. Parmenion lost even the substance of his last command held at Gaugamela.

Although he had come to advanced age and might have expected retirement, the meaning of the change must have been brought home by the fact that he also had been given a palace at Susa,[4] and finally was left in Media in charge of communications and supply.[5] His last apparent combat assignment had been to precede Alexander to the Caspian Gates after bringing the treasure from Persepolis to Harpalus in Ecbatana.[6] He returned to Media shortly afterwards.

Conversely, Craterus' importance had steadily increased. At the Granicus he had commanded a battalion of the phalanx, but at Issus he led the combined infantry battalions of the left wing. He was in charge of building the mole at Tyre, and with Perdiccas took over command of the entire siege while Alexander was away. At Gaugamela, he was again in charge of the phalanx on the left, and he was the man placed in command before the Persian Gates while Alexander turned the pass. Philotas must have watched this advancement with growing irritation, for Curtius says they were acknowledged competitors.[7]

The King apparently had some inkling of difficulty with Philotas as early as the campaign in Egypt, but he brushed the thought aside. Parmenion's oldest son was still young, and he was overbearing toward those beneath him, which apparently included a number who considered themselves his equals. Nothing is said of his thoughts about Alexander's policies, but he could not have failed to resent his father's decline. Curtius devotes much space and lurid detail to the homosexual complications between two unimportant figures that lay behind the affair, to Philotas' failure to report their conspiracy to assassinate the King, and to his subsequent torture and death on accusation by Craterus. However, Ptolemy (in Arrian) simply says that the King accused Philotas of concealment and that the army declared him guilty and cut him down with javelins along with the other conspirators. Alexander Lyncestis, dragged along in chains for five years, was also executed. Parmenion, off in Media, was assassinated on orders from the King.

All this may be rationalized to some extent, as Arrian does, by suspecting either complicity with his son or the possibility of revolt after his execution. Parmenion, isolated from the army, was impotent to revolt, but astride Alexander's communications he could have done a great deal of damage at Ecbatana. One result of the trials was the King's decision to let no one again rise to

Parmenion's position of power. Philotas' command was split between Hephaestion and Cleitus the Black, two whom the king most trusted. A further result was the replacement of one of the suspected bodyguards by Ptolemy Lagus. The promotion put him within the inner circle of the King's confidants, giving him access to information from which Arrian's *History of Alexander* profits.

As the King continued south, he passed through the land of the Ariaspians. They received special favors because of their previous help to Cyrus the Great. He then ranged through the countryside receiving submission from the Drangaians and Arachosians. There was no settling into winter quarters that year, 330-29.[8] The army underwent such hardship in the deep snows that even Ptolemy must admit to the seriousness of the situation. To make matters worse while he was in the southeastern part of Iran, Alexander learned of a second revolt by the Areians. Satibarzanes had returned with 2,000 horse from Bessus. Arsaces was unable to withstand the onslaught. Erigyius and Caranus went back with a message to the Parthians, ordering them to help. A severe battle followed; it ended only with the death of Satibarzanes as Erigyius drove a lance through his face. The rest of the winter was spent in moving towards the Hindu Kush Mountains. Another Alexandria was founded in the foothills among the Paropamisadae, where there was a short halt for sacrifices and the appointment of a Persian satrap who, as usual, would serve with Macedonian overseers. By late March of 329, Alexander had begun to ascend into the higher altitudes of the main range of the Hindu Kush.

2. *The Bactrian Campaigns*

The detour away from the borders of Bactria the preceding summer meant that now Alexander must cross the mountains his original line of march would have avoided. Arrian[9] has confused the orientation of the Hindu Kush; these mountains actually run from southwest to northeast, and the King was approaching them from the southeast. On the other side, Bessus had enjoyed almost a full year in which to get his resistance organized. He had 7,000 Bactrians along with an unknown number of Persian fugitives and other allies. His plan was to ravage the countryside ahead of Alexander as he came down the ridges in the melting snows of spring (late April). But the Macedonians came on despite the resulting short supplies, and Bessus with Oxyartes and Spita-menes retired north across the Oxus River into Sogdiana, burn-ing the bridges as they went. The Bactrians, apparently disgusted at this flight, returned to their homes while Alexander came to the cities of Bactria. He took the most important, Bactra-Zariaspa (modern Balkh), without trouble.

The weather was warm by the time Alexander got to the Oxus. Its depth and swift current would make crossing difficult in the absence of bridges. The King paused to send home the elderly Macedonians in his army, starting them back under Stasanor, one of the Companions whom he ordered to take the place of Arsaces in Areia because he had "heard the Arsaces bore him ill-will." [10]

Attempts at integration were not working in the critical area between Bactria and the west. Arsaces had been persuaded, or forced, to enter into this third instance of nationalist reaction among the eastern Iranians under his charge. The kings of Persis had also had difficulty in the area, and now Alexander had inher-ited the problem.

The Macedonians got across the Oxus on straw-filled skins, such as they had used at the Danube. Once over, Alexander got word that Bessus was under arrest. He dispatched Ptolemy with nearly half the army to meet with Spitamenes and receive his sur-render of Bessus. With the Bactrian in his custody and Spita-nemes flown, Ptolemy requested further orders from Alexander, who told him to bring back his captive bound, naked, and with a wooden collar about his neck, and to station him alongside the road the army would take. When the King approached, he stopped his chariot and asked Bessus why he had seized, then murdered, Darius. The reply was that all in their company had decided to do it in order to receive pledges of safe conduct. The King then ordered him scourged while a herald walked in front of him proclaiming his misdeeds against Darius. Finally, Bessus was sent back to Bactra-Zariaspa to await judgment.

After using the resources of the area to bring his horses back up to full strength, Alexander left Bactria for northern Sogdiana and Maracanda, modern Samarkand, from which he conducted a number of forays in all directions. The expedition that went up to the Tanais River, now the Sayhun, ran into some trouble. The natives attacked, and Alexander was wounded in the leg. The enemy then fled into the mountains. The King remained in the area to found the "farthest" Alexandria, Alexandria Eschate,

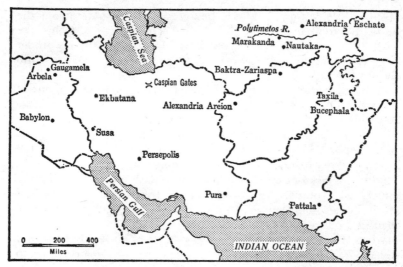

Modern Chodjend. While the city was being laid out, a party of Scyths from beyond the Tanais appeared offering peace, and the King reciprocated with an embassy of his own, which was also designed to get a glimpse of the territory to the north.

But trouble was brewing in the hot summer weather of 329. Bactrians had joined Sogdians in seizing the towns that lay between Alexandria Eschate and Maracanda, itself now under siege by Spitamenes. To make matters worse, more Scyths had appeared to aid in pulling down the Macedonians' latest conquests. The King divided his forces to retake the cities. This concluded, he sent a detachment on to Maracanda to relieve the besieged garrison.

The King then returned to the river where a party of Scyths were massed on the other side. To silence their taunts he crossed the stream and promptly encountered a new kind of warfare. The Scythian cavalry formed a circle to race around his troops. The Parthians later used the same technique to wipe out a Roman army at Carrhae, and our sources are not clear how Alexander met the difficulty. Presumably, he ordered a cavalry charge of his own, relying on the reserve strength of the Bactrian horses he had recently acquired to break up the circle. However, in the heat of late summer, the King drank some polluted water after the battle was over and had to be carried back to camp suffering from diarrhea and dehydration. There, he received an apology from the Scyths for their insults. The weakened King accepted with grace rather than prolong the expedition; Maracanda still lay under siege behind him, and the force sent to relieve it had run into serious trouble.

Alexander apparently had not clearly given command to one of the three officers sent to Maracanda with this party. They were Andromachus, Caranus, and Pharnuces, a Lycian interpreter sent along because of his familiarity with the language. As they approached Maracanda and Spitamenes' besieging forces to find the Persian retreating to the northwest along the Polytimetus River, Pharnuces' lack of experience led him to dash ahead thinking the enemy was routed. The result was a trap. The Macedonians crossed to an island only to find themselves ringed by Spitamenes' men. All but a handful were cut down while Pharnuces, Andromachus, and Caranus each tried to evade responsibility now that disaster had overtaken them. Some time later, the King came up to Maracanda on forced march and attacked Spitamenes, who had returned to the siege. The Persian again fled down the Polytimetus River until it disappeared in the desert sands now cooling under autumn skies. There, Alexander left the chase and returned to bury the Macedonians lying dead at the island ambush. The problems that had brought him south from Chodjend now had been solved, but the effort had been expensive, and Spitamenes was still at large among the desert Scyths to the west.

Alexander returned to Bactra-Zariaspa, south of the Oxus, for winter quarters of 329/328 where he met several late arrivals from the west. Nearly all brought troops, which were greatly needed, for the difficult summer had worn most units far below paper strength. There also appeared a second embassy from the northern Scyths, whose new king offered friendship, marriage alliances, and submission. All offers were courteously declined. Alexander also declined the offer of Pharasmenes, the Chorasinian king, to supply and guide an expedition against Colchis and the Amazons east of the Black Sea. His reply to Pharasmenes is a clue to his thinking: with India he would have all Asia and then could return to Greece, from where he could make a full expedition into Pontus. The statement was made in good faith, for such a campaign might hope to solve the problem of Persian action in Asia Minor. The Chorasinian king was asked to wait till then to fulfil his promises. The King now turned his attention to Bessus. The

Bactrian's nose and ears were cut off, over which Arrian sorrowfully observes that conquering a world is nothing alongside the loss of self-mastery. Bessus was then sent to Ecbatana where, some say, he was split in half.

With spring came Spitamenes. The King heard that the Sogdians were gathering at strong points. Just as Areia had needed taking three times, Sogdiana apparently was not going to remain passive. With the warm weather, the King moved back over the Oxus, leaving a holding force in Bactria. Once on the other side, he determined upon a new strategy to avoid the pitfalls of Areia. He split his troops into smaller tactical bands with mixed weapons.[11] These combat groups could then occupy the whole area and keep Spitamenes from friends and supplies. Hephaestion, Coenus, Ptolemy, and Perdiccas commanded four of the detachments, with orders to spread out. Alexander took the fifth towards Maracanda. It was long, hard work and it filled most of the summer of 328, but taking their homes and sources of supply finally enabled the Macedonians to end resistance from the Sogdian cavalry.

At Maracanda there was a drinking party, probably while the King awaited the arrival of the other combat groups. Alexander usually had sacrificed to Dionysus at this season, but this time he was sacrificing to the divine twins, Castor and Pollux. During the heavy drinking afterward, flatterers got the King's ear with observation that Castor and Pollux, even Heracles, were nothing beside Alexander. Only envy kept the living from receiving divine honors due such exploits.

All this distressed Cleitus the Black, Alexander's boyhood friend. His sister Lanice had been the young Prince's nurse, and he had saved the King's life at the Granicus. He was upset by Persian barbarism and Greek flatterers who belittled gods and heroes to overrate Alexander. He thought the King could have done nothing without his Macedonians, and he said as much. Alexander was hurt at the outburst. The flatterers tried to cover the incident by overriding it. They began to draw invidious comparisons between the King and his father, Philip. Too drunk to see the signs, Cleitus interpreted this as a challenge and began to minimize Alexander in even stronger terms, ending with the observation that the King owed his life to him. Alexander jumped up in a dark rage but was restrained by friends standing near. Cleitus, past sensitivity from the combination of rage, alcohol, and chagrin, railed on. The King called for his bodyguard, whom the appalling episode had turned to stone. Muttering that he was little better than Bessus, led about by those under him, king in name only, Alexander grabbed a pike while Cleitus was hurried out. Cleitus got away from his friends when he heard the King screaming his name and dashed back, to be run through by the pike in Alexander's hands.

There are some who say Alexander propped his spear against a wall with the thought of falling upon it, believing it improper for one to live who had killed a friend while drunk. But many who have written about Alexander do not follow this account, but say instead he lay lamenting on his couch, calling out the names of Cleitus and Cleitus' sister Lanice, daughter of Dropides, who had been his nurse. He bewailed the wonderful gift he had given her now that he had become a man. The very brother of the one who had seen her own children fighting and dying for him he had killed with his own hand! He continued to call himself slayer of his friends, refusing to eat or drink for three days or to care for any of his physical needs.[12]

This went on until all about him were as frightened of losing his leadership as they had beeen horrified at the murder of Cleitus. Some blamed the outburst on the god Dionysus, jealous at having been slighted in the sacrifices. Anaxarchus, the philosopher, argued that no crime had been committed since the king was above Justice, a point Arrian severely censors. Finally, the King roused himself and went on. But what his covert enemies had seen as early as Tyre, his closest friends now saw: no one could trifle with Alexander. Direct exchange of free opinion with him was no longer possible.

Once all the parties were together at Maracanda, various detachments went to plant settlements in Sogdiana and to secure the north against the Scyths. This worked well for Sogdiana, but now the King learned that Spitamenes had managed to get together some 600 of the Massagetae Scyths of the west and had slipped behind the Macedonians into Bactria. He attacked several Bactrian forts and then moved to Bactra-Zariaspa itself. The city was held for Alexander merely by some work parties and a number of sick. Those who could took up arms and sallied forth against Spitamenes, only to find themselves ambushed. Craterus was the first on the scene, but Spitamenes was able to flee back into the desert, leaving 150 dead Scyths behind.

Then the summer was over, and Alexander ordered Coenus

into winter quarters in Sogdiana with a major part of the army and Bactrian and Sogdian allies. His assignment was to stop Spitamenes if he should come during the cold season. Alexander took the rest of the army to spend the winter of 328/327 at Nautaca. Spitamenes did come. Isolated from the strong points of Sogdiana by Macedonia garrisons, he decided to drive directly against Coenus. His fighting force consisted of 3,000 Scyth riders. There was a severe battle, but as soon as the Scyths began to realize they were not likely to get the loot promised them by Spitamenes, they turned to looting their own allies and then left for the desert with the Persian in tow. They announced their disengagement from Spitamenes' now hopeless cause and empty promises by sending his head back to the Macedonians. It was the end of one of Alexander's most able opponents, a man who had held up the Macedonians for a year and a half, making them purchase both Bactria and Sogdiana at a high price.

The following spring saw the last of Alexander's campaigns beyond the Hindu Kush. The one remaining outpost of resistance north of the Oxus was the Sogdian Rock, held by the forces of Oxyartes, who had accompanied Bessus and who still led the scattered remnants of resistance. He had sent his family to a position of safety atop the rock, where they thought they had an unassailable refuge. The settlement lay in a saddle just under the highest summit of the peak, and below it the walls were sheer on all sides. The deep snows of early spring at these altitudes made the Macedonian approach all the more difficult while supplying the defenders with abundant water. The King arranged for a parley, and was told the defenders would surrender when Alexander found men who could fly. Furious, the young King offered handsome prizes to the first twelve who could reach the summit behind the town. Three hundred mountaineers with iron pegs and ropes volunteered to try it. The 270 who managed to make the peak above the town waved flags to show Alexander they had arrived. The King sent word to the tribesmen to turn and look at his winged men. They capitulated.

Among the people in the settlement was Oxyartes' beautiful daughter, Roxane. The King fell in love with her, we are told, and in due course they were united in marriage by a ceremony of slicing together a loaf of bread. Alexander was a complicated person, and his falling in love cannot have been a simple event, but must have had political overtones. The marriage might help with the task of reconciling Sogdians, Bactrians, and Persians to Macedonian rule. Certainly Oxyartes was won over, and he swept into camp to participate in the happy ceremonies. Two of his sons joined the Macedonian forces along with contingents of Bactrian, Sogdian, and Scythian cavalry, which the King was quick to accept, long since having learned of their effectiveness.

It is also true that Alexander had been leading an increasingly lonely life. His dreams of unified empire might be echoed by flatterers but were shared by none, least of all by those of his ranking subordinates whose abilities would have been the greatest help in realizing the dream. Our sources are nearly silent about Roxane. She meekly followed Alexander, bore him a son after his death, went to the final imprisonment and death the King's hostile successors fashioned for her and her infant son without once giving hint of the strong personality characteristic of the family from which she had come.

Paraetacene, to the east, was the next problem, and its defense hinged on the Rock of Chorienes. This was an even more formidable position that the Sogdian Rock, alleged to be some 10,000 feet high, and seven miles in circumference. Its perimeter consisted entirely of a series of deep ravines that would need bridging before either the one narrow trail or the blank rock faces could be reached. There is almost no agreement as to how the King actually bridged the ravine; he may have filled the entire chasm with trees and brush, or he may have fixed pegs in the rock and built a bridge of trees and brush anchored to the pegs before putting earth over the top. Furthermore, there is a strong possibility that the whole story is a doublet of a later campaign on the borders of India. One likely thing is that Oxyartes was able to persuade Chorienes, once he saw his defenses crumbling, to negotiate on the promise of treatment as fair as Oxyartes himself had received. Craterus was sent to receive the submission of those Paraetacae who had not yet surrendered. Now, all Sogdiana had been secured. The King returned to Bactria in the spring of 327, having solved his problem of the Bactrian and Sogdian cavalry the same difficult way he had solved the problem of Phoenician ships: by taking their stations and wearing them down by attrition.

3. *Trouble Among the Leaders*

In late spring of 327, after all the troops had gathered in Bactria, the King detailed Peucestas to train some 30,000 young Persians, including Bactrians and Sogdians. His purpose was to incorporate them into the army once they had received adequate training, and the Companions, who perhaps alone knew of it, did not relish the prospect. The trial of Philotas, however, kept them quiet. Later at Opis, when the infantry got confirmation of these efforts at amalgamation, they mutinied. Nevertheless, the King began to work other new appointments of easterners into the line of his troops, and henceforth a fixed percentage of each squadron was made up of non-Macedonians. There were also some new Persian administrative appointments at this late spring assembly in Bactria.

Alexander was actively engaged in directing the affairs of a vast and many-faceted empire. His mints were striking Greek, Persian, and Macedonian coins all the way from Amphipolis to Babylon. He was leading and supplying field and garrison troops that together must have been at least twice the size of his original expeditionary force. For Persian business, and on the days when he held audience for easterners, the King became a Persian monarch, using the royal ring of Darius with which to seal documents, dressing in Persian robes with the cap of the Achaemenid kings upright on his head. He must have done everything but speak Persian.

Macedonian resentment against Persian airs and ceremony boiled up into a troublesome episode during this spring sojourn in Bactria. The King and those immediately about him had been long wont to gather for drink and discussion in emulation of the symposia described by Plato. Of late, a frequent topic of conversation had been the comparison of Alexander's exploits with those of Heracles and Dionysus, and the many ways in which the Macedonian far surpassed all eastern kings, or Greeks for that matter.

The King apparently decided to employ the symposium for the solution of an increasingly difficult problem. Persians were accustomed to show their king the deference, strikingly odd to Greek and Macedonian eyes, of falling to one knee in a deep bow that may also have included grasping the king's hand to kiss it. It is likely the Persians in Alexander's company were willing to show him the same deference; it is possible they even expected him to demand it and would have interpreted the failure to do so as a sign of weakness. But to accept such obeisance could only add to Macedonian resentment of the Persian airs the King already had adopted. The death of Cleitus had shown that tides of distress ran only just below the surface. Whether Alexander saw it or not, the mutilation of the Mede bowing before the king on the Persepolis reliefs was some indication that strong Macedonian opinion had already formed against such obeisance.

All this necessitated some careful staging. Alexander and his most intimate friends agreed that *proskynesis,* the making of obeisance, should begin in the presence of all. Perhaps the argument was that the sight of Persians performing *proskynesis,* would be more palatable to Macedonians and others if they also saw Greeks and anyone else who might volunteer also doing it.[13] Alexander would respond to the act by granting the kiss of equality to those who performed it.[14] Thus, he apparently thought to handle the hostility he well knew existed in his men. And he would be receiving heroic honors before his death, unlike earlier heroes.

With the stage set, the scene began with a number of Persians making their obeisance. The Macedonians, of course, demurred. They were under no compulsion to show such deference to the King: they were his social equals, and they had shown nothing of the sort to his predecessors. Clearly, they regarded *proskynesis* as only the latest and most extreme form of the King's Persian affectations, and they would have none of it. With the Macedonians who refused to bow in their present mood, Callisthenes seized upon the opportunity to deliver a speech against the ceremony.

Since he had been expected to approve, the historian's reaction is interesting. Callisthenes claimed that he, more than deeds, had made Alexander famous, for the public would know only what he included in his history; he, more than Olympias, was making Alexander divine by what he said about him. However, he went on to say, a great gulf separates things human and divine, and Greeks, of all men most free, could give such honors only to a god. His argument was based upon two premises, that *proskynesis* implied deification, and that however impressive, Alexander was merely human.[15] Since the King frequently gave indication of his own resentment at the suggestion of divinity, and since this act of obeisance cannot have meant acceptance as deified king among the Persians, who accorded the honor to their human kings, it is fairly clear that the question of deification was introduced by the opponents of *proskynesis.*

Whether this strategy was Callisthenes' own or was devised by one of the generals cannot be known, though the King's fury against the historian afterward might be a clue.[16] The King had neither intended deification by *proskynesis,* nor did he want it. He may even have resented Callisthenes' writing with its exaggerated claims for him, though he must have thought the historian was compromised by what he had published and so would be forced to support the ceremony. But Callisthenes was not suffering from megalomania, and he could still tell the difference between what he had written about the King and the truth. By equating *proskynesis* with divine honors, he had voiced the thought of many minds. What was worse, he had outsmarted the King. Although Alexander wisely dropped the matter, the episode admirably underscores the difference, among the members of the King's inner circle, between those who held genuine power or influence with Alexander—and those who dared have neither.

Callisthenes now had unaccustomed favor with the Macedonians, but the King soon got his chance. That not all Macedonians were behind the historian quickly appeared when one of the Companions informed on the historian's failure to make the gesture of obeisance before the King. Soon, a story began to circulate that Callisthenes had said Athens would grant ready shelter to a tyrannicide. At Susa, Alexander himself had called attention to Athens' veneration of Harmodius and Aristogeiton when he sent their liberated statues back to the city. The historian might well have made the observation at any time with no thought of its application to the King, but now the statement had an ominous ring. Alexander's next step was to ruin Callisthenes with his new-found Macedonian friends by tricking him into an oration in which he disparaged their accomplishments.

Not long afterward, the King was out hunting with a number of pages, one of whom, Hermolaus, spent his free time with Callisthenes studying philosophy. During the course of the hunt, a boar charged Alexander, who waited with studied casualness for the animal to get close. Hermolaus lost his head and, in violation of protocol, cast a spear, killing the boar before the King could throw. Alexander had the young man flogged. But the pages were the ones who lived closest to the King. Because of their birth, they had the greatest reason to anticipate ultimate elevation to the commands and councils of the King, yet of late they had instead to suffer increasingly arbitrary commands. Hermolaus seems to have found ready company in a plot to assassinate Alexander, who inadvertently foiled the attempt by failing to retire on the night for which the deed was planned. Instead, he returned to the party he had just left and drank until dawn. The conspiracy was discovered. Callisthenes was implicated by his friendship with Hermolaus. Our literary sources take sides on the question of Callisthenes' guilt directly in relation to their hostility to the King. Ptolemy and Aristobulus agree (in Arrian) that the historian had mentioned assassination; other sources lack reference to any such suggestion.

During the course of Hermolaus' trial the whole list of grievances came out: tyranny that could forget its friends and imagine its enemies had produced the deaths of Cleitus, Philotas, and Parmenion; ostentation that could ignore the strengths and traditions of ancestral Macedonian monarchy had produced a king with a fondness for Persian pomp and delicate fabrics; megalomania that saw itself larger than life demanded the debasement of *proskynesis*. The bitter recital hurried Hermolaus to his death. Callisthenes also was executed, reminding those sympathetic with him of what the aroused King was capable. The historian's connections with the philosophers and his family relationship with Aristotle did not go unnoticed, and the intellectuals secured revenge in the hostile literary tradition of the Vulgate. Still, Hermolaus' recital was larger than the truth in its implications. Alexander's successors in the East were soon to learn that they too must adopt Persian ways to govern an empire made up largely of Persians.

As significant as they are for the problems of Alexander's reign, these plots and intrigues cannot have occupied very much of the King's time in this final stay in Bactria. Much more time was spent on receiving and integrating large numbers of reinforcements. The army was built back up to 20,000 foot and 7,000 cavalry, including the Iranians.[17] Some 10,000 infantry plus 3,500 mounted troops were to be left behind in Bactria and Sogdiana, the largest occupation force used by the King so far. The multiple foundations left behind and the policy of occupying every possible strong point made this mission a success. Bactria remained Greek far longer than Alexander's lifetime, and even longer than many an intermediate spot between the Hindu Kush and Babylon.

These changes accomplished, the army crossed the mountains again at the beginning of summer, 327, and headed eastward.

4. *India*

When Alexander left the southern slopes of the Hindu Kush in early summer of 327, he turned east through the Paropamisadae. It came as no surprise, for he had told the Chorasinians he would invade India. But in the end, the King's successors failed to retain the area, and his own troops refused to go farther than western India with the result that he had to turn back.

Why did Alexander make this effort? Military problems offer some of the answers. Two major lines of communication lay between the West and the recent conquests in Bactria and Sogdiana. These were, first, the route directly east from the Caspian area; and second, the southern route leading down through Areia, Drangiana, Arachosia, and back up to the passes over which the King had just returned. There are other passes to the south. If this southern route was to be held permanently, it must be protected against attack from the east; already three separate campaigns in Areia had shown the necessity of securing the northwestern flank of that land. And beyond the Paropamisadae the Khyber Pass provided ready access to an invader from due east. The King's own military difficulties, as he campaigned in the mountains north of the Khyber during this summer of 327, underscore the force of the argument. The pass destroyed the potential function of the mountains as a natural boundary. Furthermore, since leaving the Euphrates, the King had shown a disinclination to accept the notion of natural boundaries in any case.

Might not a simple military demonstration in these mountain areas have been enough to keep the empire safe? A demonstration had successfully stopped the Getae at the Danube, and the Indians were already sufficiently impressed to have returned Barsaentes to the King for execution. As so often happens in our sources when actual causation is insufficiently understood, Arrian—with others—appeals to the gods for a rationale of this last and easternmost conquest. Heracles and Dionysus both had come this way in legend, and the King wished to show his troops that they had surpassed the exploits of these two gods; it would be a conquest that even Cyrus and Semiramis had failed to accomplish. Later while going down the Indus, Alexander's "yearning" is again cited: a yearning to go on to the east and to see Ocean, where he could sacrifice as directed by Ammon. But this eastern territory was so quickly lost after Alexander's time that Arrian was not sure why the young King had taken it.[18]

The King sent a herald to Taxila and the Indians west of the Indus River. Ordered to meet him at their earliest convenience, Taxiles, king of Taxila, and others responded to the summons with alacrity, offering gifts that included some twenty-five war elephants. Alexander then divided his forces only recently reformed from the combat groups used beyond the Hindu Kush. Hephaestion and Perdiccas, with half the phalanx and Companion Cavalry but including all the mercenary horse, Taxiles and the Indian envoys, were to make directly through the pass towards India, receiving—or taking—the towns along the line of march. Once at the Indus, they were to make ready for the King's crossing. Their progress was delayed for thirty days in a siege of Peucelaotis, but then they went on to the river. There they built a bridge, which Arrian supposes must have been a pontoon structure.

Alexander led the other half of the troops. Before entering the Khyber, they were met by envoys from Nysa, modern Jalalabad, who requested peace. The ivy growing at Nysa was the first the Macedonians had seen since leaving home, and because the god Dionysus was identified with this plant, the King's party were more than willing to believe that the town represented the farthest penetration of the god.[19] Alexander granted the Nysans the peace they requested and even relented on the usual demand for hostages. Homesickness and propaganda may have combined as motives for a Macedonian Dionysiac revelry at Nysa in celebration of surpassing the exploits of Dionysus, though Arrian has his doubts about it.[20] Leaving Nysa, the Macedonians campaigned in the mountains to the north and east of the Khyber. There was much serious fighting, but it opened the road between the Paropamisadae and the Indus. The summer of 327 had ended by the time Alexander reached the Indus River at a point considerably north of the bridge built by Hephaestion and Perdiccas.

Some of the King's advance information concerning the river system of western India, recently acquired from his new Indian friends, is revealed by the fleet of boats he now ordered before proceeding down river to the bridge. When all were ready, they sailed downstream with the baggage train following along the shore. At the bridge, the transport vehicles and animals crossed to join the troops. More gifts from Taxiles also arrived. They included 200 talents of silver, a number of animals for sacrifice and provisions, and some 700 cavalrymen.

Once across the river, the Macedonians were in India. Arrian relates the wonders of the land in a separate monograph, the *Indika*. However, most of the information in this work comes from the period of Alexander and afterward. What the King already knew was that the Indians were formidable. Their war elephants represented a technological advance the Macedonians spared little to acquire. The Indian fighting man, tall of stature, personally brave, effective in combat, was superior to any the King previously had encountered. At great personal cost in wounds and fatigue, he did some of his toughest fighting during the Indian campaign.

Moving eastward, the army made for Taxila, the largest city between the Indus and the Hydaspes River (modern Jhelum). Taxiles, the official name of the city's ruler, had already been in contact with Alexander ever since meeting him in the Kabul Valley with troops, elephants, and promises of aid. The promises had been fulfilled to date, and at Taxila the King learned a possible reason for such friendliness: beyond the Hydaspes was Taxiles' own enemy, Porus, and beyond him still other hostile states. To the south, down river, the cities had formed a loose confederation. All were actual or potential enemies. Confronted with this information, the King reorganized his troops once again at Taxila.[21] He now placed under his own personal supervision the special squadron of the cavalry, the *agema,* which once Philotas had commanded. He then divided the remainder of the cavalry into five hipparchies of 1,000 men each, commanded by Hephaestion, Perdiccas, Craterus, Coenus, and Demetrius. Iranians had acquired sufficient importance that the first four of these hipparchies were only one-third Macedonian, the rest former Persian troops. The fifth, Demetrius', was largely Iranian. The phalanx battalions, in which easterners had a much lesser role, were commanded by Antigenes, Meleager, Polyperchon, Alcetas, Attalus,

Gorgias, and Cleitus the White. Seleucus commanded the hypaspists, and Tauron the archers. The remainder of the combat forces
were a few mercenaries and men from Arachosia and the Paropamisadae. This list of commanders, plus Antigonus, Antipater,
Ptolemy, and Eumenes of Cardia, is the roll-call of the important
figures in the dissolution of Alexander's empire after his death.

While at Taxila, the King also received a number of other Indian princes and envoys. Alexander's party found there an Indian
holy man, Calanus, who impressed the Macedonians with his
"Stoic" submission and wise advice. They were even more struck
later when, suffering from old age and illness, he burned himself
alive in Indian fashion. The arrangements at Taxila occupied
the winter of 327/326, and only in June of 326 did the King leave
the city for the Hydaspes on the next leg of his invasion of the
Punjab. He knew Porus was waiting for him at the Hydaspes, and
he sent Coenus back to the Indus to cut up the boats used there
and bring them overland in sections. Philip, son of Machatas and
brother of Harpalus, was left at Taxila as satrapal overseer with a
garrison of troops and a party of invalids. As the Macedonians
departed, they were joined by Taxiles and 5,000 of his troops plus
an unknown number of his Indian allies.

Arriving at the Hydaspes, the King pitched his camp near
modern Haranpur, across the river from Porus. Alexander, casting
about for an adequate battle plan, immediately began a series of
diversionary tactics. Parties ran up and down the riverbanks, in
and out of boats and rafts, with loud cries as though engaged in
mighty preparations. Each time, a covering detachment on the
opposite shore would attempt to stay even with the foray until
finally Porus discovered the ruse and simply posted an extended
permanent guard. Then Alexander announced he would wait all
summer if need be. It was obvious he could not attack across the
river in the teeth of Porus' defenses. Worst of all, Porus had elephants. The Macedonian cavalry, already at a disadvantage in
the deep stream, simply could not cope with the elephants,
against which horses had to be specially trained to charge.

Finally, Alexander picked his crossing, a headland opposite an
island some seventeen miles upstream from Porus' camp, near
modern Jalalpur. He next placed men at intervals short enough
for them to shout to each other all along the way between his
camp and the headland. These were to keep up a continual
shouting and bustle night and day, with intermittent fires, until

after the crossing was completed. Preparations for the crossing began openly in the camp. Craterus was ordered to take up a station at the main camp, directly opposite Porus' position. The general had his own hipparchy plus a number of southeastern Iranians and the phalanx battalions of Alcetas and Polyperchon. Five thousand Indians provided further support, for a total of 8,000 infantry and 3,000 horse.

As the King moved up to the crossing, another strong detachment was left between the camp and the headland. These were the mercenary cavalry and the foot under Meleager, Attalus, and Gorgias, 500 horse and 5,000 foot. Their orders were to cross whenever they saw the battle under way. The result was that when Alexander finally reached the headland, his forces were heavy in cavalry, the ratio with infantry being 1:3 instead of the usual 1:5 or 1:6. He had the *agema* in addition to the hipparchies of Hephaestion, Perdiccas, Demetrius, and squadrons of horse from Bactria, Sogdiana, the Scyths, and Dahae mounted archers. On foot were the battalions of Antigenes and Cleitus the White, as well as archers and javelins. All of them moved north, away from the bank and in silence, to a position behind the headland and opposite the island.[22] As they pulled up behind this screen, a tumultuous rain and thunderstorm broke.

The crossing began. Porus' scouts discovered it almost immediately and raced back to their king with the news. Truly remarkable staff work occurred in the transport and marshaling necessary for such a crossing in the doubly difficult conditions imposed by the storm. But all this is passed over in silence by Arrian, who certainly would have relished such an account had he found it in Ptolemy. The movement proceeded well except that it had been discovered. Then it was learned that the narrow channel on the other side of the island led only to a second island beyond which raced a swift and flooded channel. Time was lost in finding a ford, adding to the difficulties as 15,000 men and 5,000 horses got across three separate channels of the river.

Porus' scouts had time to return the fifteen or twenty miles separating the crossing from the Indian camp, but he cannot have known, upon receiving the news, just how far the crossing would have proceeded by the time his own troops could arrive on the scene. The Indian king faced a dilemma that has become a classic in the annals of warfare. If he went north, Craterus would cross against his rear. If he went south, both contingents could use their fast horse to advantage in a cavalry pursuit. His only hope lay in sending a small force, which he could spare without moving his elephants, to oppose Alexander's crossing while it still might catch him partly in the river. Porus' son left with 2,000 cavalry and 120 chariots to drive Alexander back into the stream while Porus himself held the elephants in position against Craterus. But it was too late. The Macedonian cavalry struck; the chariots mired down in mud near the river; and Porus' son was killed amid heavy losses. Probably at this point, Meleager, Attalus, and Gorgias crossed from their position south of the headland to join the King. He then had full infantry support for his horses and better than half his total command in full combat group.

Porus must take action. He left a small part of his army and a few elephants in the hope of keeping Craterus on the other side of the river while he went upstream moving inland where he could find firmer soil suitable for a battle site. When he reached a position offering the space and footing he needed, he deployed his forces on line. The elephants were in front with the infantry in the second line. On the banks were more foot, one battalion each, and beyond them on each side, two squadrons of horse. The order was good. Enemy cavalry could not attack the elephants directly, and his opponent's infantry could be contained by the Indian foot while the elephants trampled them.

Alexander had been proceeding south toward the Indians as fast as his cavalry could move. When he was close enough to make out the battle order established by Porus, he paused to let his infantry catch up. Frontal attack against the elephants was impossible. From the twenty-five elephants Taxiles had given him, the King had had ample opportunity to observe the value of these animals and the way horses reacted to them. There was no experimenting with Porus in this regard. Instead, Alexander decided on a cavalry attack against the wings. This would permit his infantry to attack the elephants, provided the enemy cavalry were removed with sufficient speed. Timing was crucial, for either failure to engage or a pitched battle on either wing would allow Porus to take the Macedonian phalanx in flank. But how to make a cavalry engagement immediately decisive? Alexander had not been able to do this either at Issus or Gaugamela. The plan he chose, while profiting immensely from the terrain, shows that he had given some real thought to what he would do the next time he was confronted with menacing cavalry wings. He directed all his cavalry except two squadrons against the Indians' left flank (Alexander's right). He sent the two remaining squadrons off under Coenus towards his own left, the enemy right. The success of this maneuver depended upon the existence of a rise or trees to hide these troops from enemy view until the right moment. Behind this screen, they moved off towards Porus' right, while the Indian king watched the rest of the Macedonian cavalry mass for an attack on his left, thinking it was the entire force.

When Coenus and Demetrius, the commander of the accompanying squadron, were in position but still hidden from view, Alexander sent his horse archers out to the right to cover, then two squadrons of cavalry directly against the Indian's left wing cavalry. Porus, seeing no more horse, thought that Alexander intended a straightforward cavalry engagement to turn his flank and get past the elephants. In order to prevent this, he ordered the cavalry on the right wing to come around behind his line to help the left. Soon all four Indian squadrons had engaged Alexander's three, well ahead of the Indian line. At this point, Coenus burst into view from off to Porus' right and took the Indian cavalry in the rear. Alexander had solved the problem of a heavy enemy cavalry wing. The Indians were driven back on the elephants and infantry. The elephants began to advance on Alexander's horse, but now the Macedonian phalanx had no worries from the opposing horse, and they moved in.

The time for sweeping maneuvers was over, and action became confused as a furious fight developed around the elephants. Javelins and archers had gone in ahead of the infantry, their targets the animals' mahouts. This was only partially successful, and the huge beasts were able to break the phalanx formation. However, they re-formed before Indian troops could be upon them. Porus' foot then were driven back among the elephants, which without their mahouts had begun to wheel and mill about, trampling friend and foe alike. Discipline returned first to the riderless elephants. They formed a curved line, trumpeting with trunks raised and tusks tossing, and backed away from the battle. But the rest of Porus' forces were surrounded, and in the meantime Craterus had got his men across, fresh and ready for the pursuit. Porus, however, was no Darius, though no longer a young man. He refused to flee despite a serious wound and simply directed his elephant off the field with majestic slowness.

Alexander, almost awed by this foe, first sent Taxiles to persuade Porus to return to honorable capitulation. It was the wrong choice; the two were enemies long before Alexander had come on the scene, and Taxiles was nearly killed. Next, the young King sent a man known to be Porus' friend to ask him not to throw away his life. So the Indian king, stately and tall and still of superb physique, returned to the scene. Alexander asked him what he would like. "To be treated as a king," came the answer. He was. Porus became Alexander's trusted ally, with his territory greatly enlarged. The result was that Taxiles and Porus, though reconciled, each had new territorial acquistions to keep from the other.

5. The End of the Road

The Macedonian king founded a new Alexandria, Nicaea, where his own camp had stood. It is probably present-day Jalapur. Also, on the field of battle, he established another town, Bucephala. For there the beloved horse Bucephalus, named from the oxlike blaze on his head, died. All the years since the day the boy Alexander had alone been able to ride him he had allowed no one on his back but the King. They had been together for thousands of miles until this battle of the Hydaspes, during which from old age and exertion the horse died. Other Macedonian losses are concealed. But they must have been severe to judge from the lasting impression made by elephants. Alexander immediately added a number to the twenty-five he already had.

The next step beyond his own land cleared, Taxiles was dismissed with great liberality as a faithful ally. The Macedonians were irritated, and Meleager is reputed to have noted audibly that at last in India Alexander had found a man worthy of 1,000 talents.[23] The King was stung by it, but remembering Cleitus, did nothing.

Alexander left Craterus on the Hydaspes to prepare vessels and supplies for moving down river. With the rest of the army he went eastward to cross the Acesines (modern Chenab), where he left Hephaestion to fortify a city. As the troops proceeded they received submission from some, had to fight others. But the signs are clear that the King thought it not much farther to Ocean, just beyond the last of the tributaries of the Indus. This would join the Hyrcanian (Caspian) Sea with the Persian Gulf. He would have taken the eastern end of the world, he thought, and he said as much later when at the Beas River his troops refused to go farther.

The disposition of his forces would have kept him from going on in any case: already his line was thin from leaving soldiers behind for garrisons, bridgeheads, occupation forces; and the two most important commanders were back at the Jhelum and the Chenab where each prepared for the long return that was to begin by going down the Indus. The terrain he was overrunning added to the argument. The town of Sangala offered serious resistance and was won only with the timely arrival of Porus. Alexander was acquiring responsibility for far more people than he could hope to govern in this area where the cities were unorganized, but the people tough and warlike. The army continued east through tropical rains to the Hyphasis River (Beas). The King was determined to cross this stream as well in the light of reports of fertile lands and strong peoples on the other side. More than that, Ocean must surely be somewhere over the next ridge; Alexander saw himself within reach of the end of the world.

Here at the Beas, however, his journey eastward ended. The Macedonian army was showing unmistakable signs of weariness as the King assembled them for another address of the type that so often before had aroused them. He would either persuade them of his view or be persuaded of theirs, he said, but the rest of the day showed he meant only the first. He recited the list of lands now theirs by right of conquest of enemies so easily defeated. Ocean itself was just ahead, and they would see how it formed one with Hyrcanian and Persian waters. From there one could sail all the way to the Pillars of Heracles (Gibraltar) and to Libya (ignoring the extent of Africa to be negotiated by such a voyage). Already they had surpassed the labors of Heracles and Dionysus, and every step of the way the King personally had led and participated in every danger. Apparently noting little encouragement in the faces of his audience, he ended his speech with a promise of rewards beyond their greatest dreams.

Once the King was through, there was a long and uncomfortable silence. The soldiers were tired in mind and body, homesick, and worn. The seventy days of unrelenting tropical deluge through which they had come approached the dimensions of personal insult. Though they had surpassed all others in their mighty exploits, they had continually been deprived of the fruits of victory. Rest came only to those unfit to go on, left at some forgotten station for the purpose of securing Alexander's communications, forwarding Alexander's supplies, occupying Alexander's empire. The army had gone along in the face of conservative resistance by such as Parmenion, because it could see the reasons for doing so. The troops could be persuaded that eastern Iran was needed for the security of the West. But here they were in an area not even the Persians had controlled. The importance of India to Iran was less than clear; the necessity of anything east of the Indus for the security of the West was not credible. And subsequent history was to prove them right. The territorial conquest of eastern Iran proved valid when Bactria and Sogdiana continued under occupation by Macedonians and Greeks for another century and a half, even though the King's successors failed to solve the administrative problems of so vast a state, and it fell apart. And in India, nothing remained save Alexander's name attached here and there.

At Tyre, the King's speech had been accepted. It seemed obvious that Phoenicia was vulnerable to Persian attack unless Egypt was under control and it was arguable that Mesopotamia was equally important. But here the case was not nearly so clear. The King's attempt to duplicate the adventurous decision of Tyre met with failure.

The troops looked at the ground in strained silence until Coenus, old and probably ill, spoke up. He was the one with the least to lose. Craterus and Hephaestion were not present. Relying on position and his successful charge at the Hydaspes against Porus, the old soldier made his points. The line of Alexandrias stretching from the Nile to the Indus had become prisons whose inmates were rapidly being decimated by illness and discouragement. All longed to return home, as indeed Alexander himself should. Coenus may not have known, but Alexander was soon to learn that there were signs of local resurgence in various parts of the empire. In Phoenicia and Cyprus coins appeared minted with regnal dates and local kings' names, which may well have been permitted by the Macedonian king,[24] but the nearly microscopic engraving of the name Nicocles on Alexander coinage from Paphus on Cyprus suggests that all was not entirely well.[25] Coenus finished by pointing out that once Alexander had returned to his responsibilities at home and to his men, he could come back to the Indus with fresh troops and go as far as he liked, or even to

Carthage.[26] The most kingly virtue of all, he said, is self-restraint.

Alexander would have to face the facts. The troops had not mutinied; they had been invited to speak. He clearly had intended only a short campaign to the east to find Ocean because he thought it only a short way. The men's refusal to go farther meant that they were more willing than he to admit that stories of powerful peoples beyond might mean that the great body of water surrounding the earth was farther away than he supposed. The King was furious. He sulked three days in his tent, testing their resolution. But the army was already broken; the views expressed by Coenus were those of desperation. Next Alexander announced he would go without them, but sacrifices in preparation for his departure all went wrong. With this mandate from the gods of what he could not properly accept from mere soldiers, he changed the announcement. He would return. There was a touching scene of general weeping and reconciliation.

King and army retraced their route to Craterus. The territory to the east of the river was turned over to Porus after an elaborate ceremony of sacrifices made on twelve huge altars. Once back at the Hydaspes, Alexandria Nicaea and Bucephala were discovered damaged by tropical storms and were repaired while the army made final preparations to return home. But they were not to go back the way they had come. Alexander's previous orders to Craterus meant he had always intended to go down river to the mouth of the Indus. He would see Ocean one way or another.

Craterus had a fleet of nearly 1,000 ships ready for the voyage. Nearchus was to command the entire company; Onesicritus to steer the royal barge. Before departing, the King carried out Ammon's orders in sacrificing to the rivers, to Poseidon, and to Ocean. During the course of these activities, Coenus died and was buried with elaborate ceremony befiting his service.

The trip down river began in November of 326. As the lines were cast off, libations to the gods were poured over the bow. Alexander had the pick of the troops with him on board. Phoenicians, Cypriotes, Carians, and Egyptians made up the crews. Craterus followed along on the right bank with one infantry battalion and the cavalry; Hephaestion was on the left with the remainder of the troops and all the elephants. The river between these rivals would ease the friction that recently had brought the two nearly to blows.[27] Hephaestion was older in years and in the King's affections and resented the younger but more able Craterus. Philip was ordered to bring along the baggage after an interval of three days, and behind him came a vast host of Indian princes and their retinues, women, children, and traders.

The trip began with boats carefully spaced. The high banks and woods rang with the sound of the oars and the calling of the count. At the confluence of the Hydaspes (Jhelum) and the Acesines (Chenab) the party nearly met disaster in the narrow rapids. There was some damage to the larger vessels, and the King's ship was whipped around in violent fashion thoroughly alarming all on board including Alexander, who could swim. Once through, the fleet pulled up, and the army camped on land. At this point Alexander left the river. The Malli, who lived in this area, were reported hostile, and the King intended to drive them back towards the river to Hephaestion by outflanking them from the north. Accordingly, he struck out eastward across the desert, with Ptolemy behind him. This route of march across the strip between the Indus and the Ravi was not expected by his enemies, and they were routed in the course of a long campaign of several months.

However, at one of the cities east of the Ravi there was trouble. The city itself was easily taken, but a large number of its defenders took refuge in the citadel and prepared to hold out. By this time, Alexander's troops were again faltering. With the town under control, the citadel could be isolated and left. The soldiers were near actual mutiny at the King's arbitrary decision to drive the defenders from the citadel too.[28] Seeing this hesitation and realizing how much another disagreement would endanger his control over the men, Alexander met the problem with the forcefulness and dispatch that had safely brought him this far. He impatiently grabbed a ladder and raced up it to the top of the citadel wall. Stung into action, Peucestas, Leonnatus, and Abreas followed to protect the King. The consequently very nervous bodyguard had also been goaded into movement, but their combined weight broke the ladder. The four were isolated atop the wall where they made ideal targets. Alexander jumped down, followed by the others. Arbreas was killed almost immediately, and Alexander was stunned by a blow on the head. As he sagged he was severely wounded by a long arrow that pierced a lung. He lay on the ground while Peucestas covered him with the shield of Achilles, and Leonnatus threatened any of the Malli who might care to press their advantage. By this time, the nearly frenzied army outside had burst through the wall. All defenders were killed.

Alexander was carried out more dead than alive. The troops, impossible to persuade that he still lived, were near panic for several days. Finally, Alexander ordered his attendants to carry him on board ship to return to the main camp. The army lining the banks could see him pass, but still they insisted it was only his corpse until he waved to them. As the boat docked near his pavillion he disdained a stretcher, summoned a horse, and with iron will rode to the tent. He then dismounted and walked inside, probably to faint once the flaps had closed behind him.

All, including his historians, have disapproved the bravado of these rash actions, but they ignore the threat of mutiny that drove him up the wall, and the worse threat of panic that put him on his horse. Perhaps exertion at this crucial point hastened his death, but his later march through the Gedrosian desert makes this doubtful. Of more lasting importance was the reaction the episode provoked among the Indians. Capitalizing on the animosity engendered by these campaigns, Chandragupta and his son Asoka united North India and blotted out Alexander's settlements.[29] Another result appeared in Bactria when the Greeks there heard of Alexander's "death" and separated themselves from their Macedonian colleagues in preparation for mass defection in order to return home. Their sweep westward, however, came after the King's actual death and was defeated by Seleucus only at great cost to Macedonian control of the eastern provinces.

But for the moment, the Malli had submitted. Alexander left Philip in charge, adding to his responsibilities for all the land west of the Indus in the north. When the south was given to Peithon, the King's pattern was clear: Philip in the north and west, Porus in the north and east, and Peithon in the south. From a point halfway between the Malli and the Indus Delta, Alexander detached Craterus to lead the baggage, camp followers, and all but the soundest troops directly west through the Mulla Pass and on towards Babylon by the southern route. Craterus' selection probably was due to his growing physical difficulties.

There were many more minor conflicts as the army made its way slowly south in the winter of 326/325. During one of them, Ptolemy was hit by a poisoned Brahmin arrow and lay near death. Alexander said he had dreamed that a snake showed him a plant whose leaves and roots would cure the dying general and all others suffering from the same thing. The remedy was immediately applied, and Ptolemy began to mend. Since the discovery of *rauwolfia serpentina,* the first of the modern tranquilizers but used in India for thousands of years to cure snakebite, among other things,[30] it has become evident that Ptolemy's wound and unusual recovery are facts. The story, however, appears only in those authors most heavily influenced by the hostile literary tradition stemming from Callisthenes through, probably, Cleitarchus.[31] It is not mentioned in Arrian, who not only is our best source for Alexander, but dependent on the very Ptolemy who here was cured. The general suppressed the story, but those most hostile to Alexander report it in a form that makes him peculiarly a recipient of near-divine information.

When the army reached Pattala, it had been making its way down river for nine months. Alexander determined to employ this town on the lower river, where the stream split to go east and west through the delta, as a base on which to organize his return to Babylonia. He found the settlement deserted and had to round up those hiding in the countryside with promises of security and reward before he could gain enough laborers for his construction plans. Then, while the harbor was being cleared and docks were going up, the King explored the western arm of the Indus toward Ocean. There his party was caught in a tidal bore, something Macedonians had never seen, since the Mediterranean has almost no fluctuation. But here the long and nearly level lift of the delta brought the rising water sweeping up channel in a flood. Alexander's ships were almost swamped, then beached. When the water returned again, the vessels were floated and repaired. Then the party put out to sea to be clear of the next tide. The King had found Ocean at last; he busily sacrificed to Poseidon and all the other gods as Ammon long ago had directed.

As Alexander pondered the Indian Ocean and its connections with the Persian Gulf, he could see the possibilities for trade between East and West offered by this easy link between India and Babylonia. Some who believe that the King had ideas of ruling the world consider the mouth of the Indus to be the place where these ideas became conscious policy. It is, however, possible that he here grappled only with the need for tying together East and West within the sphere of his own conquests. In this form, the problem was formidable enough; he had outstripped the Persians, outdistanced his own intelligence services, and outreached effective ability to control his vast empire. As he and the Indian wise man Calanus spoke of these things, the old seer took a dried and wrinkled oxhide and cast it on the ground. Each time he stepped on it near an edge, the hide would pop up elsewhere refusing to lie flat. But once he put his weight in the center, all of it lay straight. Babylon, he said, was the center of Alexander's empire, from which all else could be managed. And Alexander had already decided to return to the West.

Before leaving, however, he explored the eastern arm of the Indus where the tide was not so hazardous. There, he left most of his ships and Nearchus with orders to wait for the monsoon before setting sail for the Persian Gulf. They would maintain contact with each other along the shores of Gedrosia and Carmania and thus return to Babylonia together. Alexander then moved out while Nearchus awaited the changing winds of October (325). He was constantly harassed by the natives of the region and had to put across the sound to wait through September near the site of Karachi in modern Pakistan.

CHAPTER VI

Return to Destiny

1. The March Back

WHILE NEARCHUS' FLEET STOOD OFFSHORE AWAITING THE MONSOON, and Craterus' support units toiled through the Mulla Pass toward Arachosia and Drangiana, Alexander swept westward through the land of the Oreitans, his command divided into the combat groups that had worked so well beyond the Hindu Kush. He chose the largest of the Oreitan villages, Rombacia, for a new city foundation. Its location might become important should Alexander succeed in opening the area to commercial penetration. Once all Oreitans had surrendered, Apollophanes was left as satrap. With the army once again reunited, Alexander pushed westward into Gedrosia, the more difficult portion of his return march.

Whatever the King had planned, the Gedrosian trek was a journey through a fiery hell. The intent had been for the army to establish supply depots along the shore for Nearchus' fleet, which would remain several days to the rear, but almost immediately the forbidding terrain made the plan seem doubtful. For, although they found some familiar aromatic desert plants, salt-water vegetation and bushes with strange thorns told the soldiers they were entering upon unfamiliar territory.

Many unpleasant surprises came as the march progressed. The broiling sun forced them to march at night, but often the weary dawn brought the army only to poisoned water or none at all. A mountain range (the Taloi) appeared at the edge of the sea and drove the troops inland, where heat, sand, sun, and the lack of food began to decimate the noncombatant members of Alexander's train and the baggage animals. Reports came of settlements of people along the coast on the other side of the mountains, but almost no one was seen. On one occasion, when supplies arrived from the satraps, Alexander attempted to leave them for the fleet, but his men broke the seals, and he could only ignore them; the alternative was to lose the army. Finally, those baggage animals that still remained were killed and eaten; again the King looked aside. On another occasion, the army came to a dry wash where they thought to spend the night. Unknown to them as they set up camp, a violent storm was raging in the high country to the north, out of sight and sound, its first sign a wall of water roaring down the draw. Large numbers of the remaining women and children who could not scurry to safety were lost along with the royal pavillion. Then to make matters worse, the survivors desperately gulped too much of the subsiding water, and a number died. Thereafter, all bivouacs were a full twenty stades from any wadi. The story is told that once during a particularly long and dry stretch, a small quantity of water was found and brought to the King, who promptly poured it out on the ground rather than drink what others could not have. Finally, they made it back to the seashore and, for a time, were supplied with springs they discovered under the sand beneath some of the cliffs. Then came a period of wandering for seven days before the guides rediscovered the interior road that would take them to the capital of Gedrosia. When they arrived, having saved almost nothing of baggage or camp followers, but with the army itself fairly intact, they had taken sixty days to cover the 500 or so miles between the Oreitans and Pura, the capital of Gedrosia. "Most historians agree," says Arrian, "that no other trials of Alexander were worth comparing with this one."

The march was sufficiently difficult to raise questions about the King's motives in going through Gedrosia. Nearchus (in Arrian) alone says that Alexander did not know what he was getting into when he made the decision. Most ancient writers credit the King with a desire to go where the Persians had got through only with seven survivors, and with trying to best Semiramis[1] who had emerged from the desert with just twenty. Moderns have observed that the route was feasible, if difficult, for a small party; near suicide for a full army. During the course of the march, the King was constantly concerned about his inability to supply the fleet with which he had almost immediately lost contact. This and the scene of wild jubilation when Nearchus finally appeared at Pura make it clear that Alexander had thought the fleet could not make the voyage without land support, and therefore that the voyage rather than the march was the thing uppermost in his mind. He wished to determine whether economic penetration and contact between the Indus and Mesopotamia was feasible. Even his instructions to Nearchus concerning the scientific data he was to collect are sufficiently vague as to indicate that detailed exploration was not his motive.[2] That Apollophanes, the new satrap of the Oreitans, had been expected to provide supplies during the course of the march is shown by his removal from office as soon as the Gedrosian capital was reached.[3]

While Alexander had been fretting about Nearchus and the fleet, the Cretan had been successful in making the voyage even without supplies and despite severe hardship. As the army came to the Halil Rud, the river marking the boundary between Gedrosia and Carmania, Nearchus also had reached the mouth of the river, left his fleet, and was coming overland to find Alexander. A party sent out from the King to seek news of the sailors nearly missed them by mistaking them for tramps because of their worn condition, but all finally came together so that the King could be sure of the safety both of his friend and of the entire fleet.

During excited celebrations, the admiral told of his adventures. They had met strange people who ate only fish, either raw or ground into meal after drying, and who lived in huts made of large (whale) bones. There was a whole fleet of black sea monsters that dove out of sight when the ships sounded the battle-cry and charged. Onesicritus, the man who had guided Alexander's own ship down the Indus as far as the rapids, had nearly been responsible for the loss of the fleet when they approached Ras Mussandam, the modern name of the sharp cape that protrudes northeastward from southern Arabia at the end of the Persian Gulf.[4] Onesicritus had said the open water between the shore at their right and the point they could make out in the distance was only a bay, and they should save time by cutting across its mouth. Nearchus had replied that his orders were to explore all the coastline, and they must enter. Later they learned the "bay" was the Persian Gulf. Still later, Alexander learned that if they had proceeded west from Ras Mussandam, they likely would have been lost in an unknowing attempt to sail clear around the Arab peninsula. The King wanted Nearchus henceforth to stay with him, but the admiral persuaded him to let him return to the ships and bring them the rest of the way to Babylonia. A new Alexandria (now Gulashkird) was founded at their place of meeting on the Halil Rud.

Also on the way into Carmania, Alexander learned that Philip, his satrap for the northwestern part of his Indian conquests, had been killed by a group of his own mercenaries. The Macedonian guard had cut down the culprits, and the king sent orders to Eudamus and Taxiles to take care of the administration of the district until he could make a new appointment.

A number of officials from Iran met the King as he entered Carmania proper at the end of November 325, bringing with them supplies and draft animals. Craterus also appeared with the rest of the army and the elephants. From Media and Parmenion's old command came Cleander, Sitalces, and Heracon, bringing with them the greater part of their forces. Cleander and Sitalces, along with Menidas, were the men to whom the King had sent orders to assassinate Parmenion. When natives from their province of Media appeared right behind them with accusations of malfeasance, arrogance, and graft, many must have waited to see if their former special assignment would earn them particular favor now. It did not. The first two were executed for plundering temples, violating tombs, and for overbearing injustice. Heracon later was accused by the people of Susa of sacking temples there, and he also was punished. Arrian says that these executions were in part an effort to put fear into the other satraps and succeeded more than anything else the King did to keep various tribes from revolt.[5]

In Carmania, the army had a chance to rest. Stories of drunken revels, which have the King moving in besotted majesty through the land atop two chariots lashed together, have now been effectively relegated to the hostile Alexander tradition. But there was time for athletic games and artistic contests, and doubtless a few parties. During this period, Peucestas entered the royal bodyguard, its number now increased to eight in order to accommodate the appointment. The hero who had saved the King's life inside the wall of the Malli fortress was being groomed for the satrapy of Persis.

On into Persis went the army in early December of 325. Hephaestion and the greater part of the troops went along the coast south of the higher mountains to take advantage of milder weather and better supplies. Alexander proceeded directly to Pasargadae with light infantry, the Companion cavalry, and part of the archers; a fast and maneuverable combat group. Once the King had come into Persia proper, he learned of more difficulties with the officials he had left in charge. Phrasaortes, the satrap the King had left behind at Persepolis, was dead from illness and had been replaced by the self-appointed Orxines. Atropates the satrap of Media, whose Macedonian overseers Alexander had just executed, appeared with Baryaxes, a Median rebel and his fellow-conspirators. Atropates was reinstated as satrap, the rebels were executed. Most disturbing of all to the King was finding the rifled tomb of Cyrus. After torturing the magian priests who had been guarding the tomb in an unsuccessful effort to learn the guilty party, he directed that the damaged monument be restored.

Probably also at this time the King learned of the flight of Harpalus from Babylon. Alexander's minister of finance may have been dipping into royal funds to finance his own profligacy; he is reported to have imported expensive courtesans from Athens; he may have been preparing for a favorable reception at Athens for some time, though the details of any such favors from him to Attica are missing. In any case, the fleeing official appeared in Athens with an embarrassingly large amount of the King's funds, was imprisoned while a request for his disposition was sent to Alexander, then escaped only to meet his death on Crete.[6]

At Persepolis, the King felt some remorse at having burned the magnificent palace.[7] Perhaps it had not been the right decision, for he had received more trouble from defection in Susa, Media, Areia, and the areas to the east than in Persis. At Persepolis, even the self-appointed Orxines had kept the land for him. Perhaps, however, this point is better as an argument that destruction of the capital had kept the area from rebellion, for Orxines was quickly accused of rifling temples and oppressing the Persians under his command. Alexander ordered him executed, in growing impatience with those who had not kept pace with his intention to create responsible government and who had taken his prolonged absence in the east as indicating failure to return.

To forestall further difficulties, the King ordered all the satraps of southern Iran to disband their personal armies of mercenaries.[8] Finally, Peucestas was made satrap of Persia. Alexander regarded him as especially loyal and had steadily shown him favor since the Malli episode. But equally important was the fact that Peucestas alone of the Macedonians followed the King with relish into a Persian manner of life. Once he became satrap, he adopted

Persian dress and began to use the Persian language. Both made him especially acceptable to the Persians.

Alexander moved back through the Persian Gates towards Susa, where there were more executions, this time the satrap Abulites and his son Oxathres. The charge against them was overbearing behavior and graft. All the way from Carmania to Susa the King had been primarily engaged in meting out vengeance against defectors he had appointed to high office and removing the means of rebellion from others. Most, but not all, of the offenders were non-Macedonians. The association of all this with the death, albeit by disease, of Coenus, the later replacement of Antipater and demise of Hephaestion, apparently from alcoholism, has led some to suspect Alexander of conducting a reign of terror.[9] Certainly, the administration of the empire needed serious thought. Alexander's long absence in India clearly was the occasion for the defection,[10] just as his return provided opportunity for adjustment.

2. *Alexander's Government*

Although the King was yet to initiate a few changes of policy, the general form of his government was well established by 325. It deserves special attention. Following Persian administrative organization, its basic division was the satrapy, usually defined by geographical elements or ethnic and linguistic lines, or all three.

The satrap was responsible for the stability of his territory and for its defense, and as long as these local needs were met, the main problem of central administration consisted in imposing limitations of the powers of the satraps. The Persians earlier had sought to profit from Assyrian experience with powerful territorial governors who used their positions to challenge the authority of the royal government, and employed both an open and a secret system of inspectors as well as the device of turning military commands over to especially named generals in order to limit the power of the territorial officials.[11] Alexander expanded this notion by carefully attending to the separation of powers among those he named to important civil and military commands.

The western satrapies, whose Persian commanders fought the Macedonians at the battle of the Granicus, were retained with almost no change. Alexander named his Macedonian generals as the new satraps, but from the very start he also appointed separate financial officers. The two divided the chief responsibilities of defense and tribute, each directly subject to the King. In the eastern portion of the empire, where Persians and others administered the satrapies, the King divided authority three ways: the satrap as the chief civil official; an officer in charge of finance (Greek or Macedonian); and a military overseer (invariably a Macedonian). The satraps were further limited by establishment of key fortress positions within the satrapy, whose commanders also were responsible directly to the King. Finally, the existence of cities had the same effect. Most of the evidence for special treatment of cities by the royal government is western and later than Alexander. However, the value of cities for defense and stability can readily be seen, and they performed valuable services in return for the local freedoms they were allowed. That the device was a favorite one with Alexander is shown by the frequency of his city foundations in the eastern areas where previous to his coming there had been none or only few,[12] though it is likely the eastern "cities" were little more than garrisons or fortresses.[13]

The other major problems of the central government were the handling of finances and occasional supervision of imperial interests in local affairs. To these ends, the King established some financial, and possibly also administrative, districts within the empire. He had already grouped Phoenicia with Cyprus, Syria, and Cilicia under Coeranus at the time of the Battle of Gaugamela. Asia Minor west of the Taurus Mountains was under Philoxenus; the interior was under Antigonus; Egypt, with Libya, Gaza, and the Sinai Arabs was under Cleomenes. Perhaps there also was a grouping of provinces in the east as well.[14] With the possible exception of Cleomenes, whose Egyptian territory was largely stable, all had military commanders associated with them.

Central finances were entrusted to Harpalus until the consequences of embezzlement and high living forced him to flee.[15] Under his administration were the imperial mints, of which the most important was the one at Amphipolis. Other mints began striking imperial coinage in Asia Minor, Phoenicia, Palestine, and Babylon during the years when the King was east of Mesopotamia. As noted at Persepolis, the East may have still been on a barter economy, thus not requiring the presence of a mint. A measure of imperial policy is given by the fact that some of these mints issued the silver coins of Alexander alongside a continued series of Persian coins and some issues with locally significant mint marks.[16] Both points are a comment on the importance and privileges of the cities. For general circulation in the back country west of Persis, imitations of earlier Athenian coins were continued by Alexander, as they had been previously allowed by the Persians.[17] We can assume these non-Macedonian coins were primarily for the purpose of local trade and tribute; imperial finance continued to be Alexander's province alone.

Of primary importance to Alexander's administration were his techniques for gathering and disseminating information. His intelligence services were many-sided. We have already considered the argument for his having used literary materials,[18] and we have seen many examples of his astute surveillance of the terrain through which the army passed.

Staff work capable of getting his army across the Hydaspes at night in a violent storm when there was one more channel than anticipated; training that permitted his phalanx to drill, then charge, near the Danube, move on hand signals at Issus, open at Gaugamela to allow the scythe chariots through without damage and almost without advance notice; careful attention to geography and political structure; all would lead us to expect that Alexander's methods for gaining intelligence of enemy movements, dispositions, and resources were equally sophisticated. The King insisted upon the interrogation of prisoners and noncombatants whenever possible. The fact that our authors give so many successful instances of gaining information in this way argues more for some procedure for analysis than it does for exceptional luck in forever finding people who were both honest and well informed. Such interrogations are cited before Gaugamela and prior to entering the Persian Gates, and they may be assumed in most other cases.

Although the items purported to come down to us from Alexander's archives have been greatly debated, and we may in fact have almost nothing of the material he used, the existence and extensive use of written materials by the King seems clear. A daily journal was kept of the army's activities, and there were orders to and reports from officials, private and public communications, correspondence and reports of the King's officials to each other, political pamphlets addressed to the King, and possibly the King's own growing file for his personal memoirs.[19] Ultimately, he had the Achaeminid archives as well.[20]

What we know of Alexander's dissemination of information is confined almost exclusively to his propaganda. He could rationalize seizures and executions, blaming them on hostility to Darius when rebellion against his own government was the real reason. The young King's use of titles and references to divine advantages is also instructive. His coins, like those of Philip, issued in Macedonia, and intended for circulation in Greece and the eastern Mediterranean, have him only as Alexander. No title was needed for the Macedonians; the use of one would have limited him to Macedonia as far as the Greeks were concerned. But in a temple dedication of the year 330, he appears as Lord of Asia,[21] a claim he long since had made in speeches and his letters to Darius from Syria and Palestine. In Asiatic territories, the title of king proclaimed his succession to the Great King Darius, and so it began to appear on coins issued for circulation in these areas as early as 327, perhaps as early as 329. In Arab tradition, he remained Lord of Kings for nearly two centuries after his death.[22]

The understatement that characterized his pronouncements to Greeks obviously was not carried over to his dealings with Asiatics, nor was it even used with his own troops. Curtius has the story that a much-needed spring came up inside the King's tent near the Oxus River, and that Alexander expressly wished his men to believe it the gift of the gods.[23] Further, the hostile literary tradition ascribes to Alexander a deliberate effort to delude posterity by exaggerating the proportion of constructions left behind in India.[24] Arrian knows nothing of an attempt to deceive, but his statement that altars of great size were prepared lends some support to it.[25] A clear example of the King's willingness to play upon the credulity of his men is the eclipse of the moon just before the army fought at Gaugamela. While rumors as to the meaning of the eclipse ran through the camp, Alexander's sacrifice to Moon, Sun, and Earth shows he understood the actual cause of the eclipse, though seers were brought in to allay the fears of the troops.[26]

This brief survey of the King's administration has pinpointed some of his policies. Local governments were left unchanged for the most part.[27] Democracies were encouraged among the Greek cities of Asia Minor, in contradiction to previous Macedonian policy of the Greek mainland, but in keeping with the fact that the Persians had supported oligarchical or tyrannical governments. The Macedonian king was well aware of the value of aiding Persia's enemies among these Greek cities. In Phoenicia, the King favored monarchies; and in Jerusalem and Babylon, theocratic governments were encouraged.

Alexander's policy of amalgamating Persians with Macedonians in the personnel of his government provided his greatest difficulties; so much so that some modern authors have seen it as a mistake on the part of the King: he should universally have employed Macedonians. However, the available administrators within his ranks were simply too few. The King had no choice but to turn to easterners, despite the fact that many of the able Persians remained hostile to Alexander because of their greater stake in the previous government. Mazaeus was a notable exception; most of available eastern managerial talent seems to have been alarmingly inept, unable to adjust to the administrative responsibilities to which Alexander had named them. As a result, his government was organizationally sound, but weakened by some of its personnel.

Although functioning, Alexander's government thus faced many problems at the time of the King's second visit to Susa. In India, where it is noteworthy that his arrangements should have endured longer than the time it took for his army to disappear from sight around the first bend in the river, they were holding firm enough for him to turn over to Taxiles the command vacated by the death of Philip. Macedonian holdings were later of sufficient strength and value to be considered worth 300 war elephants by Chandragupta. The area of greatest difficulty was Iran, where maladministration among the Persians had necessitated sudden and violent changes. Rebellion had broken out in Media, and the King thought the situation serious enough to put Ecbatana next on his line of march as soon as this visit to the edge of the Mesopotamian plain was over.

The King's use of Macedonians in Iran and areas to the west had been little more successful. For arrogance and looting, Cleander, Sitalces, and Heracon must die; Harpalus must flee. It is worth noting, however, that all of these officials were accused of being arrogant to their inferiors and looting property belonging to gods and the King. None save Baryaxes of Media was accused of outright rebellion against the government of Alexander. The

King seemed to fare little better with Greeks. Mercenaries left in his multitudinous city foundations of the East were already restive enough to kill their commanders, and to plan a sweep westward that Perdiccas would have to stop with military action after the death of Alexander. Even the Greeks of the West were showing signs of disagreement, if the surreptitious inscription of Nicocles of Paphus is any indication.

Elsewhere in the West, things were in better shape. Antigonus was successful in holding Asia Minor open for the King's communication and supply. Cleomenes was arrogant and grafting in Egypt, but with limited troops at the disposal of the Egyptian governor, the King could afford to wait. In Greece proper, affairs apparently were considered quite stable after Antipater's success against the Spartans. At Susa, Alexander turned his attention to some of the basic policies of imperial administration. These efforts were to continue to the time of his death in Babylon.

One important way in which the King sought to implement the policy of amalgamation between Persians and Macedonians was the mass marriage ceremony at Susa. While the King may have absorbed enough Mesopotamian royal lore by this time to have consciously included in his preparations the notion of union with a goddess that underlay earlier Babylonian royal marriage ceremonies, the wedding at Susa makes sense enough simply in terms of Alexander's hope for union of ethnic groups. He took a second wife, the daughter of Darius.[28] Hephaestion, Craterus, Perdiccas, Ptolemy, Eumenes, Nearchus, Seleucus, and seventy-two more members of the high command took Persian and Bactrian wives. The ceremony, Persian in its outlines, began as the grooms seated themselves at dinner. Afterward they engaged in a round of toasts, while the troops outside the royal pavillion were informed of each new development in the five-day festivities by trumpets.[29] Finally the grooms were joined by the brides, who came to sit alongside. Alexander furnished dowries for all. Those Macedonians among the troops who also were married received their discharges at this time. They proved to be over 10,000 in number, but the King gave wedding presents to all.[30] The wedding is a comment on the ways of kings and soldiers alike; all save Seleucus repudiated their wives after the death of the King.

The mass weddings at Susa have also been taken by modern commentators to indicate the King's thinking on some of his most far-reaching policies. Opinion varies between seeing the ceremonies as the first careful, public pronouncement of a notion of world brotherhood that was to receive stress at least twice again before the army reached Babylon, and seeing them only as part of the King's necessary effort to integrate Persians with Greeks and Macedonians within a government organization that stood desperately in need of the services of all three. Alexander was dreamer enough to invest a wide-sweeping, though practical, change with sufficient idealism to make it palatable to all who must participate. He had frequently turned to mystic devices to rationalize his motives. The marriages at Susa might well have been the result of imbuing biological necessities with mystical overtones for the practical purpose of getting Macedonians to accept Persians in their government once they had accepted them in their beds. What this incipient idea of world brotherhood might have become in a statement issued to rationalize a functioning empire that joined Arabs, Egyptians, and North Africans with Babylonians, Iranians, Greeks, and Macedonians, is an interesting question, but it may not be pertinent to Alexander. He did not live that long, and his empire was not yet functioning as a successful amalgamation of these varied peoples. His problems in organizing a viable state are sufficient motive for what he said at Susa; he had not yet seen the world, and he knew it.

More than once, Macedonians had expressed dissatisfaction that the King was more generous with his former enemies than with his own men. After the wedding, he determined to shift the balance by offering to pay the debts of the entire army. The soldiers need only step forward and state the amounts owed, but they held back for fear of being thought extravagant. The air was tense with suspicion that the offer was a trick to learn who had overspent. Alexander chided them for their lack of faith in his honesty, stated that kings never should lie, and that their subjects always should believe what they heard from them. After this neat tribute to what long since had passed, he promised to cover all accounts without recording any names. The troops flocked to take advantage of the revised offer, and the episode cost Alexander a reputed 20,000 talents. The Macedonian army was a traveling market pursued by camp followers, including dealers in the special products of artificers, dealers in horses and slaves, and by those engaged in the world's oldest profession. The troops and their concubines, some of whom became their wives at Susa, had no doubt acquired both children and goods. Such families were traveling households, belonging to conquerors whose successes invested their nomadic existence with a degree of luxury equaled by few in history. It could have been frightfully expensive, ample reason for the debts the King now was paying off.

For the commanders, able to support their own tastes and obligations, if Philotas' arrogance and luxury are at all typical, there were rewards. Peucestas was crowned with gold for saving the King's life at the city of the Malli, and Leonnatus for his campaigns among the Oreitans. Others followed: Nearchus and Onesicritus for their naval expedition, then Hephaestion and the remainder of the bodyguard.

When in the Indus region, the King had included Iranians with Macedonians in four cavalry squadrons and then added a fifth that was almost entirely oriental,[31] the mounted Companions were annoyed. But now there came to Susa the 30,000 Persian youths whom Peucestas had trained and whom Alexander promptly accepted into the army, calling them his *epigonous,* "Acquisitions," a word intended to give them a place with the "Companions of the King." The young men were uniformed like the rest of the army and trained in phalanx drill. Now all the Macedonians were annoyed, foot and mounted alike. Such new blood indicated the King might be able to dispense with their services in the future; he had just discharged 10,000. They already had been greatly pained to see the King affecting Persian dress and mannerisms. Not even the marriages with dowries supplied by Alexander had done a great deal to alter the growing displeasure, though the form of the ceremony had made much of raising the eighty or so in the headquarters command to the social level of the King. They were equally indignant with Peucestas' success in learning Persian and his gleeful adoption of barbaric dress and ways.

3. *Trouble with the Army*

During these months at Susa, Alexander issued his famous edict requiring the cities of the Greek mainland to receive back their exiles. This was in direct agreement with, and required by, his previous order to the satraps to disband their mercenary troops. These released soldiers, who had taken service in the East largely because they had been exiled from their homes, now promised to flood the free ports of the eastern Aegean, a ready market for peddlers of revolution and trouble. The measure had other implications as well. Most of the exiles had been driven from Greek states where Macedonian policy as administered by Antipater for the King supported aristocratic governments or tyrannies. The displaced were obviously democratic in sentiment, and their return indicated a changed Macedonian policy for the mainland. The new policy required a new man in place of Antipater, so thoroughly identified with previous conservatism. Hence, the edict is often associated with the order, issued later at Opis, for Craterus to replace Antipater in control of the Macedonian regency at home. There is no substance to ancient rumors echoed in many a modern publication that Antipater was in disgrace.[32] Despite Olympias' many complaints against him to the King and the weariness Alexander may have felt from the regent's answering charges, there was no hostility between the two. But as Arrian says, Antipater needed to be replaced before animosities in Greece grew beyond the King's power to heal them.[33] The government was to have a new look, and the general had earned an honorable retirement.

Finally, sometime during the stay at Susa, Calanus, the wandering Indian holy man whose wisdom had found special favor with Alexander, decided he was dying and wished to be burned alive. Unable to dissuade him, the King agreed, as impressed as his troops when the old man calmly went up in smoke. He had said goodbye to the Macedonians, but had told Alexander that he would see him again in Babylon.

King and army finally left Susa for the south in early summer of 324, while Hephaestion went west toward the Tigris with most of the infantry. Upon reaching the mouth of the Tigris, the King and his company proceeded upriver towards Hephaestion's camp. On the way, they destroyed the blocks the Persians had left in the river to discourage navigation. These apparently were low dikes over which the water flowed in a cataract, and which the King's men dredged out. The work cannot have been too difficult, for there is no indication that the ships could not get through after a minimum of delay. Arrian[34] and Strabo[35] agree that the cataracts served the purpose of hindering possible naval invasion up the Tigris, which flowed at a lower level, faster, and deeper than the Euphrates, the lower reaches of which were choked with marshes. After rejoining Hephaestion, the reunited force proceeded upriver to Opis on the Tigris, almost due north of Babylon.

At Opis, the King announced his intention of retiring superannuated or infirm troops for honorable return to Macedonia. He would, he promised, give them reward sufficient to make them the envy of all at home, an effective advertisement for his campaigns. The announcement had come on top of the discharges at Susa and the arrival of Persian troops, and it may have threatened to reduce Macedonians to a minority in the infantry; they all demanded their release. If Alexander wished to continue fighting, they said, he could use the help of his father. Arrian makes sure we will not mistake their meaning by pointing out that this was a reference to Alexander's alleged descent from Ammon.[36] It was a direct allusion to the notions of deification that had lain just beneath the surface ever since the confrontation between Callisthenes and the King. Alexander, who always reacted against such suggestions, flared up immediately.

He rushed into the crowd, singling out the ringleaders for immediate execution. The amazed soldiers fell silent, and the King mounted a stand to make a speech.

"Go if you wish," he raved, "but know the truth first!" And he began with his father *Philip* as a direct counter to their slur and an outright rejection of deification. Philip had found them helpless victims of bandits from the hills and had changed their rags and hides for clothes, making them strong and giving them laws and customs that had yanked them into civilization overnight. Then he had added Thrace to Macedonia, relieving their fears of further plundering from that direction, and permitting them to mine in peace the precious metals of the coastal range. From there, he had gone on to open Greece to them, in the process changing Athens and Thebes from overlords to suppliants. By this time, he said, those present had begun to participate with Philip in this grand venture, as he went on into the Peloponnesus from Central Greece to become overlord of all the Greeks, authorized by them to conduct the war against Persia.

Yet, Philip's deeds were small compared to those of Alexander and his men. He had inherited only a token or two from his father: a few gold and silver cups and less than sixty talents, but a debt of 500 talents, to which he immediately had to add another 800 talents upon coming to the throne.[37] But moving from this penury, they together had conquered almost without limit. "I took," he went on, "the Persian forces at the Granicus." This gave him Ionia, Lydia, Aeolia, both the Phrygias, and allowed him then to lay siege against Miletus. Thereafter followed Egypt and Cyrene without a blow, and then came Syria, Palestine, Mesopotamia, Babylon, Bactria, Susa. "The wealth of Lydia, the money of Persia, of India and the Exterior Sea all is yours; it belongs to you generals and colonels who are becoming satraps as a result." For himself, the King had taken nothing, considering himself only their safeguard, providing them with better food and peaceful rest. If any should doubt, had he rested while they toiled and suffered? He would match wounds with anyone—at least in the front part of his body! He had been hit by every conceivable weapon. And all the way, he had led them to glory and wealth. In proof of this he had shared all with them: marriages, blood relations, debts, and rewards.

So if they all wished to go instead of allowing only the elder and weak veterans to be discharged, let them go. At home, they could brag of having deserted the conqueror of so much, who would have gone farther if they had not stopped him at the Hyphasis (Beas) River. They could tell how they had left him in the keeping of the wild tribes they had conquered. Tell it and be proud.

Alexander jumped down from the podium on which he had been speaking and strode off to his tent. This was not the gamble of a man desperately afraid of rebellion. On the contrary, it was the troops who were high and dry: their rewards had vanished in the flush of the moment; they had no organization; the Companions made no move to come to their aid. The army was forced to await the King's action, just as it always had been when issues between them arose, well aware that the vast distance between themselves and home, the lack of leadership among their own numbers, and the tendency to compete with each other made them helpless without him.

The young King sulked in his tent for a day, then sent for his Persians. He delivered an address to them in which he gave assurance of his favor and his intent to abolish all distinction between them and everyone else.[38] He then began to name them to positions of command and to put them within the ranks of the phalanx. His Persian relatives by marriage now were permitted to receive the kiss of fellowship. This ended what remained of Macedonian reserve: the soldiers broke down, circled his pavillion casting their arms to the ground, many of them in tears as they complained of his new Persian commanders and of having been deprived of the royal kiss.

Cearly preferring his Macedonians both as fighters and friends, Alexander came out immediately. Again, the reconciliation was tearful for all concerned. They were granted the kiss of fellowship as among kinsmen and equals. Sacrifices and a feast followed, during which the King prayed for harmony and fellowship between Macedonians and Persians in the government.

The retirement of aging soldiers at Opis, coming on the heels of the discharge of newlyweds and the arrival of Peucestas' 30,000 Persians at Susa may have provided the spark for mutiny, but its real causes were many and deep, as surely Alexander knew.

The gifts, debt-cancellation, and rewards at Susa had a breathless character about them as though they were a conscious, hurried, though far from thoughtless effort to forestall growing hostility among the Macedonians. Alexander's treatment of important commanders must have rankled. The deaths of Philotas, Parmenion, Cleitus, and Callisthenes made it obvious that no position was secure; it also must have shown the wide range of areas in which it was fatally possible to offend the King. Where once the army could listen to its leader and shout out advice or disagreement from the ranks, there now was a growing separation between King and men. The complications of government had taken away the time once employed for the gracious use of personal names and the initiative that brought the King out to his men. The bodyguard had been joined by a palace guard. But perhaps the greatest psychological barrier of all had been the attempt to establish *proskynesis* in Bactria. Was that what Alexander wanted? The question was pertinent when a soldier wished to approach with a petition. Better to stay away except for emergencies. Persian dress, grand entourage, spacious court combined with the concern about protocol placed a barrier between King and troops that could never have been really erased had Alexander tried, which he did not. All erected a gulf across which it was increasingly difficult for any but the highest officials to go. All kings have reasons for their actions; it is the refusal to communicate these reasons or justify the actions that is the first step toward tyranny. Alexander was not immune to the plots and suspicions that inevitably followed.[39] He would find it difficult to avoid the third step, actual oppression. The army, remembering Permenion, knew it.

A failure of communication lay at the bottom of these growing difficulties; Alexander's Macedonians just did not see the picture of his developing government and policies. Even Ptolemy, who, as Altheim points out, had been with the King since youth and had the added advantage of succeeding to some of the dynastic problems that faced Alexander, gives little information about the man and about his ultimate intentions. The "system in its manifold aspects, in its magnificent unity and simplicity remains quite unknown." [40] Ptolemy may have had his reasons for retaining the secrets of a king,[41] but the difficulties Alexander had with his other commanders indicates that they all were in the dark to some extent.

Perhaps the most important of the reasons for the failure of communication is the fact that under Alexander the Macedonian monarchy radically changed in character. Philip had been a king who, for all his ability, was subject to the wishes of the free citizens and whose word was absolute only on the field of battle. Otherwise, he was judge in those cases of legal dispute which were referred to him, and he represented the state before the gods; he was, in short, first among equals. For practical considerations, in that afterward he would have to live with decisions taken on the battlefield when the army returned home, he was subject to advice and counsel at all times. The chief limiting factor in the citizens' exercise of their prerogatives as his peers was the King's success in his military and political decisions. Few care to question a successful administration, especially when its actual competences have been only haphazardly defined. For Philip and his predecessors there was always the easy and practical limitation of having to consult about its advisability with those who would bear the brunt of an action. Under Alexander, in the space of one decade, this government had changed from a limited to an absolute monarchy. The phenomenal success to which Alexander's strategy had led and his increasing intolerance of dissent contributed to a change that must have come about much faster than the ability of the Macedonians to grasp it. They saw their Alexander, whom they had heard refer to himself as though he were the whole army after the Granicus battle when he dedicated the captured armor from "Alexander and the Greeks, save Sparta," become King Alexander. The sound of it rested uneasily.

Yet, to keep the winds of resentment from sweeping westward off the Iranian plateau, a strong government was needed. It would require actual direction by the King and his lieutenants, with whatever help they could gain from Persians. But this kind of administration had not been required even by the conquest of Greece, and previous experience therefore failed to condition his commanders for responsibilities of imperial rule. For, non-Macedonians were among the officials of this new government. Greeks had been involved since the start; but, first in Asia Minor, then in Babylon, and finally in apparent utter abandon, Persians were used wholesale for the administrative needs of the vast areas east of Mesopotamia. A necessary step in designing this government was the appearance of 30,000 Persians in Susa; necessary, but not any more palatable to the Macedonians.

A final reason for the inability of the Macedonians to grasp what their King was about was that some information was deliberately withheld from them. Information the King made every effort to gather can at best have been distributed to only a small company;[42] it would have been physically impossible to do otherwise. Moreover, that Alexander realized that one important secret to personal power lay with keeping as much knowledge as possible to himself is shown by several things. He chided Aristotle for revealing the reasoning of philosophy by publication,[43] and he claimed knowledge of the remedy for Ptolemy's wound from a poisoned arrow as the result of a dream. Some scholars have been quite sure that the King particularly kept his plans for the future a secret, the more so since he knew his troops were hostile to the idea of extensive further campaigns. Possibly only Hephaestion was taken into complete confidence.[44] An interesting light on the secrecy of the King has been noted, [45] when Heracles, Alexander's alleged son by Barsine, the widow of Memnon, appears and disappears on the world stage after the King's death like a wraith still defying identification and proof. His difficulties, if there really was a Heracles, or the possibility of putting forth a false son, were alike the direct result of the King having made his family relationships a secret.

Once the mutiny was past, Alexander discharged some 10,000 willing to leave and sent them home with full pay for their entire service from the time they left home until they should return. Alexander detailed Craterus, his most loyal and trusted follower, though perhaps not his most intimate friend,[46] to guide them home. Craterus was ordered to replace Antipater, and to relay orders to the old regent to come to the King with new Macedonian replacements. Because Craterus was ailing, Polyperchon went along.[47] Both the weakening Craterus and the jovial Polyperchon[48] seem to indicate that Alexander had decided the situation in Greece was fairly stable[49] (he once had referred to Antipater's conflict with the Spartans as a "mouse-war").

In the fall of 324, Alexander moved his army over the Zagros Mountains and north to Ecbatana. He remained there until the spring of 323. Since he was to engage in a busy round of activity upon arriving at Babylon, involving further exploration among other things, it would appear that much of the planning was done while at this Persian capital.[50] Again, there were games and sacrifices, which Arrian says were usual after a period of trial and success.[51] Now that he had been reconciled with the army, the King felt he had surmounted the major difficulties in devising his government and was ready for its implementation.

During the course of this rather extended celebration, Hephaestian fell ill. It seems likely he had become an alcoholic. After seven days, he died. Arrian can make little of the stories of Alexander's excessive grief, though seems ready to admit that by this time almost anything could be believed of the King. He wanted his dead friend honored as a god and sent off to Siwah for Ammon's permission to do so. There was an elaborate funeral costing some 10,000 talents, and general mourning when the King was present; Craterus' animosity towards Hephaestion might indicate what transpired behind Alexander's back. The King perhaps consciously emulated Achilles' funeral for his beloved Patroclus in another round of athletic and literary contests. Hephaestion's troops henceforth would serve nominally without a commander, though in fact Peucestas led them. Finally, before heading toward Babylon, Alexander embarked upon a campaign against the Uxians and Cossaeans, still restive in the area east-southeast of Ecbatana.

4. Babylon Again

At last Alexander was on his way back to the city that he and Calanus had agreed was the center of his wide domains, and where the Indian seer had ominously said that he would see Alexander again. On the way through the mountains near Ecbatana, embassies from the far west met the King. Libyans appeared with a crown to celebrate his conquests. Southern Italians approached to offer their congratulations, privately concerned about his attitude toward their treatment of Alexander's relative, the king of Epirus, recently engaged in Italian wars. From Africa came Carthaginians and Ethiopians; from Europe, Celts, Scyths, and Iberians. Carthaginians and Ethiopians might be expected since they occupied lands nearly contiguous with some of those Alexander had touched in Egypt and Cyrene, and he had met Scyths and Celts in his northern campaigns. Before reaching a point too far away from the Caspian, Alexander dispatched Heracleides to prepare ships for the exploration of the Euxine and Caspian seas. Although his plans went in other directions, he had not idly promised the Chorasinian king to undertake a later campaign in the area of the Black Sea.

The army came out of the mountains and crossed the Tigris. A party of Chaldean wise men from the city of Babylon met the troops at the river. They warned Alexander that it would be fatal to enter the city. Apparently, the reconstruction ordered for the temple of Bel had not been proceeding as the King had directed. Rebuilding it would require the revenues from the immense farmlands belonging to the temple and which were being used by the priesthoods for their own purposes.[52] When Alexander refused their advice, they besought him at least not to enter the city from the west, but to choose an eastern approach instead. He had a moment or two of nervousness, for he proceeded to within some forty miles of the city and sent a party of friends to consider the situation before he entered. He further made some effort to approach from the east until the marshy land forced him to give it up and enter the city from the west. We are told of no further remonstrance on the part of priests. Diodorus, however, is quite positive that the king was disturbed by the request.[53] Only the arguments of the philosophers relieved his anxiety when they said that proper philosopher-kings were above the superstitions of common men.

This episode has much that is enigmatic. The priests can hardly have been shortsighted enough to object to the reconstruction of the temple and the resulting power this would restore to them. Equal darkness shrouds their efforts to keep the King from the western side of the city. Although the city's fortifications were strongest to the east, and had been since the time of Nebuchadrezzar,[54] the desire to protect valuable priestly farm holdings from the feet of thousands of soldiers and horses is also possible. The King later was to seek rest in a pleasant garden on the west bank. That something was concealed there is not likely; Alexander later made no inspection of the land to the west as he did that to the east. The King's alarm, stressed by Diodorus and allowed by Arrian's account of hesitation to enter the city, is equally noteworthy for one who so often had used the pronouncements of seers to further his own policies.

Perhaps part of the explanation of the Chaldeans' warning and the King's response can be found in the history of this city, which so long had proved difficult to manage for Assyrian and Persian kings alike. As noted previously, Assyrian kings tried one method after another to stabilize and control this city to their south. The effort ended in the destruction of Babylon by Ashurbanipal, after the rebellious city had called even upon Arabs for assistance. Assyrian fears of independence for Babylon proved well-founded when the local Babylonian dynast Nabopolassar aided Medes and others in pulling down the Assyrian Empire between 612 and 605. The city's period of independence, which included the reign of Nebuchadrezzar, was, however, ended by Persian conquest. The last king of Babylon, Nabonidus, may have hastened his own end by aiding the Persian king Cyrus against his Median overlords. That he was aware of the rising cloud in the highlands to the north and east is shown by his interest in opening the Arabian Desert to the west to Babylonian arms and, possibly, trade. He claims to have taken the desert city of Teima by force and destroyed it before rebuilding it as a rival even of Babylon's greatness. He must, however, have decided the attempt to move Babylonian interests westward was futile, for he returned to the city at the time the Persians were taking it peacefully, let in by Babylonians dissatisfied with Nabonidus' absentee reign and his intolerance of their religious ideas and festivals.

The convivial relationship between Persians and Babylonians found Persian kings taking the title of King of Babylon until the old problem of Babylonian nationalism and desire for self-determination again cropped up. Thus, Persia took up Assyrian practice in repeated attacks on the city, ending with its destruction by Xerxes.

Alexander had learned enough from the people in Babylon to be aware of the problems posed by the mountains to the east and to follow Persian practice in avoiding the title of King of Babylon. His information must also have made him capable of fairly sophisticated analysis of Babylonian political moves when aided by intelligence gained then and later from Persian archives and officials. If he knew much at all of the background we have been considering, the request that he refrain from entering the city must surely have given him pause. Was this a revival of Babylonian self-determination? He had learned in Iran, Bactria, and Gedrosia that problems the Persians had been unable to solve were not likely to yield in a moment. It was a sobered Alexander who entered the city in defiance of the Chaldeans' warnings.

Once in the city, the King entered upon a round of activity as if to discredit the priests' warnings by the energy of his directives and plans. Envoys came from the Greeks with more messages of congratulation, but the King's attention was focused on his plans for a changed Babylon. Efforts centering around the construction of a huge flotilla of ships showed that there had been purpose in his destruction of the navigation blocks in the lower Tigris. Part of the new fleet were the ships Nearchus had lately brought in from the Persian Gulf. Part was brought in pieces across from the Mediterranean to Thapsacus, then assembled and floated down the Euphrates. Part was built of cypress wood right in Babylon. The King sent for more Phoenicians to help man the fleet and gave orders for the building of a harbor at Babylon of sufficient capacity for 1,000 vessels.

Arrian gives two reasons for all this attention to maritime ventures: the first, his story that the Arabs worshipped two gods,[55] the sky because it contains all the stars, and especially the sun, and Dionysus because he journeyed to India, becomes inept when he suggests that Alexander could be a third god. The second is more creditable in pointing out that the Arabian Desert was rich in spice, its seacoast extensive, and its many offshore islands with good harbors all would permit the growth of wealthy cities. Alexander intended to colonize the shore along the Persian Gulf and to enter the Arab world, showing much greater appreciation of the Arab-India trade than did his successors until almost the Roman period, when his vision was fulfilled. Arrian's accuracy is attested by the Danish excavations on Failaka, Arrian's Icarus, where Greek foundations seem to be datable to the time of Alexander or his immediate successors.[56]

Since the Macedonians had only just returned from India, the unknown factor in these thoughts of widening trade was the Arabian peninsula itself. Alexander had more than one reason for being interested in the area. In addition to the possibilities of trade, he may by this time have learned of the part Arabs had played in late Assyrian and Neo-Babylonian affairs, from the time of their help to Babylon's last unsuccessful bid for independence from Assyria to the sojourn of Nabonidus in the Arabian Desert at Teima. It is certain that Alexander now realized that Arabs were to be met at both ends of the Fertile Crescent, for he had been involved with them himself in his minor campaign into the mountains from Tyre and in his siege of Gaza, where Arab mercenaries were important for Batis' defenses. Now he was again meeting their potential military threat as well as potential trade competition in southern Mesopotamia.

The King determined to implement this interest in the Arabs by a two-pronged attack. He dispatched three successive naval expeditions, the last of which brought back the report that the Arab peninsula was of greater vastness than any had anticipated, as great as India. The historians of Alexander have taken this to mean that the opinion of the time considered Arabia impossible to circumnavigate. This, however, is not reported of the King himself.

While these explorations and the construction of the harbor at Babylon were under way, Alexander began his own explorations of southern Mesopotamia. He sailed some ten miles down the Euphrates to the mouth of the Pallacopas, a canal dug for purposes of flood control. Its function was to divert Euphrates flood waters into the swamps of the southwest from which they could slowly drain into the sea. When the river was low, the canal could be closed and the river still used to irrigate part of the higher plain between it and the Tigris. However, the mouth at which this process was controlled had been excavated in soft earth and required enormous amounts of labor to keep it open. Alexander solved the problem for the Babylonians by going some four miles farther down the river where he found a spot with stony soil. There, he cut a new channel, facing it with stone to cut down erosion and silting. This begun, he sailed down the Pallacopas to a body of lakes lying at the edge of Arabian territory. There, he sought out a favorable site and founded a garrison city with fortifications and Greek mercenaries.

Next he returned upriver and went into the marshlands east of the city of Babylon, now rather pleased to note that he had come in and out of the city without the mishaps prophesied by the Chaldeans. Perhaps his greatest concern was trouble from Arabs, but he had moved up to their borders and founded a city without difficulty. In the marshy lands east of the city where he spent much of his time examining the tombs of older Babylonian kings, an episode occurred that may have reawakened concern for his safety. Alexander's hat with its royal diadem blew off his head in a freshening breeze and was caught in a patch of reeds some distance away. Someone on board ship promptly dove in to retrieve it. The sailor, returning with the hat, put it on his own head to keep it dry. Many later remembered the episode as another portent of the fact that, as Arrian says, the King's end was not far off.

5. *Alexander the Great*

Upon returning to Babylon from his explorations to the south and east, Alexander again threw himself into the administrative tasks that had accumulated during his absence. Peucestas appeared with another 20,000 Persians for whom the King had sent him back to Persis from Susa, and reinforcements arrived from the west. All were integrated within the army, which Alexander was in the process of reorganizing. He ordered a full staging of his forces, with Persians enrolled among Macedonian units, as soon as the reorganization was complete.

A reply from Ammon also arrived, authorizing Alexander to honor the dead Hephaestion as a hero, but not as a god. It was accompanied by a rising tide of complaints concerning Cleomenes' administration in Egypt. He was guilty of exploiting famine in Greece, only the latest depth to which his grafting had sunk. Alexander responded by ordering Cleomenes to honor Hephaestion with shrines in Alexandria and on Pharus and with coins inscribed with the dead man's name. The King was too clever to drive a person in Cleomenes' position into rebellion by attempting to deal with the situation at a distance. His efforts to discover a way around the Arabian peninsula are possible indication that he intended soon to deal with Cleomenes in person.

New embassies also came from Greece, bearing golden crowns as though they had come to some god;[57] evidence that at least a few Greek communities had indeed declared him divine. The decree issued at Susa, for all Greek cities to take back their exiles, has frequently been cited as further evidence for the deification of Alexander the Great, on the grounds that being king in Asia gave him no authority over Greeks and his position as Hegemon of the League of Corinth not only lacked this authority, but the constitutional provisions of Philip's peace and alliance had expressly forbidden political interference with member cities. The decree, it is therefore argued, was based upon his new authority as a god. The most recent brush with the question of deification, however, had come with the mutiny at Opis. The question merits scrutiny.

Despite clear knowledge that Alexander did not like it and the fact that many had sought to avoid the subject for some time, the soldiers at Opis had brought the question into the open with their challenge to the King to discharge them all and fight henceforth with his father (Ammon). Plutarch tells us the King once pointed to a wound and observed that it was spouting blood, not the ichor of the gods.[58] It is doubtful that he ever did request anyone to deify him.[59] Inscriptions written after his death refer to King Alexander, never to a deified Alexander.[60] The King had his own very good reasons for rejecting the idea of deification. He lived too close to his men even yet. Moreover, for Alexander, the suggestion of divine parentage must have called up uncomfortable questions about the legitimacy of his birth, once a very sore point. His reaction at Opis indicates continued sensitivity.

Of greater interest is the possible source of the thought of deification for Alexander. By the time of the Macedonian conquest, the notion clearly was not Babylonian.[61] There were instances of deified rulers in the earliest periods of Mesopotamian history, among the Sumerians and Babylonians before 1300 B.C.,[62] but the practice had died out. Certainly the Persians had no such thoughts about their kings.[63] The fact that strong Assyrian kings did not use the device despite being honored with prostration and foot-kissing, while relatively weak earlier kings were promoted to the rank of gods,[64] leads to the suspicion that early Near Eastern deification of rulers might have been a device of the priestly hierarchy for the purpose of interposing a sacred palace guard between King and people rather than a symbol of monarchical strength.

With Greeks, however, the situation was somewhat different. To begin, before the time of Alexander they were under the mistaken impression that Persian kings were deified.[65] Clearly the misconception was due in part to the honors the Persian king received, but also it may have stemmed from the fact that Greeks themselves had promoted a few imposing individuals to the rank of gods. Among them were the Spartan king, Lysander; Clearchus of Heracleia; and even Philip, the father of Alexander. By and large, these divine honors were voted in out-of-the-way places, and certainly in the case of Philip, by people who were not in frequent contact with the object of their attentions. And Alexander's growing megalomania might well have encouraged the army to think him guilty of planning his own divine honors, particularly as they may not have heard or understood the fine points of Callisthenes' opposition to *proskynesis* on the grounds that it amounted to deification.

It seems clear, therefore, that the deification of Alexander was a Greek idea; it was done by some cities at their own instance, not at his request, and it expressed itself in time by the construction of a temple or two, though perhaps much after his death.[66] Even though Alexander did not request it, and did not therefore plan to utilize it in fashioning his government, it remained a precedent to be used by the great kings of the Hellenistic age who were, or sought to be, more insulated from their subjects than he was.

Part of the reason for the confusion surrounding the question of deification stems from the nature of Alexander's complex personality, the analysis of which is the most tangled question of all, necessarily put off as long as possible. Before we can consider it, we must yet again contend with the hostile tradition of most of the accounts of Alexander's life. What is known about the persons involved in this earliest literary tradition can be gained from a number of modern works.[67] The views of these ancient authors seem to have been influenced primarily by the Peripatetic philosophers around Aristotle and his disciples and by the Stoics.[68] Usually they are thought to have acquired their hostile flavor from the fact that Alexander executed one of their number, Callisthenes; the virulence of their hatred, however, cannot be explained alone by the death of Callisthenes.

One possibility is that the Macedonian king clearly violated cherished Greek beliefs that no person's career, accomplishments, or methods should violate the Golden Mean. Superior ability, but more, superior achievement, could only be realized at the expense of others. A team should have no star performers, and the person who rose above his fellows was automatically suspected of *hubris,* the "overweening pride" of classical Greek authors. And when ostentation revealed genuine pride and arrogance, suspicion could quickly turn to conviction. Now, this idea of the Golden Mean, which philosophy sought to express as a carefully regulated life free of desire and pride, had already been placed in considerable disarray by such giants as Themistocles, Pericles, Socrates, Aristotle, and even Alexander's father, Philip. All had changed the life of the body politic, even its thought, by their highly creative individualism. Nevertheless, among these philosophers who operated below the heights reached by Socrates, Plato, and Aristotle, the Golden Mean as basis for the regulation of life continued to be the goal through the entire period of ancient Greek history.

Moreover, Alexander had shown some concern of his own for philosophy, which undoubtedly encouraged its practitioners to take a proprietory interest in him. Socrates had suggested that only a philosopher-king, immersed in the quest for understanding of Justice and the Good, could know what is best for his people. Similarly, his appreciation of the true worth of the Soul and its hoped-for refinements would place him above temptation for self-aggrandizement. And the Macedonian king, in a sense, conformed to this view of reasoned and reasoning responsibility. As recently as his speech to the mutinous troops at Opis he had stressed his own disinterest in personal gain as he pointed out the enrichment of his men and their commanders by his efforts and vigilance. None could deny their profit, though the luxury of his court and its ceremonies may have caused some to wonder at his vaunted lack of personal interest. Yet, the fact that he would use the argument shows his continued sensibility to the point.

Nevertheless, Alexander had gone beyond the reach of philosophy in a number of ways. Total war, with its considerations of tactics, strategy, politics, geography, economics, and his own administration had moved him into areas on which the philosophers were ill-informed. These things lessened his susceptibility to academic arguments about Justice and Right. He now had an empire to run, and its overriding practical necessities made him engage in things that contradicted many of the positions of the philosophers, almost seriatim. Barbarians, Aristotle said, were best fitted for subjugation; Alexander placed them in his government. Secrecy, necessary to the security of his plans, denied the use of logical argument to those it kept uninformed. Appeals to personal deities to rationalize if not to form decisions was contrary to the nature of philosophy, and this had had to be pointed out to the King when he was half fearful of entering Babylon. Unexplained decisions, under the guise of "desire" alone, excluded philosophers from his counsels. His awareness of his own worth, upon which he could trade when necessary, could at times substitute the rule of personality for that of reason.

Above all, Alexander's success, like that of previous imposing individuals but on a much greater scale, seemed to prove that something other than philosophy could realize superlative accomplishment. In this sense, the Macedonian king was too good to be true, at once the more irritating and the more susceptible to criticism because of his interest in the life of the mind. And when the philosophers, who after Alexander had themselves begun to slip from the earlier rigor of Plato and Aristotle, found in him instances of pride, arrogance, and despotism, they pounced upon them with greater avidity than accuracy. Their intent may have been to hold the King to a standard that had never existed in fact, but the technique of the writers following their lead was to accuse Alexander of a number of things that could not possibly have been true.

Two other factors promoted this process. One was the hostility of some of his successors toward the King. Past the end of the fourth century, veneration of Alexander was tantamount to support for those who were striving either to maintain or reconstitute his empire. Consequently, the enemies first of the regents Perdiccas and Antipater, later of Antigonus, could only favor propaganda hostile to the dead King as they jockeyed for positions of control over parts of his territory. Ptolemy, writing his *Memoirs* while king of Egypt and therefore unwilling to give information that could be used to rationalize a unified empire, is probably the best example. With some, the hostility was sharper because of personal antipathy toward Alexander stemming either from association with people like Parmenion or uneasiness about the King's intentions just before his death when he called Antipater to him. The second factor aiding the hostile tradition was Alexander's lack of confidants. After the death of Hephaestion there were few around who could present the opposing view. The official journals and histories were either suppressed or lost.[69]

The result of these factors so prejudicial to accurate history is that Arrian must try to revise the picture for the reason given by Plutarch: that no one so debauched could have done so much.[70] It was a good clue; and Arrian, Tarn, Schachermeyr, and others have done much with it. Yet, the fact remains that the character of ancient sources makes it difficult to come to grips with the personality of the Macedonian king.

As with many important figures, one may ask whether Alexander personally initiated the plans and decisions of his campaigns. Beloch's statements crediting Parmenion with Alexander's military successes[71] suffer alike from Curtius' hostility[72] and an academic preoccupation with plans and ideas to the near exclusion of direction and control. Being king of Macedon was more than planning battles. Further, argument concerning credit for staff plans works both ways. It is as easy to say Alexander planned Parmenion's capture of Damascus as to say Parmenion planned Alexander's success at Tyre. The general had been defeated by Memnon at Magnesia while Alexander and Philip were still in Greece, but Alexander defeated Porus by solving the problem of heavy enemy cavalry wings after the assassination of Parmenion.

Aside from the advantages of the well-articulated machine that was the Macedonian army in combat, the chief ingredients of Alexander's military successes were planning and courage. Time and again the King's personal leadership in the thick of the fray supplied the latter. His troops always gave evidence of near panic when they thought they had lost him. Yet, the King was no dull pugilist, driven to doubled bravery in battle to maintain his own usefulness as a figurehead. The ability to remember personal names down to the lowest ranks; his facility for making speeches; his exalted claims for his own strategical capabilities; and his occasional quick rejection of advice are among the things that are out of character for a man whose sole talent was courage.

Broad questions of strategy may, however, be another matter, and many have believed that Harpalus was certainly the financial and possibly the political wizard who guided the King's hand. The opinion is within the realm of possibility. As Alexander's director of finance, Harpalus had charge of minting the coins whose types, quantity, quality, minting sites, and purposes were matters of considerable care. The question of political advice is more difficult to manage. Silence on the subject in the literary sources cannot be used to argue that the King received no such advice, since many other obviously important and interesting aspects of Alexander's reign also are passed over in silence. But after the second disgrace and flight of Harpalus, there was no obvious difference in the King's administration, except perhaps growing signs of difficulty within the command structure itself. But along with this, some of Alexander's most ambitious and sophisticated plans for the future were worked out after Harpalus' departure. The King very likely was an able enough administrator to use talent wherever he found it.

Moreover, if Parmenion—and Harpalus—were the brains behind the King, he either had to find new talent when they were gone or let his associates be sure of what they would long since have begun to suspect: that Alexander was incompetent. Always new talent to take over a sensitive function is more expensive than the original incumbent. A strong man's reaction is to decrease the importance of the post, precisely what Alexander did. After their deaths, none were allowed as close as Parmenion and Philotas had been. Hephaestion and Craterus were kept in positions of less power. We are not dealing here with a Merovingian-like king, docile captive of a palace guard. In all the literature there is no hint of derision for a sham king. On the contrary, petulant criticism abounds of a man grown too large, his understanding of others' desires too slight, his power too autocratic. Alexander was his own chief of staff, and always had been.[73]

Few have suggested that Alexander was limited by being over-modest.[74] In public and in private, his life and statements evidence an almost steady assurance of his own ability to meet all obstacles, even those not yet on the horizon. Though assurance may later have become pride, even arrogance, in the eyes of lesser men with opposing views, Alexander knew how to temper it with courtesy and generosity when he chose. He early had established the policy of using his wealth to reward others; his practical answer to those, like Olympias, who scolded him for depleting his resources too greatly, was that gifts made friends and secured their loyalty. The problem was not to give less but to acquire more. It is not difficult to see how some resented being purchased by this young man so anxious and able to excel.

Many of Alexander's attitudes did not change during his meteoric career. He continued his intellectual interests, gathering information, disputing with the philosophers in his train, and applying the insights he gained to his administration. As success came, and with it more leisure, the symposia became more frequent. They probably also witnessed heavier drinking and intellectual adulteration by the attentions of flatterers; but they do not indicate lessened intellectual interest. The young King was, however, capable of arresting behavior in several directions. The man whose rage impaled Cleitus, who ordered the assassination of Parmenion, massacred the Malli, kept Darius' family from even the concern for evil, and pardoned a woman guilty of killing a Macedonian soldier who had raped her, inspired loyalty among his men sufficient to lead them knowingly to death when they had long since failed to understand his purposes.

Alexander's attitude toward sex has been ably disposed of by Tarn.[75] He married only Roxane and a daughter of Darius and left only one heir, Alexander IV. He resisted suggestions of living with other women, sent home Scythian women warriors lest they be molested by the troops,[76] persuaded 10,000 of his men to marry their concubines. Despite the fact that our sources do not permit us to be absolutely sure about his private life, we may note his constant insistence upon moderation and the subjection of the body. He voiced this view as late as the trying days in Bactria, well after the death of Darius, which the hostile tradition takes as the turning point in Alexander's deterioration.[77] The episode, reported by Athenaeus, occurred when the King was passed a cup of undiluted wine. He refused it with the curt remark that there was no need for an Alexander who required medical attention for alcoholism.[78] We can be sure his detractors would have proved clandestine liaisons if they could. His aggrieved question as to what Philoxenus could have seen in him to suppose he would welcome the present of a beautiful boy, if genuine, puts him a step ahead of his Greek contemporaries.[79]

There were things about Alexander, however, which did undergo change during his campaigns. His manner of dress and the protocol governing the functions of his court became more elaborate under the necessity of governing the Persian Empire. The need for maintaining separation from his people for an increasingly absolute monarch required a jealous vigilance that could easily appear as, and might in time become arrogance, especially as it was accompanied by growing luxury. We cannot be sure that his ostentation was not solely for public display. Clearly, the King was by this time operating on a different scale of personal conveniences than the one on which he had begun.

Alexander also showed signs of increasing timidity before the pronouncements of seers. The ease with which he had used the gods to pacify the troops at the Guagamela eclipse had slowly changed so that the King required philosophical assurances in the face of Chaldean warnings against entering Babylon. Luxury, arrogance, separation from his men, the palace guard and the flatterers, and policies hard to fathom and explained only in propaganda and slogans, approach the substance of despotism. All that remained were the measures of repression designed to force the situation upon an increasingly restive army. The ominous round of punishment encouraging further infraction was already sufficiently started to substitute attitude for action as grounds for accusation in a sequence where hatred of Alexander could become the only crime, subservience the only virtue. It is a measure of the King's good sense that the progression went no further than it did by the time of his death.

This is a picture of a man, lonely and successful, whose failure to communicate was better than most men's success.[80] The King whose techniques of rule and vision of empire had left his friends behind may have begun to suffer anxiety from the increased risk of failure built up from so long a series of successes and the inability to distribute the risk in conversations with others who understood the problems. He was realist enough to know that the best of calculations cannot assure every outcome. The issue had been in doubt too many times even in the face of his own maximum effort. He knew that another day's warning, another thousand of the enemy, a moment's charge instead of retreat, another breath of wind across an arrow's flight could have turned victory into defeat. Whether his faith was in his own genius in the later sense, or whether, in keeping with his time, he feared the jealousy of the gods, Alexander shows signs of suffering from the psychology of success in a man aware of the imponderables in human effort. Few have got so high to see the yawning chasms below.

At one point during the course of these days spent in making military arrangements, the King happened to become thirsty. He left the throne room with his Companions. While they were away, an unknown man came up and without a word seated himself on the royal throne. The courtiers wailed and beat their breasts but did not drag him from the seat because of some Persian law. When Alexander learned of the commotion, he hastened back and ordered the man tortured to learn his reasons for the act. The only reply elicited was that it had entered his head to do so. The seers then declared this, too, portentous of some impending catastrophe. It has been suggested that it was a Babylonian attempt to employ the device of a substitute king, but if so the Macedonians obviously were not aware of it for the man was not feted and then killed as the standard formula demanded.

Shortly thereafter, the King returned to his quarters early one morning, burning with fever. He had spent the preceding two nights in heavy drinking parties, and fatigue had lowered his resistance to the point where he was little able to resist the sudden onslaught of acute infection, probably pneumonia. The next day, June 5, 323, he issued orders to the officers to make final preparations for departure on the eighth. The army would leave, to be followed by the fleet one day later. Then he rode in a litter down to the river and sailed across to rest in a pleasant garden on the western side. On the sixth, he performed the usual sacrifices, still from his litter, and ordered the commanders to another meeting on the following day. The meeting was held after sacrifices on the seventh, with special attention to Nearchus' instructions for the fleet. On the eighth, the sacrifices were all he could manage, though he summoned the officers again to direct that they see that all was in order for the expedition, now already one day delayed apparently without the King realizing it. This order was repeated on the ninth, and again on the tenth. On the eleventh, he was too weak to converse and directed that officers down to the rank of captain stand before the doors as he was carried from the garden into the building. On the twelfth, the troops, already well aware from the delay that something was seriously wrong with the King, virtually broke into the palace to see him. He was only able to raise his eyes in greeting as they filed by, in their grief as speechless as he. In an all-night vigil, officers and men waited until dawn on the thirteenth.[81] As the sun rose, Alexander died.

Notes and References

CHAPTER I

1. This point must depend to some extent upon the source we employ for the episode. Plutarch (de Alex. fort. ii. 11 and Alex. v. 1) says the Persians were ambassadors. Curtius (v.9.1; vi.25; 5.2) and Diodorus (xvi.52.3) say the Persians were refugees from a war against Darius and had with them the Rhodian Greek admiral Memnon. Curtius says Alexander was seven at the time.

2. Isocrates was a teacher of rhetoric and writer of legal pleas in Athens during the time of Philip; he died in 338 B.C., shortly before Philip's own death. In his later years Isocrates became interested in the need for unity in Greece as an aftermath of the Peloponnesian War and the subsequent failure of both Sparta and Thebes to provide effective political leadership. He had come to see in Philip of Macedon the only hope for sufficient unity to launch a war against the Persians, who for decades had been interfering in local Greek affairs on the mainland and for centuries had subjugated the Greek cities of western Asia Minor.

3. Neither date nor circumstances for Philip's change from regent to king are precisely known. His deposed nephew, Amyntas, remained on the scene in Macedonia until after Philip's death.

CHAPTER II

1. Justin D. Prášek, *Dareios I* (*Der alte Orient* XIV, 4 [1914]), pp. 11–15. The career of Harpagos (Herodotus i.108–110) provides an example of a general whose position was independent of the satraps, subject directly to the king. See also Olmstead, *History of the Persian Empire*, 1948, p. 59, for a list of the checks against the powers of the satrap in the form of several officials who reported directly to the king.

2. The discussion to follow uses Tarn, *Alexander*, 1948, for the numbers of troops.

3. Alfred R. Bellinger, *Essays on the Coinage of Alexander the Great* (*Numismatic Studies*, No. 11, 1963), p. 48.

4. Arrian i.17.8. Memnon's territory might well have been the uplands to the south, from which once before he had struck down a Macedonian army commanded by Parmenion; it cannot have been the Phrygian territories through which Alexander had just passed, for they had belonged to Arsites before and now were the responsibility of Calas.

5. Tarn I, p. 19; Diodorus, xvii.22.5.

6. Attested by literature and material remains alike: cf. Carl Roebuck, *Ionian Trade and Colonization*, 1959, p. 65 and n. 15.

7. D. J. Wiseman, *Chronicles of Chaldaean Kings*, 1956, pp. 39 and 87. That Pirindu was as far west as Pamphylia is perhaps possible, but not likely.

8. Harpalus may have had an important part in the creation of these arrangements, although he fled from Alexander at about this time. His disgrace and second, final flight, with its complicated problems, has caused baffled interest in this first hint of trouble with the King. Known facts are few: the departure occurred just before the Battle of Issus when Harpalus was persuaded to flee by Tauriscis, but the two separated in Greece (Arrian, iii.6.7). Alexander was both surprised and grieved to learn of the flight (Plutarch, *Alex.*, xli), finally persuaded him to return, and reinstated him in charge of the finance administration (Arrian, *loc. cit.*). His oft-mentioned connection with the trial of Alexander of Lyncestis is tenuous at best: Calas, nephew of Harpalus, accompanied the Lyncestian on the reconnaissance in force by expendables (Arrian I.17.8 and p. 46 above), yet Calas remained in trusted military command until his death in combat in 327 B.C., six years after Alexander's own demise (Berve, *Alexanderreich* II, 1926, No. 397).

9. Arrian places the appointment of Balacrus after the Battle of Issus.

10. Cf. D. Schlumberger, "L'Argent grec dans l'Empire achéménide" in R. Curiel and D. Schlumberger, *Tresors monetaires d'Afghanistan* (*Mémoires de la Délégation archéologique française en Afghanistan*, Vol. XIV, 1953, pp. 1–64), p. 24.

11. Bellinger, *Essays on the Coinage of Alexander the Great*, p. 48.

CHAPTER III

1. *The Lost Histories of Alexander the Great*, 1960, pp. 81 f.

2. XII.18.

3. Actually, Myriandrus was on the coast south of Iskanderun, an impossible location for the events leading up to the Battle of Issus.

4. Polybius, xii.18.

5. The smaller number 29,000, used by many scholars, would merely mean that Alexander reached full deployment earlier, and probably that the space between the two armies at the time of the halt was broader. Since we do not know the exact strength of Darius' forces, it might mean nothing.

6. One of Darius' daughters also was named Statira. The two are discussed in Berve, *Alexanderreich* II, Nos. 721 and 722.

7. Not entirely accurate; see below.

8. Arrian, ii.17.1–4. The suggestion that Alexander's "speeches" are more what Arrian or others thought than what Alexander actually said has often been made. Without insisting upon the wording, the assumption made here is that Arrian at least reports substantially what Alexander said. The inclusion of the main thrust of this speech at Tyre in Aristotle's argument (see n. 15 below) shows that the relationship between Egypt and Mesopotamia was understood in the period of Alexander. It was not the general Roman view, for the Roman policy with regard to Mesopotamia usually accepted the Euphrates as the boundary of western interest. Assuming Arrian to offer the best text of Alexander's speeches, it may be noted that these are the only ones we have for Alexander. If they reflect anything not the King's own sentiment, it would be the view of Ptolemy, Arrian's source, but we shall later see the disparity between the propaganda of Ptolemy as king of Egypt and Alexander's broad strategy.

9. G. Driver, *Aramaic Documents of the Fifth Century* B.C., 1954, p. 6.

10. *Alexander*, xxix.

11. This rough estimate is based on a comparison with those later operated by 1,000 men each in Demetrius' siege of Rhodes in the second century B.C.

12. Tarn says he did not (*Alexander* I, p. 86).

13. E.g., *Evagoras*, lxii; *Panegyricus*, clxi and following.

14. *Antipater Epist.*, vii.

15. *Rhet.*, xi.20 (1393a.31–1393b.4).

16. Cf. G. Goossens, "Artistes et Artisans étrangers en Perse sous les Achéménides," *La Nouvelle Clio* 1–2 (1949), pp. 33–44; G. Richter, " 'Graeco-Persian' Seal Stones," in *Archaeologica Orientalia, in Memoriam Ernst Herzfeld*, 1952, p. 194 and *passim*.

17. G. Cameron, *Persepolis Treasury Tablets*, 1948, *passim.*; R. Kent, *Old Persian, Grammar, Texts, Lexicon* (*American Oriental Series*, XXXIII, 1953), *passim*.

18. S. Smith, "Greek Trade at Al Mina," *Antiquaries Journal*, XXII, 2 (1942), pp. 87–112.

19. Seton Williams, "Preliminary Report on the Excavations at Tell Rifa'at," *Iraq*, XXIII, 1 (1961), p. 78.

20. Cited, with bibliography, by A. Tcherikover, *Hellenistic Civilization and the Jews*, 1961, p. 41.

21. Cf. C. Roebuck, *Ionian Trade and Colonization*, 1959, pp. 69 f.; S P. Noe, *Bibliography of Greek Coin Hoards*, 2nd ed., (*Numismatic Notes and Monographs*, LXXVIII) for pertinent areas. There is a vast journal literature on Greeks in the Near East; a recent and popular treatment of the general problem is J. M. Cook, *The Greeks in Ionia and the East*, 1962 (U.S. edition, 1963).

22. Polybius, xvi.22; cf. F. Kienitz, *Die politische Geschichte Aegyptens vom 7. bis zum 4. Jahrhundert vor der Zeitwende*, 1953, p. 33 n. 6.

23. Tarn, *Alexander* II, pp. 265–270.

24. The brief survey of Egyptian history between 600 and 332 B.C. to follow is based on Kienitz, *op. cit.*, for the most part.

25. Xenophon, *Agesilaus*, ii.27.

26. E. T. Newell, *Miscellanea Numismatica: Cyrene to India*, p. 68.

27. J. Pirenne, *La Grece et Saba*, (Extrait des Mémoires présentés par divers Savants à l'Academie des Inscriptions et Belles-Lettres, Tome XV [1953]), p. 90, with references.

28. Solon, *Fragment 6* (No. 30 in J. M. Edmonds, *Elegy and Iambus I*, Loeb Classical Library).

29. Discussed at length by F. Zucker in "Athen und Aegypten bis auf Beginn der hellenistischen Zeit," *Aus Antike und Orient*, 1950, pp. 146–165.

30. J. Milne, "Trade Between Greece and Egypt Before Alexander the Great," *Journal of Egyptian Archaeology* XXV (1939), pp. 177 ff., especially p. 182.

31. Herodotus mentions Darius' campaign to the Danube (iv.139 ff.), an Egyptian compaign against Tyre (ii.161), Heracles' temple at Tyre (ii.44), and the failure of Cambyses' troops to reach Siwah (iii.26), all points that have already appeared in Alexander's information. Moveover, some information to be cited later also can be found in Herodotus: that the Arabs worship only two gods (i.105, 131; iii.8), that a line of oases extended westward across the desert

from the Nile toward Gibraltar (iv.181–185), and that Amazons were inclined freely to extend sexual favors to chance acquaintances (iv.110–117). As far as such evidence can go it would indicate the possibility that Alexander did read Herodotus, especially where our sources repeat Herdotus' inaccuracies.

32. *Griechische Geschichte* (2nd. ed.), II, p. 193.

33. Cf. Tarn, *Alexander* II, pp. 349–352.

34. The evidences are discussed at length by Zucker, *op. cit.*, pp. 163 f.; Kienitz, *op. cit.*, pp. 83 f.; A. T. Olmstead, *History of the Persian Empire*, pp. 510 f.; Tarn, *Alexander* II, p. 349.

35. XVII.49.2–3.

36. Most of the evidence is well known. Kienitz, *op. cit.*, pp. 83 f., discusses the activity of the pharaoh Hakoris at Siwah to show that the contact went both ways.

37. Herodotus, iv.181–185; C. Rathjens, "Die Weihuauchstrasse in Arabien," *Tribus, Jahrbuch des Linden-Museums*, NF II and II, (1952-3), p. 295. J. Milne, *op. cit.*, p. 177, finds this western trade much earlier.

38. Cogently argued by C. B. Welles, "The Discovery of Sarapis and the Foundation of Alexandria," *Historia* XI, 3 (1962), pp. 276–298.

39. Arrian, iii.4.1–4.

40. Aristotle makes the point in the *Politics*, iii.13 (1283b.37–1284a.11); it cannot have failed to come up when the two were together at Mieza. Cf. Tarn, *Alexander* II, pp. 366 f.

41. Cf. F. Altheim, *Alexander und Asien*, 1953, p. 115.

42. G. Posener, *La Première Domination Perse en Égypte*, 1936, pp. 180 ff.; Herodotus, ii.158.

43. Their remains have recently been discovered in the Wâdī Dāliyeh. See F. M. Cross, "The Discovery of the Samaria Papyri," *The Biblical Archaeologist* XXVI (December, 1963), pp. 110–121.

CHAPTER IV

1. Curtius, iv.10.34.

2. J. F. C. Fuller, *The Generalship of Alexander the Great*, 1960, pp. 167 ff., on which the tactical portions of the following description rely.

3. Arrian, iii.11.3.

4. Curtius, iv.13.36.

5. Xenophon, *Anabasis*, i.8.9–20.

6. Xenophon, *Hellenika*, iv.1.18 f.

7. Kent, *Old Persian, Grammar, Texts, Lexicon*, pp. 136 f. (DPe and DPh).

8. F. Altheim, *Alexander und Asien*, pp. 54 f.

9. M. Sprengling, "From Persian to Arabic," *American Journal of Semitic Languages* LVI (1939), p. 180.

10. Altheim, *op. cit.*, p. 40.

10a. E. W. Marsden, *The Campaign of Gaugamela*, in *Liverpool Monographs in Archaeology and Oriental Studies*, 1962, was not available to me.

11. Curtius, v.1.3–6.

12. F. Wetzel, "Babylon zur Zeit Herodots," *Zeitschrift fur Assyriologie* NF XIV (42[1944]), pp. 45–68, especially p. 50, where the language difficulties and cultural decline are overstated, as is shown by the continuation of cuneiform documents in Akkadian into the period after Alexander.

13. Cf. D. J. Wiseman, *Chronicles of Chaldaean Kings*, 1956.

14. S. Eddy has collected many of the instances in *The King is Dead*, 1961, pp. 104–06 and nn. 10–12.

15. E. S. G. Robinson, "A 'Silversmith's Hoard' from Mesopotamia," *Iraq* XII (1950), pp. 44–51, especially p. 49.

16. E. Porada, "Greek Coin Impressions from Ur," *Iraq* XXII (1960), pp. 228–233.

17. Cf. Curtius, v.4.10–11.

17a. L. Legrain, *Ur Excavation Texts X. Seal Cylinders*, 1951, nos. 722 and 821, pp. 48 and 52 and plates 39 and 42. Note also nos. 717, 810, and 823. All these seal impressions were found in a single collection, buried about 450 B.C.

18. Strabo, xvi.1.9; Arrian, vii.7.7.

19. V.1.34.

20. F. Wetzel, *Das Babylon der Spätzeit* (*62. wissenschaftliche Veroffentlichung der deutschen Orient-Gesellschaft* [1957]), p. 20.

21. Altheim, *op. cit.*, p. 66.

22. A. T. Olmstead, *History of Assyria*, 1951, p. 251.

23. Cf. Wiseman, *op. cit.*, pp. 15 f. and Kienitz, *Die politische Geschichte Aegyptens vom 7. bis zum 4. Jahrhundert vor der Zeitwende*, p. 19 n. 7, where the identification of the Umman-Manda with Medes or Scyths is much discussed. It is possible that the confusion is due to the fact that the earlier Umman-Manda were a mixture of peoples, including Scyths and Medes, but by the time Babylonian scribes could obtain better information, Medes predominated.

24. V.1.40–42.

25. Curtius, v.2.13–15; Diodorus, xvii.66.3–7.

26. Cf. E. Schmidt, *Persepolis I* (*Oriental Institute Publications* LXVIII, 1953), p. 164.

27. Arrian, *Indika*, xl.6–8.

28. Curtius, v.5.5–24.

29. G. Cameron, *Persepolis Treasury Tablets*, p. 11.

30. F. Altheim, *Zarathustra und Alexander*, 1960, p. 70.

31. Cameron, *op. cit.*, p. 12.

32. Schmidt, *op. cit.*, p. 164.

33. XIII.37. Athenaeus was a philosopher of the second century A.D., who wrote an extensive work entitled "The Banquet of Philosophers," in which many philosophic notions and anecdotes are included. He also has collected various bits of information concerning banquets and convivial occasions in general; hence his references to Alexander's parties.

34. Schmidt, *Persepolis II* (*OIP* LXIX, 1957), p. 5.

35. III.97. Herodotus calls attention to the fact that he has not included the territory of Persis in the list of satrapies just given, as noted by Cameron, *loc. cit.*

36. A. Pope, "Persepolis Considered as a Ritual City," *Proceedings of the 22nd. International Congress of Orientalists*, held at Istanbul, 1951. *Communications*, Vol. 2, pp. 58–66.

37. F. Altheim, *Die Weltgeschichte Asiens* I, 1947, p. 147.

38. Altheim, *Zarathustra und Alexander*, p. 70.

39. *Phocion*, xvii.

40. *Alexander* I, p. 55.

41. Altheim, *Alexander und Asien,* p. 32; Kent, *Old Persian,* . . . , *passim.*

42. Curtius, vi.3.1–18.

CHAPTER V

1. Cf. Berve, *Griechische Geschichte* (2nd ed., 1952), II, p. 201.

2. *Alexander* I, p. 61.

3. Cf. Welles, *Historia* IX, 3 (1962), p. 287.

4. Plutarch, *Alexander,* xxxix.

5 Curtius, vi.9.11; Arrian, iii.26.3.

6. Arrian, iii.19.7.

7. VI.8.2.

8. A debatable point, cf. T. B. Jones, "Alexander and the Winter of 330–329 B.C.," *Classical Weekly* XXVIII (February, 1935), pp. 124–125. The fixed points are the departure from Zadracarta in October of 330 and Alexander's success in reaching the northern slopes of the Hindu Kush early enough to witness the height of the growing season, but late enough for sufficient snow to have melted in the passes to allow his march through them (late April). During these seven months the army had marched more than 1,500 miles, turned back from Bactria, campaigned against Satibarzanes twice and against Barsaentes once, tried and executed Philotas and others, assassinated Parmenion, and conducted campaigns in the hills south of the Hindu Kush under severe winter conditions. If they rested with the Ariaspians for the two months of December and January, only some forty-five days would have remained for the rigorous hill campaigns and the nearly 600 miles march through difficult terrain to the Hindu Kush.

9. III.28.5.

10. Arrian, iii.29.5.

11. Bengtson, *Griechische Geschichte (Handbuch der Altertumswissenschaft* III, 4, 1950), pp. 325 f., believes Alexander first hit upon this plan in Drangiana.

12. Arrian, iv.9.3–4.

13. J. P. V. D. Balsdon, "The Divinity of Alexander the Great," *Historia* I (1950), p. 376.

14. *Ibid.,* p. 380 f.

15. References to the monumental literature on the subject may be found in G. Walzer, "Zur neueren Forschung über Alexander den Grossen," *Schweizer Beiträge zur allgemeinen Geschichte* XIV (1956), p. 171.

16. T. Brown, "Callisthenes and Alexander," *American Journal of Philology* LXX, 3 (1949), p. 244, believes Callisthenes was initially thought to have favored *proskynesis* but only because Hephaestion later lied to save his own skin and implicated the historian, who actually knew nothing of the plan until the time of its execution.

17. Cf. K. Beloch, *Griechische Geschichte* (2nd ed., 1927), IV, 1, pp. 27 f.; Tarn, *Alexander* I, p. 83, and II, pp. 163 ff.

18. Tarn solves this problem (*Alexander* I, pp. 85 ff., and pertinent Appendices in II) by relying upon Alexander's initially very distorted view of Indian geography, in which the King was convinced that India was only one last satrapy west of Ocean held by Cyrus and Darius I, and bounded by the Paropamisadae in the west and Ocean in the east and south. What genuine

Persian knowledge of the area this tradition implies had been lost after the dissolution of these holdings or Xerxes' changes in policy, or both.

19. Arrian, v.1.6.

20. V.2.6–7.

21. Cf. Tarn, *Alexander* I, p. 92 and II, pp. 164 ff.; Fuller, *The Generalship of Alexander the Great*, pp. 126 f.

22. The precise location of the battle against Porus has been greatly disputed. The description of both location and general tactics again largely follows Fuller, *op. cit.*, pp. 180–199.

23. Curtius, viii.12.17–18.

24. E. T. Newell, *Alexander Hoards II: Demanhur, 1905* (*Numismatic Notes and Monographs* XIX, American Numismatic Society, 1923), p. 138.

25. E. T. Newell, "Nikokles, King of Paphos," *Numismatic Chronicle* (1919), pp. 64–65; S. McA. Mosser, *The Endicott Gift of Greek and Roman Coins* (NNM XVCII, ANS 1941), pp. 2 f. See now J. M. F. May, "The Alexander Coinage of Nikokles of Paphos," *Numismatic Chronicle* (1952), pp. 1–18, where May concludes the earliest cannot be later than 320 B.C.

26. Some historians are unwilling to accept as genuine this reference to Carthage in Arrian's word *Karchedon* (v.27.7), but reasons to the contrary will be presented below.

27. Plutarch, *Alexander,* xlvii; *de Alex. Fort.,* ii.4.

28. Arrian, vi.9.2–4.

29. See Balkrisha Govind Gokhale, *Asoka Maurya,* Twayne's Rulers and Statesmen of the World Series. Twayne: New York, 1966.

30. Personal letter from M. R. Shields, M.D., Ciba Corporation, Sept. 18, 1964.

31. Diodorus, xvii.103.7–8; Curtius, ix.8.22 ff.; Justin, xii.10.3; Strabo, xv.2.7 (who mistakenly puts the episode in Gedrosia); Cicero, *de Divinit.,* ii.66. For further information on the role of Cleitarchus, see Pearson, *Lost Histories,* pp. 212–242.

CHAPTER VI

1. Semiramis was the legendary Queen of Babylon, whose exploits and travels excelled those of all male Near Eastern rulers in Greek eyes, as noted previously.

2. Pearson, *Lost Histories of Alexander the Great,* p. 142.

3. This point is greatly disputed; Apollophanes is variously described as a scapegoat whose precipitate removal later proved embarrassing to the King, or the first victim of a purge (on which more will be said shortly). Fact is only in the terse statement that he was removed.

4. Arrian's name for Ras Mussandam is Maketa (*Indika,* 32.7).

5. VI.27.5.

6. Diodorus, xvii.108.8; cf. Berve, *Alexanderreich* II, no. 143. See also n. 15, below.

7. Arrian, vi.30.1.

8. K. Beloch, *Griechische Geschichte* (2nd ed.), IV, 1, p. 34.

9. The most recent person to see a plot here is E. Badian in his article "Harpalos," *Journal of Hellenic Studies,* LXXXI (1961), pp. 16–43.

10. Arrian, vii.4.2.

11. Memnon, Alexander's early opponent, was the latest case in point.

12. The pattern is given by E. Meyer, *Blüte und Niedergang des Hellenismus in Asien*, 1925, pp. 16 f.

13. G. Walzer, "Zur neueren Forschung über Alexander den Grossen," *Schweizer Beiträge zur allgemeinen Geschichte* XIV (1956), p. 184.

14. P. Julien, *Zur Verwaltung der Satrapien unter Alexander dem Grossen* (Diss. Lipsiae, 1914), p. 62.

15. The circumstances of Harpalus' second flight are not much better known than those of his first. Beloch, *op. cit.*, IV, 1, p. 33, sums up what can be said: he had foolishly embezzled the King's funds, imported Athenian courtesans, and had adopted airs as though he himself were king. Beloch also supplies most of the documentation for these points in ancient sources. Badian, *op. cit.*, has worked this mystery into an extreme view that ties it with wide-sweeping tendencies toward revolt among the members of Alexander's high command.

16. E. T. Newell, *Tarsos under Alexander* (reprint from *American Journal of Numismatics* LII [1918], pp. 69–115), pp. 16 ff.

17. A. Bellinger, *Essays on the Coinage of Alexander the Great*, p. 66.

18. The point is argued by Pfister, "Das Alexander-Archiv und die helle-nistische-römische Wissenschaft," *Historia*, X, 1 (January, 1961), pp. 45 f., on the basis of known works, rather than evidence from Alexander's decisions.

19. *Ibid.*, pp. 55 ff.; T. Brown, *Onesicritus*, 1949, pp. 79 f.

20. Pfister, *op. cit.*, p. 46. The statement of Hamza, that Alexander burned all Persian books of wisdom save those on philosophy, astronomy, medicine, and agriculture, which he sent to Alexandria (*Hamsae Isphahansis Annalium libri X*, ed. Gottwaldt, pp. 45 and 33), is false. It belongs to the myths of later Sassanid hostility to the Macedonian king, when the Egyptian city was famous for its library and Babylon had been forgotten.

21. The Lindian Chronicle, C. 104–5 (Chr. Blinkenberg, *Lindos II. Fouilles et Recherches 1902–1914*, Tome I [1941], p. 179), reads: "King Alexander, having become Lord of Asia after defeating Darius in battle, performed a sacrifice. . . ." The passage apparently concerns the results of Gaugamela, though written well after the King's death.

22. G. A. Cooke, *North Semitic Inscriptions*, 1903, p. 45.

23. VII.10.14.

24. Plutarch, *Alexander*, lxii; Curtius, ix.3.19; Justin, xii.8.16.

25. V.29.1. The episode argues against any intent on Alexander's part to remain in India.

26. U. Wilcken, *Alexander the Great* (trans. G. Richards), 1932, p. 133.

27. Beloch, *op. cit.*, pp. 14 f.

28. The question of Alexander's wives is discussed by Tarn, *Alexander* II, pp. 330–338.

29. Charles (Athenaeus, xii.54); Plutarch, Alexander, lxx; Arrian, vii.4.4–8.

30. Arrian, vii.4.8.

31. Arrian, vii.6.3–5; cf. p. 153 above.

32. Tarn, *Alexander* I, p. 112, ought to have dispelled the alleged animosity between the King and his regent, but the idea has been slow to die.

33. VII.12.6.

34. VII.7.7.

35. XVI.1.9.

36. VII.8.3.

37. Here he spoke with more enthusiasm than accuracy as we have seen.
38. Curtius, x.3.12–14; Arrian, vii.11.1–3.
39. Curtius, vi.2.4.
40. *Alexander und Asien*, p. 110.
41. Pearson, *Lost Histories of Alexander the Great*, p. 192, suggests Ptolemy had no interest in interpreting Alexander's political ambitions. It may in fact be true that he had special reasons for not interpreting them, as we shall see shortly.
42. T. Brown, *Onesicritus*, pp. 79 f.
43. Plutarch, *Alexander*, vii.
44. Wilcken, *Alexander the Great*, p. 227. This is primarily an argument from silence, dependent upon the fact that no other confidant is recorded.
45. Pearson, *Lost Histories*, p. 117; Tarn, *Alexander* II, pp. 330–337.
46. Plutarch, *Alexander*, xlvii.
47. Arrian, vii.12.4.
48. "Jovial" is Berve's word (*Alexanderreich, sub Polyperchon*).
49. Curtius, x.1.43 f., however, says there was trouble in Thrace and Greece at this time.
50. Wilcken, *op. cit.*, pp. 222 f.
51. VII.14.1. Arrian was very probably correct, in that pauses for games and sacrifices provide an index to what Alexander regarded as his most important trials and accomplishments.
52. Arrian, vii.17.4.
53. XVII.112.3–5.
54. F. Wetzel, "Babylon zur Zeit Herodots," *Zeitschrift für Assyriologie* NF 14(48[1944]), p. 46.
55. VII.20.1. We have already noted Herodotus as an earlier source for this information.
56. P. V. Glob, "Undersøgelser i Kuwait," KUML 1958, pp. 166–171; Erling Albrechtsen, "Aleksander den Stores Visitkort," KUML 1958, pp. 172–189; Aage Roussell, "Et Hellenistisk Terrakottavaerksted," KUML 1958, pp. 191–200; Kristian Jeppesen, "Et Kongebud til Ikaros," KUML 1960, pp. 153–197; Otto Mørkholm, "Graeske Mønter fra Failaka," KUML 1960, pp. 199–207. The excavations show Persian occupation before Alexander and Hellenistic evidence for the period almost immediately after his death. Although it is doubtful that the town is Arrian's Pallacopas settlement (see below) as Albrechtsen suggests, the evidence clearly supports Alexander's order to found cities in the gulf area.
57. Arrian, vii.23.2.
58. *De Alex. Fort.*, ii.9.
59. Forcefully argued by Balsdon, "The Divinity of Alexander the Great," *Historia* I, 3 (1950), pp. 387 f., though to list the scholars who have argued on either side of the question would be to call the roll of nearly all modern contributors to the Alexander literature.
60. Two instances are the passage in the *Lindian Chronicle* cited previously (cf. n. 21 above), and an inscription from Eresos (E. L. Hicks, *Manual of Greek Historical Inscriptions*, No. 125 1. 129). Like the inscriptions cited by Balsdon (*op. cit.*, p. 386), these were written after Alexander's death and at a time when his successors might well have used any precedent they could find in a deified Alexander.

61. Despite statements of C. McEwan in *The Oriental Origin of Hellenistic Kingship*, 1934.

62. D. O. Ezard, *Die "Zweite Zwischenzeit" Babyloniens*, 1957, pp. 58 ff. and p. 111.

63. H. Bengton, *Griechische Geschichte (Handbuch der Altertumswissenschaft III, 4)*, p. 332 and n. 4.

64. With exception of Shulgi, strong king of the Third Dynasty of Ur, and the possible deification of Hammurabi. Both of these, however, were followed by weaker kings who retained the practice.

65. Aeschylus, *Persians*, 155 ff.

66. Instances are given, with references, in Beloch, *Griechische Geschichte* (2nd ed.), IV, 1, pp. 47 f.

67. Notably Pearson, *Lost Histories;* Tarn, *Alexander* II, pp. 1–133; Bengtson, *Griechische Geschichte*, pp. 306–311.

68. Tarn, *Alexander* II, p. 131.

69. Pearson, "The Diary and Letters of Alexander the Great," *Historia* III (1955), pp. 429–455.

70. *Alexander*, xxiii, though Plutarch's point concerns drinking alone.

71. *Op. cit.*, 2, pp. 299 f.

72. VII.2.33: "Parmenion had done much without Alexander; Alexander nothing without Parmenion."

73. A. R. Burn, *Alexander the Great and the Hellenistic Empire*, 1959, p. 86.

74. Harold Lamb's novel, *Alexander the Great*, takes a different though greatly complicated view of the King's personality.

75. *Alexander* II, pp. 319–337.

76. Herodotus' assertion that Amazons freely bestowed their sexual favors, as noted before, may have been the cause of this reaction on the part of Alexander.

77. Pearson, *Lost Histories*, p. 54.

78. Athenaeus, x.44.

79. Plutarch, *de Alex. Fort.*, i.12.

80. Tarn, *Alexander* I, p. 55.

81. Parker and Dubberstein, *Babylonian Chronology 622 B.C.–A.D. 45*, (Chicago University, *Oriental Institute Studies* XXIV, 1942), p. 17 n. 3.

Selected Bibliography

No selected bibliography of sources and studies for Alexander the Great can hope to be fair; the modern literature is mountainous, and ancient references to the man who excited nearly everyone's interest can be found almost everywhere. The following is intended as a more or less current representation of the kinds of material available for the study of Alexander, from the standpoint of the special interests of this book.

I ANCIENT LITERARY SOURCES AND FRAGMENTS

Arrian. Flavius Arrianus, *History of Alexander and the Indika*. Although written in the second century A.D., Arrian's work is a serious attempt to rehabilitate the hostile literary traditions of his time. Based upon the *Memoires* of Ptolemy (now lost), it is the best single source now available to us.

Curtius. Quintus Curtius Rufus, *History of Alexander*. This is an early example of the now available major ancient sources, but it suffers considerably from the influences of the hostile tradition and from Curtius' sometimes maddening lack of care as a historian. Much information not found in Arrian can be gained from Curtius, but it must be used with care.

Diodorus. Diodorus Siculus, *Universal History*, Book XVII. The section of Diodorus' work which relates directly to Alexander also suffers in part from hostile influences, but more than that it is the result of an often uncritical compilation of material from many sources. At times this is an advantage, however, when Diodorus supplies data he himself has failed to understand; but its use requires much critical judgment.

Plutarch. In his *Lives of Illustrious Men*, "Alexander," Plutarch offers much information and many insights not otherwise available. He clearly was one of the most widely read authors of antiquity, and thus has much to say. However, Plutarch is much more interested in telling a story with a moral than in providing accurate history, and his interest in showing the decline of the Macedonian king's moral standards imparts a flavor to his work that must at times be guarded against in its implications, though most of his facts have proven accurate where they could be verified

Other direct ancient sources exist, but add little information. What is directly relevant in this material has been collected in the following works:

Jacoby, Felix. *Fragmente der griechischen Historiker* (Berlin, 1923–1958), is a comprehensive collection of nearly all the fragments to which the title pertains. Both the sections directly relating to Alexander and the commentary are invaluable for the study of special problems.

Robinson, Jr., Charles Alexander. *The History of Alexander the Great*, Vol. II (Providence, 1953–1963). Vol. I of this work is one of the many volumes on the life of Alexander available in English, but the second volume is a very valuable collection of translations of many of the fragments given by Jacoby, provided along with a comprehensive list of categories under which Alexander's life may be studied. These categories serve as a convenient way in which to gather relevant material for special questions concerning the King.

II MODERN BIOGRAPHIES

Here the problem of selection is particularly acute, for a multitude of works exists, and any selection must be arbitrary. The list, therefore, is short and is not to be taken as an indication of the relative number of works available.

Burn, Andrew R. *Alexander the Great and the Hellenistic Empire* (London, 1959). This book, typical of many modern biographies of Alexander, is a useful discussion of the King's life for undergraduates. It has the value of pointing out in particular Alexander's relation to the period following his death.

Savill, Agnes F. *Alexander the Great and his Time* (London, 1959). The particular value of this work, otherwise little different from many others, is its interest in Alexander's medical condition. It offers as good an explanation as any for his final days.

Schachermeyr, Fritz. *Alexander der Grosse* (Graz, 1949). Schachermeyr's work is the most comprehensive of current biographies of Alexander. While it lacks the special studies and bibliographical material of Tarn's work, it is a thorough study of the life and times of the Macedonian king.

Tarn, William W. *Alexander the Great*, Vols. I and II (Cambridge, 1948; Vol. I has been published in paperback by Beacon Press, 1956). Although Volume I is a relatively short account of Alexander's career, Tarn's work remains the best modern work. The first volume gives the results of Tarn's close reasoning and impressive scholarship, most of which is laid out in Volume II. The present work, and any done in the future concerning the Macedonian king, will depend on the careful work of this publication.

Wilcken, Ulrich. *Alexander the Great* (translated by G. C. Richards, London, 1932). This book is a moderate representation of the German school of Alexander biographers, thorough and at the same time quite readable with considerable emphasis on the military characteristics of the conquests.

III SPECIAL STUDIES CONCERNING VARIOUS ASPECTS OF ALEXANDER'S CAREER

The following titles represent some of the particular interests of the present volume.

Altheim, Franz. *Alexander und Asien; Geschichte eines geistigen Erbes* (Tuebingen, 1953). Altheim, as is typical of his other works relating to Alexander, discusses primarily the relationships between the conquests of the Macedonian king and the Persian Empire, both with respect to idealogical differences and, to a lesser degree, the political problems.

Altheim, Franz. *Zarathustra und Alexander* (Frankfurt a/M., 1960). This work is an extension of Altheim's earlier volume, and represents further work with the idealogical differences between Alexander's world and that of the Near East.

Bellinger, Alfred R. *Essays on the Coinage of Alexander the Great* (*Numismatic Studies*, No. 11, American Numismatic Society, New York, 1963). These essays are intended as a preliminary effort in connection with a more thorough study of the coinage of Alexander. They are invaluable in any realistic appraisal, in the present state of the scholarship on this question, of the King's monetary and general fiscal policies.

Berve, Helmut. *Das Alexanderreich auf prosopographischer Grundlage* (Munich, 1926). An indispensible tool for the analysis not only of the King's administrative organization, but also of the many important figures and the parts they played in his expedition.

Brown, Truesdell S. *Onesicritus, A Study in Hellenistic Historiography* (Berkeley and Los Angeles, 1949). A study of the role of the man who piloted Alexander's ship down the Indus River and who joined Nearchus in the naval expedition along the coast of Gedrosia to Mesopotamia, this work offers much information not only concerning these events, but the problems in interpreting the ancient sources as well.

Eddy, Samuel. *The King Is Dead* (Lincoln, Nebraska, 1961). Eddy's work concerns the legacy of Alexander in the Near East and raises many questions about the depth of penetration of Hellenic culture in that area, along with Persian reactions to it.

Fuller, J. F. C. *The Generalship of Alexander the Great* (New Brunswick, 1960). General Fuller offers a thorough discussion of the campaigns, strategy, and tactics of Alexander's conquests.

Julien, P. *Zur Verwaltung der Satrapien unter Alexander den Grossen* (Diss. Lipsiae, 1914). As the title suggests, this is a study, unfortunately not readily available in this country, of the political organization of Alexander's empire and the extent to which it was modeled after Persian practices.

Kornemann, Ernst. *Die Alexandergeschichte des Koenigs Ptolemaios I von Aegypten* (Berlin, 1935). This work attempts to reconstruct the actual text of Ptolemy's writings, upon which Arrian based much of what he says.

Newell, Edward T. *Alexander Hoards II: Demanhur* (*Numismatic Notes and Monographs* XIX, 1923. The American Numismatic Society). Newell has provided us with many works concerning the coins of Alexander, of which this one is more or less typical in its illustration of the uses to which coins may be put.

Pearson, Lionel I. C., *The Last Histories of Alexander the Great* (*Philological Monographs*, XX, The American Philological Association, New York, 1960). Pearson's work is the most recent and a very important discussion of the materials, dating problems, and significance of the historians of Alexander whose works now are lost. Its use is crucial to any attempt to reconstruct the narrative of the Macedonian conquest.

Stark, Freya. *Alexander's Path, from Caria to Cilicia* (London, 1958). Miss Stark, a consumate expositor of the significance to ancient history of modern locations in the Near East, has here a volume containing much information on the journey of Alexander through what is now southwestern Turkey. She provides fascinating material on the geography of the area and its problems with respect to Alexander.

IV MODERN GENERAL HISTORIES OF PARTICULAR VALUE FOR ALEXANDER

Altheim, Franz. *Die Weltgeschichte Asiens* (Halle i. Saale, 1947–1948). The chief value for Alexander of this two-volume work is its discussion of the background of the areas into which the Macedonian king came. Its information concerning the Persian Empire is particularly valuable.

Beloch, Karl Julius. *Griechische Geschichte,* 2d ed., Vol. IV (places of publication variable, 1927). This portion of Beloch's history is a very thorough analysis of Alexander and the Macedonian Empire. It offers a more extreme position in the German tradition than does the work of Wilcken cited above.

Bengtson, Hermann. *Griechische Geschichte (Handbuch der Altertumswissenschaft,* III, 4, Munich, 1950). The chief value of this work is the mass of bibliographical material accompanying each section of the text.

V SPECIAL STUDIES OF NEAR EASTERN PROBLEMS

Kent, Roland G. *Old Persian, Grammar, Texts, Lexicon* (American Oriental Series, XXXIII, 1953). Kent supplies nearly all known Persian inscriptions relating to the empire before the advent of Alexander, and offers much insight into the obviously propagandistic but nevertheless informative views held officially by its kings.

Kienitz, Friedrich Karl. *Die politische Geschichte Aegyptens vom 7. bis zum 4. Jahrhundert vor der Zeitwende* (Berlin, 1953). A very complete history of the three hundred years before Alexander in Egypt, Kienitz's work offers much material for the reconstruction of Greek influences and penetration into the kingdom of the Nile.

Olmstead, A. T. E. *The History of Assyria* (New York, 1923). This work remains the only complete history of the Assyrian Empire. It provides much information concerning the political problems of the Assyrian kings and is necessary for an understanding of the background of Alexander's penetration into the Near East.

Olmstead, A. T. E. *The History of the Persian Empire* (Chicago, 1948). In this work Olmstead discusses in thorough fashion not only the Persian Empire itself, but also the campaigns of Alexander from the Persian point of view. The book is the culmination of an active life of study of the ancient Near East.

Posener, Georges. *La première Domination Perse en Égypte* (Cairo, 1936). Particularly for information concerning the canal between the Nile and the Red Sea, but also for general Persian control of Egypt, this book is an invaluable collection of local texts and information.

Roebuck, Carl. *Ionian Trade and Colonization* (Archaeological Institute of America, New York, 1959). Although not the most recent such work, Roebuck provides a comprehensive collection of pertinent materials for the study of Greek penetration into Asia Minor and the Near East in the period before Alexander.

Wiseman, Donald J. *Chronicles of Chaldaean Kings* (London, 1956). Although this work is confined to recent information concerning Neo-Babylonian conquests in the West, it is included here as typical of later work being done with such materials as these.

Index

INDEX OF CLASSICAL CITATIONS